CASTLES IN CONTEXT

Castles in Context

Power, Symbolism and Landscape, 1066–1500

Robert Liddiard

WIND*gather*
PRESS

Castles in Context

Copyright © Robert Liddiard 2005

All rights reserved.
No part of this publication may be reproduced, stored in a retrieval system, or transmitted in any form or by any means (whether electronic, mechanical, photocopying or recording) or otherwise without the written permission of both the publisher and the copyright holder.

Published by: Windgather Press Ltd, 29 Bishop Road, Bollington, Macclesfield, Cheshire SK10 5NX

Distributed by: Central Books Ltd, 99 Wallis Road, London E9 5LN

British Library Cataloguing-in-Publication Data
A catalogue record for this book is available from the British Library

ISBN 0-9545575-2-2

Designed, typeset and originated by Carnegie Publishing Ltd, Chatsworth Road, Lancaster

Printed and bound by CPI Bath

Contents

	List of Figures	vi
	Acknowledgements	ix
	Preface	xi
1	From Functionalism to Symbolism	1
2	Castles, Conquest and Authority	12
3	Architecture and Power	39
4	The Castle at War	70
5	Lordly Landscapes	97
6	Experiencing Castles: Iconography and Status	122
7	Rethinking the Castle Story	151
	Notes to the Chapters	153
	Further Reading	166
	Bibliography	168
	Index	175

List of Figures

1	English and Welsh castles mentioned in the text	xii
2	Ludlow, Shropshire	xiv
3	Beaumaris Castle, Anglesey	xiv
4	Tattershall Castle, Lincolnshire	4
5	Bodiam Castle, Sussex	8
6	The view of Bodiam from the north	9
7	Distribution map of early Norman castles in Britain	16
8	Hen Domen motte and bailey castle, Montgomeryshire	17
9	Canterbury Castle motte, Kent	20
10	Exeter Castle gatehouse, Devon	21
11	Caesar's Camp, Folkestone, Kent	24
12	Beeston Castle, Cheshire	25
13	Benington Castle, Hertfordshire	26
14	Distribution map of the holdings of Peter of Valognes in 1086	27
15	Castle Camps, Cambridgeshire	29
16	The castle gatehouse at Ludlow, Shropshire	32
17	Colchester Castle, Essex	33
18	Scarborough Castle, Yorkshire	40
19	Montgomery Castle, Montgomeryshire	44
20	Stokesay Castle, Shropshire	45
21	The south tower, Stokesay Castle, Shropshire	45
22	Orford Castle, Suffolk	48
23	The fourteenth-century keep at Clun, Shropshire	49
24	Castle Hedingham, Essex	52
25	Rhuddlan Castle, Flintshire	56
26	Dolwyddelan Castle, Caernarvonshire	57
27	Caernarvon Castle, Caernarvonshire	57
28	Goodrich Castle, Herefordshire	60
29	Caister Castle, Norfolk	63
30	Cromwell's Castle, Isles of Scilly	65
31	Blicking Hall, Norfolk	67
32	Lulworth Castle, Dorset	68
33	The gatehouse at Carisbrooke Castle, Isle of Wight	69

List of Figures

34	Map indicating attacks on castles in England and Wales, 1066–1652	71
35	Graph showing the frequency of sieges in England and Wales	72
36	Distribution map of Hampshire castles	74
37	'Heynoe's Loop' at Carisbrooke Castle, Isle of Wight	77
38	Grosmont Castle, Monmouthshire	80
39	Clun Castle, Shropshire	81
40	Corfe Castle, Dorset	85
41	'The Rings', Corfe, Dorset	88
42	Conway Castle, Caernarvonshire	90
43	Framlingham Castle, Suffolk	92
44	Rochester Castle, Kent	93
45	Leeds Castle, Kent	96
46	Ravensworth Castle, Yorkshire	99
47	Devizes Castle, Wiltshire	102
48	Launceston Castle, Cornwall	103
49	The medieval dovecote at Dunster, Somerset	108
50	Clare Castle, Suffolk	109
51	Berkhamsted Castle, Hertfordshire	112
52	Raglan Castle, Monmouthshire	113
53	Framlingham Castle, Suffolk	114
54	Sycharth Castle, Denbighshire	116
55	Castle Rising, Norfolk	117
56	Tintagel Castle, Cornwall	124
57	Manorbier Castle, Pembrokeshire	125
58	Dinas Brân, Denbighshire	125
59	Carreg Cennen Castle, Carmarthenshire	128
60	Okehampton Castle, Devon	128
61	Warkworth Castle, Northumberland	129
62	A plan of Haddon Hall, Derbyshire, indicating phases of building	130
63	Ruthin Castle, Denbighshire	133
64	The deviated course of the Peddars Way at Castle Acre, Norfolk	135
65	Castle Acre Castle, Norfolk	136
66	The priory at Castle Acre, Norfolk	137
67	Dover Castle, Kent	140
68	Criccieth Castle, Caernarvonshire	146
69	Interior view of gunport at Raglan Castle, Monmouthshire	149
70	Reconstructed trebuchet at Caerphilly Castle, Glamorganshire	152

All photographs are copyright Robert Liddiard unless otherwise indicated in the caption.

In memory of Sam Liddiard, 1976–2002

Acknowledgements

This book has been long in the making and over the past few years I have accumulated numerous debts of gratitude.

I should first thank Richard Purslow who originally suggested the idea of a 'scholarly but accessible' book on castles and who has shown remarkable tolerance in the time it has taken to bring the project to fruition. Had he known how long he would have to wait I doubt he would have been so keen at the outset.

My own knowledge on the subject of castles has constantly been corrected and expanded by talking to other scholars in the field and I owe thanks to Charles Coulson, Oliver Creighton, Paul Everson, John Goodall, Sandy Heslop, Kieran O'Conor, Tadhg O'Keeffe, Matthew Johnson, Christopher Taylor and Ann Williams. I also need to thank John Arnold, Jon Finch, Kate Giles, Sarah Harrison, Ruth Harvey, Gillian Jones, Philippa Maddern, Lucy Marten-Holden, Kate Parker, Anne Rowe, Huw Pryce, George Taylor and Nicola Whyte, all of whom have contributed ideas and directed me to useful references. I would also like to acknowledge the support of colleagues at the University of East Anglia: John Charmley kindly lightened a heavy teaching load and Philip Judge, Stephen Church, Carole Rawcliffe, Christopher Harper-Bill and Jenni Tanimoto have all provided help in their own way. I should also thank Tom Williamson for his constant interest in my academic well-being.

This book would never have been finished at all had it not been for the support and friendship of a number of people. Robert Johnston, Steven Price, Geoff Spencer and James Thomas did more than they realize to keep me on track during uneasy times, as did Bellen, Gail, Geoffrey, James, Jo, Karen, Helen, Natalie and Sara. Kelvin Palmer and Stephen Robb in particular have all my thanks for their constant good counsel and companionship.

Two people are deserving of special thanks. The first is Caroline Palmer who, despite knowing this book was being produced for a rival firm, provided the very best of advice during the course of its completion. The second is my father who has offered continued support and guidance at every turn on what has been a difficult road for both of us during the past two years. Finally, I need to thank Sarah Farquharson, who came back into my life at exactly the right time.

Robert Liddiard
University of East Anglia
May 2004

Note on Welsh place-names

The English spellings of Welsh place-names which are in common use have been employed throughout (e.g. Chepstow for Cas-Gwent). The Welsh spelling is given in brackets after the first instance of each name in the text.

Note on county names

County names are given prior to the 1974 reorganisation.

Preface

Ask anyone to visualise the Middle Ages and they will, almost invariably, conjure up the image of the castle. Alongside the great cathedrals and parish churches, castles are one of the most potent symbols of our medieval past. They are 'tangible' monuments, exciting to explore and exerting a powerful hold on the imagination of children, students, the general public and academics alike. For agencies such as English Heritage, Cadw and Historic Scotland they are the jewels in the crown of the nation's heritage.

Over the past fifteen years, castle studies have been dramatically transformed. Scholars from a variety of backgrounds have not only seriously questioned, but rapidly overturned, much of the received wisdom about castles that has been handed down to us by previous generations. The main focus of this new thinking has concerned the military role of the castle. Rather than judging castles as primarily military buildings, the historiographical trend is now to see them as noble residences built in a military style. Much of this debate has been conducted in academic books and journals and has yet to reach a wider audience: certainly, a good deal of the new thinking has yet to impact on the heritage industry from which most people still derive their information about castles. Therefore, while to many experts in the field the debates (and indeed the particular castles) discussed here might seem *passé*, the content of this book has largely been driven by the sorts of questions frequently raised by students in undergraduate seminars, extra-mural classes and outreach work in the wider community. This book thus makes available to a wider audience the results of recent scholarship but also attempts to place castles and castle-building into the broader context of medieval society. At times I have necessarily drawn heavily on the work of academic colleagues, but as well as providing a synthesis of current thinking I aim to shed some new light on specific issues. In a short book it has been impossible to do justice to the subject, but the guide to further reading will help those who wish to follow up areas of particular interest.

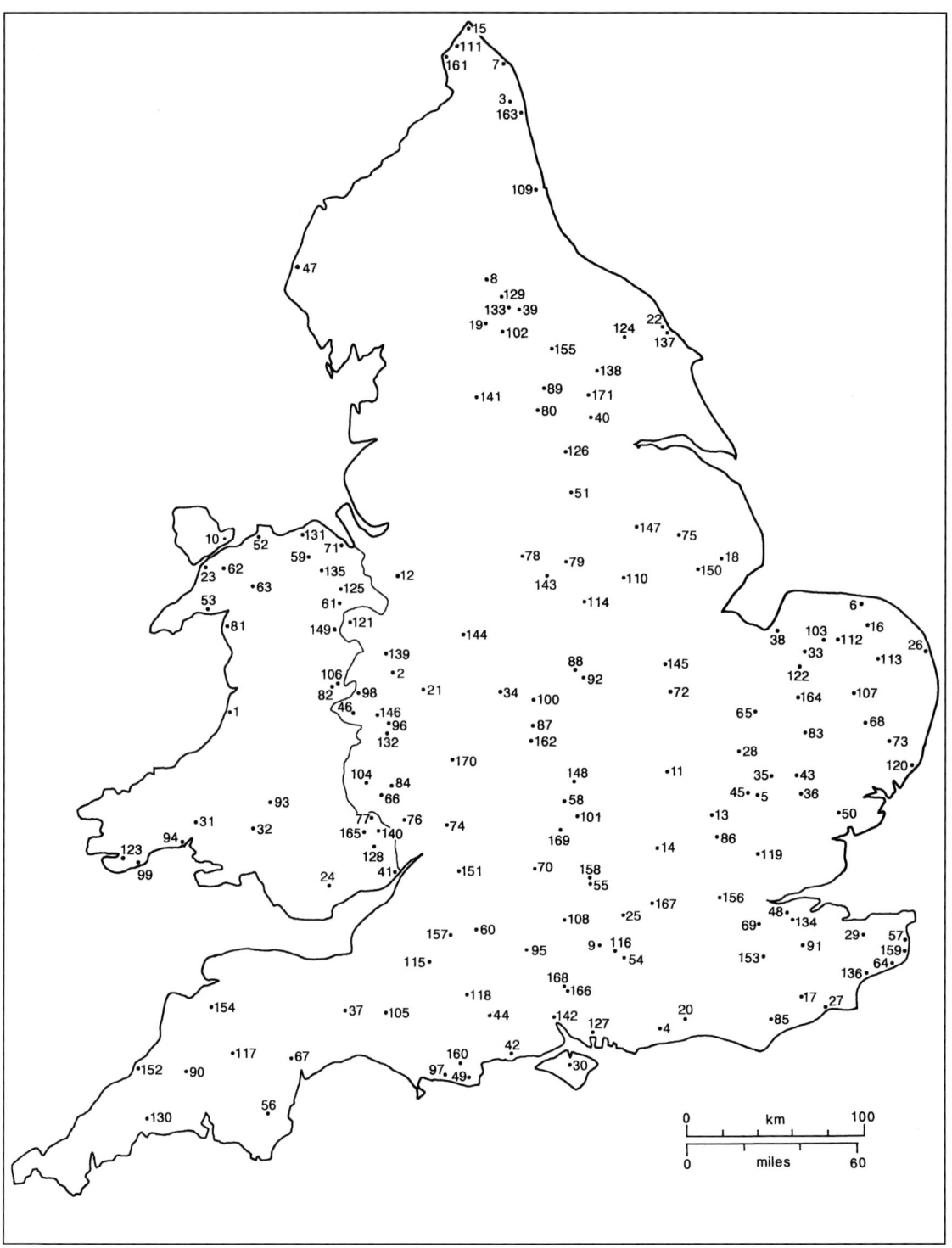

FIGURE 1 (*opposite*)
English and Welsh castles mentioned in the text.

1. Aberystwyth
2. Acton Burnell
3. Alnwick
4. Arundel
5. Audley End
6. Baconsthorpe
7. Bamburgh
8. Barnard
9. Basing House
10. Beaumaris
11. Bedford
12. Beeston
13. Benington
14. Berkhamsted
15. Berwick
16. Blickling Hall
17. Bodiam
18. Bolingbroke
19. Bolton
20. Bramber
21. Bridgnorth
22. Brompton
23. Caernarvon
24. Caerphilly
25. Caesar's Camp
26. Caister
27. Camber
28. Cambridge
29. Canterbury
30. Carisbrooke
31. Carmarthen
32. Carreg Cennen
33. Castle Acre
34. Castle Bromwich
35. Castle Camps
36. Castle Hedingham
37. Castle Neroche
38. Castle Rising
39. Catterick
40. Cawood
41. Chepstow
42. Christchurch
43. Clare
44. Clarendon
45. Clavering
46. Clun
47. Cockermouth
48. Cooling
49. Corfe
50. Colchester
51. Conisborough
52. Conway
53. Criccieth
54. Crondall
55. Crowmarsh
56. Dartington Hall
57. Deal
58. Deddington
59. Denbigh
60. Devizes
61. Dinas Brân
62. Dolbadarn
63. Dolwyddelan
64. Dover
65. Ely
66. Ewyas Harold
67. Exeter
68. Eye
69. Eynesford
70. Faringdon
71. Flint
72. Fotheringay
73. Framlingham
74. Gloucester
75. Goltho
76. Goodrich
77. Grosmont
78. Haddon Hall
79. Hardwick Hall
80. Harewood
81. Harlech
82. Hen Domen
83. Hengrave
84. Hereford
85. Herstmonceux
86. Hertford
87. Kenilworth
88. Kirby Muxloe
89. Knaresborough
90. Launceston
91. Leeds
92. Leicester
93. Llandovery
94. Llanstephen
95. Ludgershall
96. Ludlow
97. Lulworth
98. Lydham
99. Manorbier
100. Maxstoke
101. Middleton Stoney
102. Middleham
103. Mileham
104. Moccas
105. Montacute
106. Montgomery
107. New Buckenham
108. Newbury
109. Newcastle
110. Newark
111. Norham
112. North Elmham
113. Norwich
114. Nottingham
115. Nunney
116. Odiham
117. Okehampton
118. Old Wardour
119. Ongar
120. Orford
121. Oswestry
122. Oxborough
123. Pembroke
124. Pickering
125. Pickhill
126. Pontefract
127. Porchester
128. Raglan
129. Ravensworth
130. Restormel
131. Rhuddlan
132. Richard's Castle
133. Richmond
134. Rochester
135. Ruthin
136. Saltwood
137. Scarborough
138. Sheriff Hutton
139. Shrewsbury
140. Skenfrith
141. Skipton
142. Southampton
143. South Wingfield Hall
144. Stafford
145. Stamford
146. Stokesay
147. Stow
148. Sulgrave
149. Sycharth
150. Tattershall
151. Tetbury
152. Tintagel
153. Tonbridge
154. Torrington
155. Topcliffe
156. Tower of London
157. Trowbridge
158. Wallingford
159. Walmer
160. Wareham
161. Wark
162. Warwick
163. Warkworth
164. Weeting
165. White Castle
166. Winchester
167. Windsor
168. Wolvesey
169. Woodstock
170. Worcester
171. York

xiii

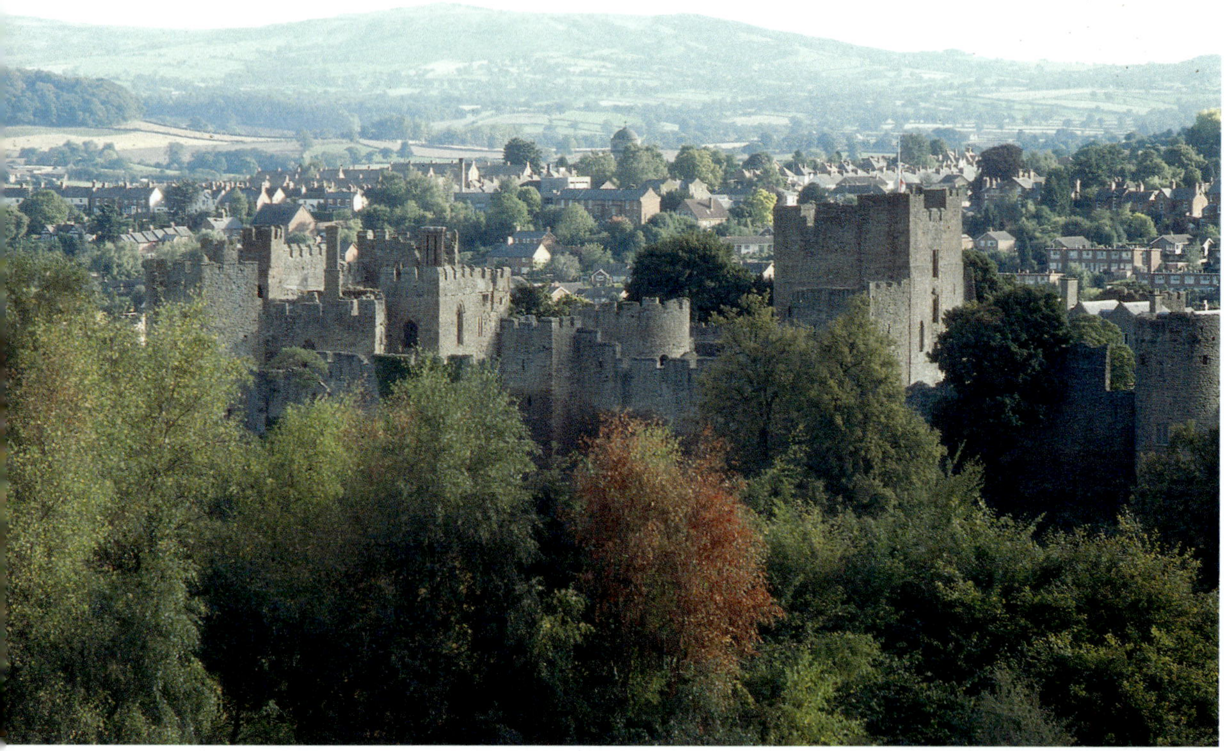

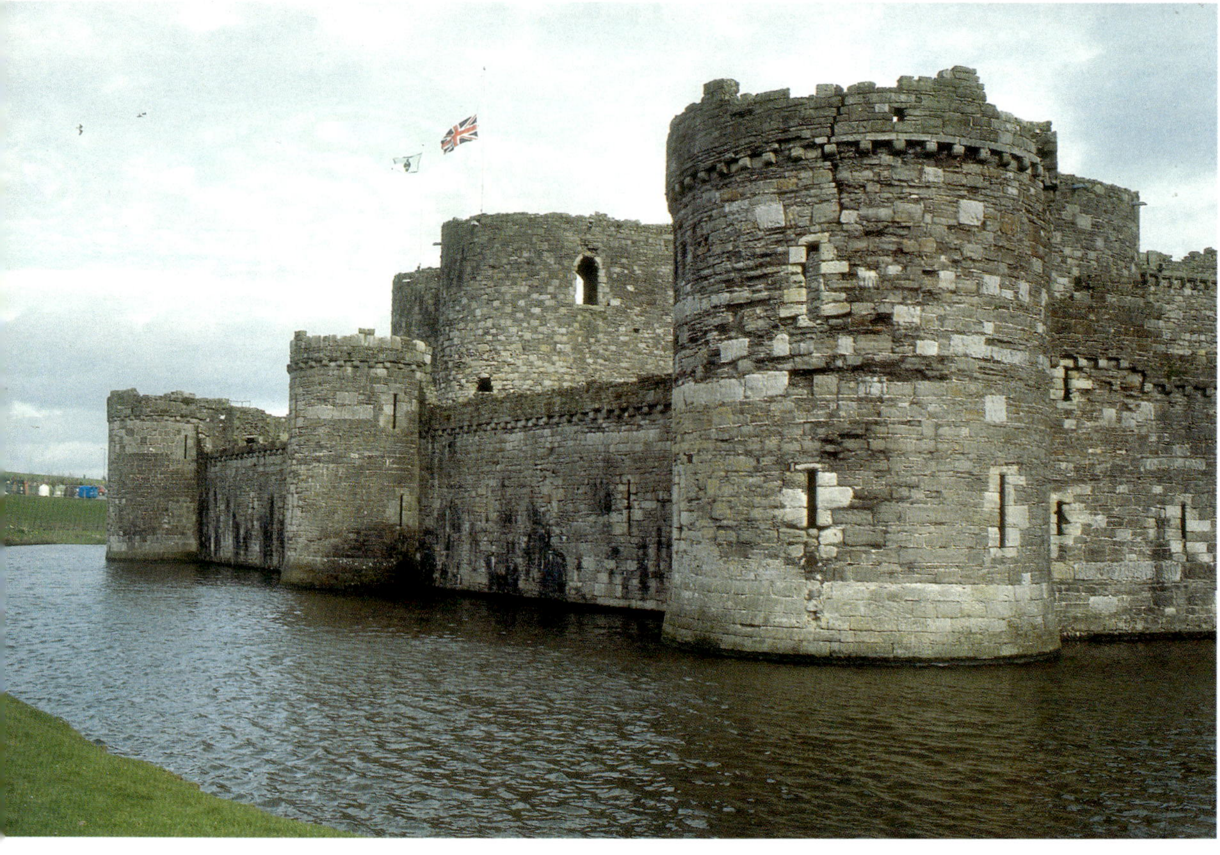

CHAPTER ONE

From Functionalism to Symbolism

The castle story

Much of this book relates the ways in which our thinking on castles has dramatically changed over a relatively short space of time and the reasons why this change has occurred. Before this can be done, however, it is necessary to recount, in very general terms, how previous generations have interpreted the medieval castle. At the risk of over-simplifying what is a complicated subject, it is fair to say that there has, for many years, been a castle 'story' that has been repeated countless times in books, television programmes and heritage displays. Certainly, it was the story that the author was led to believe as a schoolboy. Many of the premises central to this story remain influential today and some parts will be familiar to many readers.

The 'story' begins when the castle (along with feudalism, the social organisation which supported it) was introduced into England in 1066 during William the Conqueror's invasion of England. In the Norman settlement that followed the victory at Hastings, William and his followers studded England with castles in order to pacify a potentially rebellious population. These castles were chiefly of motte and bailey type (the motte being an artificial mound of earth and the bailey the adjacent enclosure) which had the advantages of being quick to build and affording good protection for the invaders. Once the immediate danger of the Conquest had passed, however, new threats emerged, this time from the Norman barons themselves, who used their castles for private war. If the monarch was not powerful enough to subdue them, barons would usurp royal authority and fight each other (and the king), using their castles as bases. It was only in the late twelfth century, as siege weaponry developed, the costs of building in stone became prohibitive, and royal authority was strengthened, that the evils of private castle-building began to be curbed.

Thereafter the development of castles became an evolutionary struggle between attacker and defender: rounded towers replaced square towers to counter the threat of mining; the development of the gatehouse (Figure 2) reflected the need to protect the vulnerable castle gate; water defences became larger and more elaborate in order to prevent attacking engines from reaching the walls; concentric tiers of defences maximised defensive firepower from the

FIGURE 2 (*top*). Ludlow, Shropshire. A complex castle exhibiting different stages of development. The highest building in this picture, the keep, was created in the twelfth century by strengthening and heightening the existing gatehouse.

FIGURE 3 (*opposite*). Beaumaris Castle, Anglesey. Raised by Edward I at the end of the thirteenth century, Beaumaris has long been held up as one of the most perfect pieces of 'Military Architecture' of the Middle Ages.

1

ramparts. These developments achieved their apogee during the late thirteenth century with the castles built by Edward I in North Wales. Castles such as Conway (Conwy) and Beaumaris (Biwmares) represented the high point of medieval military architecture (Figure 3).

Thereafter, the castle went into decline. Warfare became characterised by battles rather than sieges (seen, for example, during the Wars of the Roses), cannon made the castle progressively more obsolete, and the buildings themselves increasingly made concessions to domestic comfort (Figure 4). Later medieval castles still reflected a concern to deter the more aggressive forms of local violence, but the fortified residence of the military magnate was slowly giving way to the country house. By the early sixteenth century, the strong Tudor monarchy had curbed the worst excesses of the medieval baronage and Henry VIII's construction of a chain of artillery forts across his kingdom demonstrated that the state now had responsibility for war and national defence. The castle age, and therefore the castle 'story', was over.

The development of castle studies

As a way of explaining the changing nature of castles across the Middle Ages, the story outlined above is elegant, highly persuasive and remarkably enduring. It is, however, now open to reinterpretation at almost every turn. In order to understand why, it is necessary to examine where this story originated and why it has come to be questioned. There is a vast secondary literature on castles and what follows is only a brief examination of how the castle 'story' came into being.

The origins of castle studies

Castle studies, at least in its modern academic form, originated in the nineteenth century. Prior to this, castles had attracted the interest of travellers and antiquarian writers but were not a subject for serious academic study. For much of the eighteenth and early nineteenth centuries the image of castles was bound up with notions of the romantic and picturesque, embodied in novels such as Sir Walter Scott's *Ivanhoe*. As the nineteenth century progressed, however, general developments in the field of architectural studies, particularly in France, made castles a more acceptable subject for academic research.[1] Yet their battlements, murder holes and arrow loops ensured that castles were studied primarily as fortifications, rather than integrated with the burgeoning study of the architecture of medieval cathedrals and churches. A new category of reference was invented for them: 'Military Architecture'. Castles were the medieval equivalent of the artillery forts and bastions that appeared in Europe in the sixteenth century. This martial image of the castle also went hand in hand with then current theories about the nature of medieval society which stressed its violence: in the age of feudal lawlessness private war was the *modus operandi* of the robber baron and the castle was the brigand's lair.

In British historiography one of the first significant studies on castles to

From Functionalism to Symbolism

appear was G. T. Clark's *Mediaeval Military Architecture in England* (1884–85).[2] Much of this two-volume work comprised a detailed survey of a range of sites across Britain and France, but an extended introduction charted castle development. Clark undeniably saw castles primarily as military structures and his treatment of individual buildings was clearly influenced by his background in civil engineering. Unfortunately his book is chiefly remembered for the fact that he suggested that mottes were pre-Conquest in date and this has sometimes overshadowed what was, for its time, a pioneering study.

Although Clark's work was highly inventive, castle studies were to be dominated for decades by two books published in 1912 which set the ideological agenda for future generations. The first was Ella Armitage's *The Early Norman Castles of the British Isles*.[3] In this innovative piece of work Armitage used a combination of Ordnance Survey maps and references to early castles culled from documentary sources to demonstrate that it had been the Normans who had introduced the castle to England. This was not an entirely new idea – the historian J. H. Round had taken Clark to task on this issue some years earlier in an article published in *Archaeologia*[4] – but between them Armitage and Round exploded the idea that mottes belonged to the Roman, Viking or Anglo-Saxon period. Moreover, Armitage's work was not simply confined to the area of castle origins. She also discussed the siting and distribution of Norman sites and offered a tentative analysis of their landscape context. In this sense her work was truly groundbreaking.

The second crucial work was Alexander Hamilton Thompson's *Military Architecture in England during the Middle Ages*.[5] This was primarily a study of the upstanding structural remains of castle buildings, although it did touch on other areas, such as castle siting and morphology. In a particularly elegant argument, Thompson charted the 'Darwinian' evolution of the castle across the medieval period. He argued that the rationale behind developments in castle design was purely military: 'it is obvious that, in the history of military architecture, any improvement in defence is the consequence of improved methods of attack'.[6] This is a narrative that was to become very familiar in subsequent decades.

It is difficult to underestimate the impact of these three works on castle studies; all were, in their own way, highly influential. The disagreement over mottes aside, all three agreed on the military character of the castle. Thanks to Armitage and Round the castle was firmly established as a 'Norman import' and a tool of Conquest, while Thompson provided a template with which to explain the changing development of castles from the eleventh century to the end of the Middle Ages. It is to these great scholars that we owe the basic outline of the 'castle story'.

It should of course be noted that their conclusions were necessarily a reflection of, and conditioned by, the time in which they wrote. Britain's imperial position and global power were immense sources of pride and unusually, in British history, the armed forces were revered. Additionally, these early castle scholars were part of a general revival in interest in the Middle Ages

From Functionalism to Symbolism

that took place at the end of the nineteenth century. The military character they ascribed to the castle was a natural outcome of the Victorian view of British history, warfare and colonialism.[7] On the eve of the First World War, the military interpretation of castles was firmly in place and the central tenets of this theory would change remarkably little over subsequent decades.

Towards an orthodoxy

The inter-war and immediate post-war periods saw the further development of this military interpretation of castles. Monographs by Oman (1926), Braun (1936) and Toy (1953, 1955), while all contributing new insights, essentially reinforced the conclusions of an earlier generation.[8] In the aftermath of the two most destructive conflicts Europe had ever seen, there was little reason to question the influence that the *matériel* of war could have on society.

The decades after 1945 were dominated by the work of three scholars – A. Taylor, R. Allen Brown and D. J. Cathcart King. In the work of the latter two figures, the military interpretation of castles was, arguably, taken to its logical conclusion. The period after the Second World War was a time when new research produced significant quantities of information about castles: the publication of the medieval volumes of the *History of the King's Works* marked a watershed in terms of information on royal castle-building and Taylor and Brown both published ground-breaking work on patterns of royal castle-building in England and Wales.[9] At around the same time D. Renn published his study of Norman castles, which provided valuable new information on castles of the earlier period.[10] An enormous amount of documentary research and fieldwork allowed King to publish, in 1984, his massive *Castellarium Anglicanum*, an inventory of castle sites in England and Wales; and, later, *The Castle: An Interpretative History* (1988).[11] That the military role of the castle was 'basically the most important' was also evidenced by wider studies of medieval warfare.[12] In 1956 John Beeler put forward the idea that castle-building during the reign of William I owed much to the king's need to create a strategic 'grand plan' of castles in order to prevent insurrection.[13]

In terms of their ideas on the function of castles, Brown and King in particular closely allied themselves to the basic tenets first formulated by Armitage and Thompson. Brown's best-known work, *English Medieval Castles* (1954, 1962, published as *English Castles* in the 3rd edition, 1976) leaves no doubt as to the military rationale that he believed governed castle development. A castle was 'a fortified residence of a lord' and despite the fact that new archaeological work necessitated the re-writing of earlier chapters for the third edition, he stuck closely to the idea that the castle was both feudal and military and had come to England at the time of the Conquest.[14] The chapter titles of *English Medieval Castles* adhered to the familiar interpretation: the development of keeps is described in a chapter entitled 'The Perfected Castle', that for the Edwardian castles of North Wales is entitled 'Apogee', but hereafter the castle goes into 'Decline'. The extended introduction to King's *Castellarium Anglicanum* perhaps owed more to the work of Armitage, in that it deals

FIGURE 4.
Tattershall Castle, Lincolnshire. The restored tower was built by Ralph Lord Cromwell around 1440 and is one of the finest brick-built structures of the fifteenth century. Note the windows.

JEAN WILLIAMSON

substantially with issues such as siting and distribution, but again the military character of castles as private fortresses was not in doubt.[15]

This is not to say that the residential functions of castles were unappreciated or ignored at this time. Particularly innovative in the 1950s and 1960s was the work of P. Faulkner, who analysed castles in terms of their internal domestic arrangements and tried to relate the design of castles to their residential purpose.[16] It is also worth noting that even some of the greatest exponents of the military school were puzzled by the seeming weaknesses of even some of the most famous castles. King speculated over sites such as Portchester, where a Norman keep stands in the corner of a Roman shore fort. The Roman structure exhibited the militarily-advantageous rounded towers that allowed flanking fire, but the Norman architects ignored this design and chose to build in an 'inferior' square style. Equally, the open-backed mural towers at castles such as Dover and Framlingham seemed entirely at odds with the careful design of the outward-facing arrow loops. King concluded that siege warfare must have been in its infancy at this time if builders could apparently disregard such obvious weaknesses.[17] R. Allen Brown was also troubled by the fact that much of his own documentary research revealed that the majority of castles spent most of their time at peace and were often badly prepared for war on the few occasions that they did find themselves caught up in conflict. His conclusion was that castles were static defences that controlled the countryside and therefore did not need strong garrisons.[18] Importantly, it was the puzzles that presented themselves at this time that would ultimately be responsible for the change in attitude that would come later.

The questioning of the military orthodoxy
The military interpretation of castles first began to be questioned in the 1960s, when the discipline of archaeology began to address the problem of castle origins. As a result of systematic field survey, it was realised that many of the very earliest Norman castles were not of motte and bailey type but were ringworks (an oval enclosure with bank and ditch).[19] In 1966 B. K. Davison pointed out that there seemed to be a lack of mottes in Normandy prior to 1066 and that the motte and bailey may have only developed during the course of the Norman conquest of England.[20] In 1967 he went further and suggested (before a major series of archaeological excavations at a number of early Norman castles designed to test the point) that ringworks must have been known in pre-Conquest England and implied that if a castle was defined as a 'fortified residence of a lord' then, *de facto*, the idea of private fortification being new to England in 1066 was incorrect.[21] This provoked a fierce backlash from R. Allen Brown who vigorously restated the case for the castle being a Norman import and suggested that Ella Armitage had answered all the major questions over origins a generation or more earlier.[22] As it transpired, the series of excavations in the late 1970s did not come to any clear-cut conclusions on the issue, but an important line of future enquiry had been put on the agenda.

An article by Charles Coulson entitled 'Structural Symbolism in Medieval

From Functionalism to Symbolism

Castle Architecture' (1979) was the starting point for much of the new thinking on castles that has emerged over recent years.[23] Coulson suggested that the 'military' architectural features of castles might not necessarily have served a utilitarian function, but instead could have had some kind of symbolic purpose. While acknowledging the need for domestic protection, Coulson proposed that the construction of a crenellated building could be intended to stand as an emblem of lordly status, rather than a response to military insecurity. Moreover, it was suggested that one of the dominant themes of castle architecture was nostalgia, and not the desire to build the most perfect military structure. Not only were castles aesthetically pleasing to the medieval eye, but their construction embodied 'the *moeurs* of chivalry, the life-style of the great, and the legends of the past'.[24] The idea that arrowloops, gunports and battlements might have been designed within these frames of reference was a major departure from previous arguments. Perhaps surprisingly, however, the academic community largely ignored the implications that such ideas could have for the wider orthodoxy;[25] thus the 1980s saw a steady stream of work, yet nothing to hint at the turnaround in thinking that was still to come. Coulson continued the themes of his 1979 article, particularly on the topic of fortress customs.[26] In 1984 an important article by David Austin prefigured much of the work that would take place a decade later on castle landscapes, but it stood for many years in isolation.[27] Colin Platt's *The Medieval Castle* (1982) stuck to the traditional narrative but the chivalric elements to castle-building informed much of the discussion on the castles of the later medieval period.[28] M. W. Thompson's *The Decline of the Castle* offered a valuable survey of later medieval building, but its title reflected the orthodox view of the period.[29] King's *The Castle in England and Wales* (1988) was perhaps the last monograph that can be said to fit easily within the military mould.[30]

By the late 1980s, although important elements of the military interpretation had been queried, it could not be said that a new orthodoxy had been developed or that the wider academic community had necessarily accepted any of the new thinking. In the early 1990s, however, the debate over the military role of the castle suddenly came to the fore and crystallised over one castle in particular: Bodiam in Sussex.

The battle for Bodiam
Bodiam has always been a well-known castle; it is remarkably well preserved and its watery setting makes it extremely photogenic (Figure 5). Although its description as 'an old soldier's dream house' was coined as early as the 1960s, the castle has often been interpreted as one of the last military buildings of its kind, a final salute to a martial role that had diminished over the previous century. Bodiam was raised in 1385 by Sir Edward Dalyngrigge, a Sussex landowner, royal administrator and veteran of the Hundred Years War. He obtained a licence to crenellate (a document giving nominal permission to raise a castle) from the king 'to make into a castle his manor house of Bodiam,

near the sea, in the county of Sussex, for the defence of the adjacent country'.[31] This appears to relate, in an unambiguous way, the castle's purpose: at the time the south coast was suffering from French raids and this demanded a response from government and the local gentry. The design of the castle itself also superficially displays a utilitarian, military purpose. The moat prevents anybody gaining access to the curtain walls, the symmetrical design allows flanking fire and it also contains early gunports – its up-to-date design even allows provision for the weapons that would ultimately make the castle obsolete. Bodiam occupies a key position in the castle story in as much as it is representative of a time when the military purpose of castles was supposedly in its final stage, and any 'revisionist' interpretation of its function would have wide implications for castle studies.

The scholarly assault on Bodiam came from two directions. Charles Coulson offered a critique of the documentary evidence for the castle and its architectural remains, while Paul Everson, Robert Wilson-North and Christopher Taylor, as part of a survey of the castle for the Royal Commission for Historic

FIGURE 5.
Bodiam Castle, Sussex. In the early 1990s Bodiam became the focus for a heated debate within castle studies over its status: was it a fortification intended to deter raiding or a noble residence built in a martial style?

From Functionalism to Symbolism

FIGURE 6.
The view of Bodiam castle from the probable viewing platform to the north. From here guests could look down on the castle in its watery setting. Castle and landscape have been designed together to stunning effect.

Monuments, examined the landscape context of the site. Although working independently of each other, the conclusions these scholars reached were remarkably similar.

To begin with, the castle was nowhere near the sea in the late fourteenth century, and if it were intended to deter coastal raiding then it is sited in a very odd place. The licence to crenellate did not confer the 'right' of fortification onto Dalyngrigge and its wording cannot be taken literally. Licences were actively sought out by the recipient as a marker of a particular social relationship with the king. Its martial language is explicable given the aristocratic obsession with military culture that existed throughout the medieval period. It certainly has nothing to do with marauding Frenchmen. When it comes to the building itself the defensive provision is in fact highly suspect. The gunports and murder holes are impractical and could never be militarily effective, the battlements are too small, the moat is shallow and easily drained, access around the parapets is difficult and the whole site is overlooked by higher ground. When judged by the standards of the military engineer, these are problems indeed.

The castle's architecture is in fact deliberately nostalgic; it harks back to the thirteenth century and the perceived 'golden age' of castle-building during the reign of Edward I. Considerable effort went into improving the castle's external appearance; the provision of a moat ensures that the building looks larger than is actually the case, an impression heightened by the size of the windows and the battlements, which are proportioned to give the impression

of strength. The relatively cramped domestic courtyard is something of an anticlimax: in reality, it is a medieval manor house. Confirmation of this analysis was suggested by a survey of the landscape context of the site. Rather than a defence against mining, the castle moat now appeared as an ornamental lake, setting the building off to maximum visual advantage. In addition to the moat, the castle was surrounded by a series of further ponds. Any visitor wishing to approach the castle did so via a circuitous route from which the aesthetic appeal of the building and its surroundings could be appreciated. This latter characteristic seemed confirmed by the re-interpretation of the earthworks on the rising ground above the castle as a viewing, rather than an artillery, platform (Figure 6). Taken together, the historical and architectural evidence suggested that Bodiam castle was a residence built in a martial style – its 'military' elements part of an architectural language of display – all standing at the centre of a contemporary 'designed landscape'. This is certainly a long way from the idea of a fortress intended to inhibit French raiding.

The 'Battle for Bodiam' was a *cause célèbre* within castle studies but, such has been the pace of change, it is now something of a cliché. Nevertheless, it did bring castles back into the forefront of academic research (in other words, castles became trendy) and kick-started a serious debate.[32] Although the problems with the military orthodoxy had already been signalled some years before, Bodiam became the focus of the discussion and the general academic climate became more receptive to revisionist ideas. A particularly influential review article by David Stocker, 'The Shadow of the General's Armchair', put Bodiam at centre stage and gave credence to the revisionist line; it was suggested that what had hindered the study of castles was the retrospective application of modern tactical thinking to a period where such ideas never existed.[33]

The battle for Bodiam: victory and defeat
The early 1990s saw a steady flow of major publications on various aspects of castle studies. In 1990 John Kenyon's *Medieval Fortifications* summarised much archaeological work on castles in England and Wales and the same year also saw the publication of N. J. G. Pounds' *The Medieval Castle in England and Wales*, a massive study of castle-building largely based on documentary research.[34] M. W. Thompson's *The Rise of the Castle* stuck closely to some older interpretations but included valuable chapters on castles as settlements.[35] In 1992 Tom McNeill's *Castles* rejected a traditional chronological approach in favour of the social and cultural dimensions of castle-building.[36] P. Barker and R. Higham's study *Timber Castles* also emerged in 1992; it comprised the first major survey of earth and timber castles and dispelled the idea that such fortifications were the poor relation of their masonry counterparts.[37] The 1990s also saw a stream of progressive publications all overtly contributing in some way to the revisionist cause. Such was the pace of change that as early as 1996 warnings were sounded about a 'bandwagon effect', whereby 'status' replaced 'war' as a simplistic buzzword for the development of castles.[38]

From Functionalism to Symbolism

Considerable analysis and reinterpretation of key buildings in the 'castle story' took place at this time. One of the most influential was T. A. Heslop's study of Orford castle in Suffolk (Figure 22), in which the traditional military rationale of Henry II's keep was rejected in favour of a more ideological explanation for the design of the building.[39] Work by P. Dixon and P. Marshall has drawn attention to the influence of courtly chorography over the way guests entered and experienced the interior of castles and suggested new ideas for the function of keeps.[40] Bodiam generated a good deal of interest in the landscape context of castles and the number of medieval 'designed landscapes' identified has risen significantly. The social character of fortification again received attention from Charles Coulson.[41] One of the most significant general advances, however, has been the extension of the 'revisionist' arguments back chronologically from the later medieval to the Anglo-Norman period. Arguments made ten years ago about fourteenth-century castles such as Bodiam are now being applied to castles such as Dover, built two centuries earlier.

Very recently a series of books has emerged dealing directly with the revisionist theme. Oliver Creighton has produced the first full-length study on the neglected theme of castles and landscapes, Matthew Johnson a volume on the material role of castles in medieval society and Charles Coulson a massive historical study of the social character of fortifications in the Middle Ages.[42] A significant body of literature now exists that details specifically with the 'revisionist' agenda and it is with aspects of this very recent historiography that this book is concerned.

The following chapters will examine how this new thinking has impacted on our understanding of castles in a number of key areas: the 'military' character of the castles during the Conquest years; the architecture of castles; the nature of siege warfare; castle landscapes; and the way in which contemporaries may have viewed and experienced castles. Some of these themes have received a good deal of attention and it is impossible (particularly in a short book) to offer any grand new theories. It is to be hoped, however, that this book points up the ways in which castles may be seen in a different light. Regardless of the focus for debate among academics castles are, fundamentally, about people, those who built and experienced them. Therefore, large sections of this book are concerned with wider processes of social organisation and change in the Middle Ages.

CHAPTER TWO

Castles, Conquest and Authority

The Norman Conquest

The most famous date in English history is 1066. Quite why the events of that year took place at all, why they occurred in the way in which they did, and what effect those events had on the course of English history have been matters of debate ever since. Monuments to the conquest and settlement of England by the Normans still dominate the landscape today. In the generation following 1066 every Anglo-Saxon cathedral and major monastic church was rebuilt with breathtaking speed in a politically-charged programme of cultural modernisation.[1] In the secular world, the Norman impact on English society found visual expression in the castle. Perhaps more than anything else castles are the quintessential badge of the Conquest and have come to symbolise the way in which the new ruling class imposed their will on a subject population.[2]

The story of the Norman settlement has often been told as one of straightforward military occupation. Thus, following his coronation on Christmas Day 1066, William I had to conduct several military campaigns to counter sporadic uprisings by the conquered English. In order to secure their settlement in the face of native resistance the invaders were forced to build castles wherever they settled; along with the mounted knight, the castle was *the* crucial mechanism by which they made their gains permanent. The immediate Conquest years might therefore be compared to a modern military operation: 'the Normans had to live like an army of occupation, living, eating, and sleeping together in operational units. They had to build castles – strong points from which a few men could dominate a subject population'.[3] This overtly 'military' view still dominates popular and scholarly opinion; indeed, it is difficult to underestimate the extent to which the idea that the Norman Conquest was a ruthless military take-over is deeply ingrained within English historiography. Ultimately, this interpretation derives from historical accounts from the eleventh and twelfth centuries. The *Anglo-Saxon Chronicle* records the evils of castle-building and in the twelfth century the great Anglo-Norman historian Orderic Vitalis explicitly linked the successful Norman settlement with the lack of English castles.[4] Historians have followed the lead given by such sources and even as the role of the castle is re-evaluated there is still a reluctance to question the military rationale of the Conquest years. Indeed, in one recent account it remains fully intact, with the process of Norman castle-

Castles, Conquest and Authority

building being compared to German *blitzkrieg* in the Second World War.[5]

1066 and all that

In October 1066 Duke William of Normandy, at the head of an army best described as a Northern French coalition, invaded England and killed its king Harold Godwineson. By Christmas William had received the surrender of the leading men of the realm, had been crowned at Westminster, and had become 'king of the English'. This was not the first time in the eleventh century that a foreigner had claimed the throne by force. Some fifty years earlier Cnut of Denmark had done so, and the early years of the Dane's reign had been marked by violent bloodletting as he secured his position by the murder of his political adversaries. In contrast to Cnut, William did not embark on a policy of slaughtering his opponents; rather, there is evidence to suggest that William was anxious to rule as the legitimate heir to Edward the Confessor and to respect the rights of his new subjects. In the immediate aftermath of 1066 there was plenty of land with which he could reward his followers, and the senior English ecclesiastical and secular magnates who surrendered to his rule kept their lands and political office. However, it would be foolish to suggest that this process was always peaceful or that all English regions submitted without attempting to negotiate their position with the new king. Between 1066 and 1069 William was forced to conduct a series of itineraries around his new kingdom in order to secure his throne. There was nothing unusual about this; many Anglo-Saxon monarchs had had to undertake similar actions before their kingship was recognised by the whole English nation, but the Conqueror's progress was not only backed by an overt military presence but marked by a programme of castle-building.

In the spring and summer of 1068 William led a campaign to the South-West and the Midlands. It was this period that saw the widespread foundation of castles within urban areas, at, amongst other places, Exeter, Nottingham, Warwick, York, Cambridge, Huntingdon and Lincoln. By this time it was becoming apparent that reconciling the interests of both native English magnates and those of incoming Normans was to prove a real test. In 1069, the tensions caused by the Norman settlement erupted in a major revolt against William's rule. Northumbria and large parts of Mercia rose up in rebellion with the aim of putting the English prince Edgar *Aetheling* on the throne. It was during the course of the northern rebellion – dubbed the English Revolt – that William's attitude to his English subjects seems to have changed. The revolt ended only after the infamous 'Harrying of the North' and in the early 1070s a systematic purge of senior English secular and ecclesiastical figures took place. The pre-Conquest earls of Mercia and Northumbria – Edwin and Morcar – forfeited, along with the archbishop of Canterbury, Stigand, and other major bishops and abbots.[6] By the time of the Domesday Inquest in 1086, almost all the major landowners in England were men of foreign extraction.

The situation eventually arrived at in 1086 was in fact more a result of events between 1070–86, than of those immediately after the battle of Hastings. In many accounts, the events of the years up to 1070 are often couched in the language of 'native resistance' to the Conquest; however, this term is highly problematic. To begin with, it implies that there was only one possible (that is, unfavourable) reaction by Englishmen and women to the arrival of the Normans. Equally, it implies the existence of an English 'nation' that was determined to resist and that ultimately was unable to withstand the invaders. Thus, 'English resistance' over the years 1066–75 has been characterised as unsophisticated in scope, lacking in leadership and militarily inept, the latter partly due to an absence of knights and castles.[7]

Historians have, in recent years, re-interpreted the events of this period. Perhaps one of the most important changes in our understanding of eleventh-century society has been the rejection of the idea that, unlike pre-Conquest England, pre-Conquest Normandy was 'feudal'. The idea that a specific social structure, 'feudalism', was a prerequisite to castle construction has been undermined by a number of scholars, who have pointed out that many aspects of 'feudal' society can be found in pre-Conquest England.[8] Historians have also comprehensively revised the simplistic ethnic models of 'Norman vs Englishmen' that informed nineteenth-century novels such as *Ivanhoe* and many popular historical accounts. Rather, in recent years, scholars have stressed the continuities at social levels below the senior aristocracy and in royal government and, significantly, pointed out that much of the 'ethnic' conflict in the years 1066–75 should be seen in the broader context of eleventh-century politics and rebellion. Thus the 'resistance' of Eadric the Wild in Herefordshire in 1069 looks suspiciously like the actions of a disgruntled magnate with parallels either side of 1066; the 'English Revolt' of 1069 bears some comparison with the Northumbrian revolt in 1065; and the 'Rebellion of the Three Earls' in 1075 (only one of whom was English) appears to have been a straightforward magnatial rebellion with pre- and post-Conquest characteristics.[9] It is important here to remember that although there was much about the Norman Conquest that was peculiar and unprecedented, it is in fact extremely difficult to characterise this period as a time of military occupation in the modern sense, and this is crucial to our perception of the castle. It is more helpful to disaggregate two linked, but separate, themes: the Norman *conquest* and the Norman *settlement*. Arguably, the Norman *conquest* was achieved very quickly and was different from the Norman *settlement*, which was a more protracted and piecemeal affair. And one of the historical processes we are witnessing when it comes to castle construction after 1066 is the mechanism by which an eleventh-century elite legitimised their succession through building.

That the events of 1066 necessarily involved the forcible dispossession of the king and ultimately resulted in the almost wholesale disinheritance of the leading Englishmen of the realm is undeniable; but the extent to which the Norman settlement was made effective by a chain of military outposts in which a small number of invaders kept down a rebellious people is more open to question. While there is no doubt that the Conquest was a traumatic event as far as the Old English aristocracy was concerned, and that William the Conqueror had to go to extraordinary lengths to secure his kingdom, this does not necessarily equate with the mailed fist of Norman conquerors keeping down a hostile population in some kind of eleventh-century version of the modern-day Israeli occupation of the West Bank and Gaza Strip; a subtler picture is now emerging of how the Normans made permanent their gains and the mechanisms by which the settlement of a new elite was heralded. The simple equation of castles, militarism and conquest may not be as straight-forward as it first appears.

Pre-Conquest fortification

Before the impact of castles on the English landscape can be assessed it is first necessary to examine the fortifications in existence prior to the Conquest. The term chiefly used for fortifications in pre-Conquest England was *burh*, a word that could refer to the urban works raised by the West Saxon kings or the predominately rural residences of the Old English aristocracy. The earliest urban *burhs* owed their foundation to Alfred the Great's need to defend Wessex from the Vikings; these were large communal enclosures, surrounded by a bank and ditch and with the interior frequently laid out on a gridiron plan.[10] In the tenth century *burhs* became a mechanism of expansion as the West Saxon kings marked the re-conquest of the Danelaw by placing *burhs* in the newly-won territories, such as at Stamford (Lincolnshire) and Nottingham. Some of these 'frontier settlements' in turn became important urban centres and formed part of a wider network of *burh* or shire towns with significant economic and governmental roles. These had locally-significant concentrations of population, were provisioned with markets and housed the apparatus of government. It was these kinds of places that were the focus for royal castle-building in the immediate post-Conquest period (Figure 7).

The rural *burh*, on the other hand, was simply an aristocratic residence and must have been far more numerous than its urban counterpart.[11] Something of its character can be gauged by an eleventh-century tract by Archbishop Wulfstan, known as 'Of People's Ranks and Laws', which states that, among other indicators of status, the nobleman's residence should consist of 'church and kitchen, bell house and *burh-geat*'.[12] Where it has taken place, archaeological excavation has confirmed and added to this picture. Although only a small number have so far been examined, to judge from sites such as Goltho in Lincolnshire and Sulgrave in Northamptonshire such *burhs* were comprised of a wooden hall with outbuildings which were themselves surrounded by a ditched and fenced enclosure known as a ringwork.[13] Some significance was attached to the entrance tower – the *burh-geat* – that appears to have served as a marker of thegnly rank. These enigmatic structures occur in both secular and ecclesiastical contexts. They do not appear to be intended for military

Castles in Context: Power, Symbolism and Landscape, 1066–1500

FIGURE 7. Distribution map of early Norman castles in Britain. Although such maps can never be precise, the Norman policy of establishing castles in urban areas is immediately apparent. Based on the list complied by Harfield, 1991.

defence; rather, they seem to have served a quasi-ceremonial purpose.[14] Some of our best evidence for these structures comes from the Bayeux Tapestry, which represents several English buildings as multi-storeyed towers with window openings and possible display balconies. These features are reminiscent of those found on some extant Anglo-Saxon church towers, such as Northgate in Oxford, where they have been interpreted as openings for the display of holy relics or platforms from which clergymen could minister to their assembled flock beneath. In a secular context we should perhaps envisage lords appearing at their *burh-geat* and displaying their *dominatio* to tenants and followers beneath. At Sulgrave, Eynesford (Kent) and Portchester (Hampshire) traces of masonry buildings have been excavated that probably represent the remains of such entrance towers.[15] It was in complexes such as this that English nobles resided prior to the Conquest. They were frequently found at the centre of scattered estates and served as the focus for estate dues and renders. Such thegnly *burhs* were therefore both secure residences and centres of manorial lordship.[16]

Early castle-building

As will be seen, there are points of comparison between aspects of Norman castle-building and Anglo-Saxon fortification. The Normans can, however, be credited with introducing new two forms: the motte and bailey castle and the stone keep or *donjon*. The motte and bailey castle consisted of an artificial mound of earth (the motte), with which was associated some kind of tower or superstructure, and usually at least one enclosure (the bailey). This was different from the ringwork castle (which the Normans also raised), which comprised an enclosure defended by a bank and ditch. Eventually, motte and bailey castles were to outnumber ringworks by a ratio of approximately 4:1, although obviously not all of these were in occupational use at any one time.[17] It should not be thought, moreover, that castles made of earth and timber were the poor relation of their masonry counterparts. Excavations at Hen Domen (Montgomeryshire) have demonstrated the complexity of their design and the sophistication of their defences (Figure 8).[18] The development of earth and

FIGURE 8. Hen Domen motte and bailey castle, Montgomeryshire. Excavations here have demonstrated the sophistication of earth and timber castles in the Anglo-Norman period. The bailey was crammed with buildings and underwent several phases of rebuilding during the course of its occupation.
© CLWYD-POWYS ARCHAEOLOGICAL TRUST

timber castles is also bewildering in its variety: mottes could be added to ringworks, ringworks converted into mottes and the arrangements between mottes and their associated buildings was often idiosyncratic.[19] While the ringwork was a form of fortification known in pre-Conquest England there is, as yet, no evidence to suggest that the motte was anything other than a 'Norman import', although quite when they were introduced is open to debate.

Castle-building after the Conquest can profitably be broken down into three phases: firstly, the foundation of royal castles; secondly, the granting of lordships to individual magnates who then constructed their own fortresses; and thirdly, the process whereby lords enfeoffed their knightly tenants who themselves subsequently built their own residences.[20] The first phase chiefly concerned the placing of castles either directly in, or in close proximity to, existing urban centres, usually county towns. The majority of baronial castle-building – the second and third phases – took place in the countryside and it was here that castles impacted on the majority of the population. Historians have long tried to estimate the number of castles built at this time but the most recent assessment by Richard Eales is more sophisticated than most.[21] As the majority of Anglo-Norman castles are undocumented, the best guide to the total numbers of castles raised in the eleventh and twelfth centuries is simply the number of earthworks that are extant today; and in England and Wales there are approximately one thousand sites that we might assume were raised in the period 1066–1200. On the basis of documentary references, however, it can be estimated that there were only a few hundred castles in late twelfth-century England. As historians have tended to reduce their estimates of the numbers of castles built during the 'anarchy' of Stephen's reign, the balance of probability suggests that the majority of earthwork castles scattered across the countryside date from the late eleventh century and the period of the Norman settlement.[22] Of course, not all of these would have been in concurrent occupational use and Eales suggests a figure of around 500–600 'active' sites at any one time, with a peak around the year 1100. As there were only approximately two hundred baronies in England at this time, it must follow that considerable numbers of relatively humble lords and knightly tenants were engaged in castle-building at some point after the Conquest.[23]

Urban castles

The building of royal castles in those shire *burhs* which served as centres of local government or county towns is undeniably one of the most striking features of the immediate post-Conquest period: of the thirty-six castles known to have been built by William the Conqueror, twenty-four were connected in some way with existing urban centres.[24] This is readily explained by the function of *burhs* in this period: they were centres of shire government which were often found at major road or river junctions, and were usually provisioned with existing markets, mints and defences. It was because of their role in government that the chronicler William of Newburgh later commented that the royal castles were the 'bones of the kingdom' and thus it is not difficult to see why the Conqueror wanted to focus castle-building in the major towns of the realm.

Castles were commonly placed in the corner of the existing borough's defences. The castle could then utilise the extant fortifications, as clearly occurs at Leicester, Gloucester, London, Winchester and Wareham. The physical form that these early castles took is not clear, however; while, in due course, mottes were raised at castles such as Canterbury, York and Cambridge it is not easy to establish whether these were primary features (Figure 9). The issue of when exactly mottes were first raised in England was substantially readdressed in the 1960s when it was proposed by Brian Davison that the motte and bailey castle was a result of innovations during the Conquest itself. It was the peculiar circumstances of the Norman settlement, he suggested, that made castle-builders develop a new form of castle.[25] This idea has now been shown not to be entirely correct, as mottes of pre-Conquest date are now believed to have existed on the continent (although motte-building may have been, nevertheless, a relatively recent phenomenon at the time of the Conquest), but Barbara English has recently developed Davison's line of argument. In an incisive discussion, she suggests that it would have been impossible for mottes to be raised at the speed recorded by chroniclers.[26] At Dover and York castles were apparently raised in as little as eight days, a period of time certainly too short for the construction of a mound of any size. Rather, the form that the majority of these urban castles took in the immediate post-Conquest period (up to *c.*1070) was chiefly that of a ringwork.

The familiar narrative of castle plantation in towns at this time is one of destruction and the domination of the urban population. Both are attested in historical accounts and in the archaeological record, but need to be put alongside other evidence for the character of castles during this period. Oliver Creighton has pointed out the 'central paradox' of castle-building at the time of the Conquest: on the one hand castles appear as instruments of conquest, an imposition on the existing urban fabric; while on the other, they can be related to English traditions of fortification.[27] There is some, albeit limited, evidence that a number of these early urban castles were placed over existing high-status structures and perpetuated some kind of lordly or royal authority. The most clear-cut example is Stamford, where the Norman castle overlay the double-ditched enclosure of a pre-Conquest residence.[28] At Southampton the castle was raised over what was interpreted as a large English hall and at Newark the castle origins have been pushed back to the eleventh century and it has been shown that the castle was built in a section of the town apparently already cut off by a bank and ditch, suggesting antecedent high-status occupation.[29] In other cases, this situation may be obliquely referred to in documents; at Wallingford, for example, Domesday Book states that Miles Crispin (almost certainly the castellan of Wallingford Castle) 'holds the land where the housecarls lived', suggesting that the castle was raised over a pre-Conquest high-status structure.[30] It is not known with any degree of certainty how many urban castles may have been maintaining some kind of existing

FIGURE 9.
Canterbury castle motte, Kent. The original castle at Canterbury was built during the autumn of 1066 following the battle of Hastings. The (now much altered) motte may not have been a primary feature, however; at first the castle probably consisted of a ringwork. Early in the twelfth century a replacement stone castle was built on a new site to the west.

structure or appropriating some kind of authority but the overtly 'military' character of some of these early castles can certainly be questioned.

A particularly relevant example is to be found at Exeter, a castle that points up how difficult it is to read the idea of 'English resistance' in ethnic terms, and also how ambiguous the act of castle-building could be in the initial phases of the Norman Conquest. In the spring of 1068 the South-West became the first region to test the authority of William the Conqueror. The events concerned have sometimes been interpreted as some kind of proto-English nationalistic uprising against Norman rule, but the real cause seems to have been the desire of the men of Devon to bargain about their liability for tax. According to the later historian Orderic Vitalis, the citizens of Exeter had communicated to William that they were only willing to render to him 'the accustomed dues' – probably their retort to the Conqueror's plans to levy a 'great' geld across the kingdom that year. The response of the new king, who 'was not used to having subjects on these terms', was to lay siege to the city with an army that, significantly, included Englishmen.[31] The city submitted after eighteen days when a section of the walls was brought down by mining. The *Anglo-Saxon Chronicle* relates that those in the city surrendered 'because the thegns had betrayed them', an indication that there were some who wished to acquiesce with the king.[32] Following the surrender – the citizens were treated leniently – Rougemount (Red Hill) castle was raised in the corner of the city walls.

Castles, Conquest and Authority

FIGURE 10.
Exeter castle gatehouse, Devon. This remarkable survival dates from William the Conqueror's campaign through the south west in 1068. Rather than evoking what we might call Norman 'militarism', the design of the gatehouse in fact resembles Anglo-Saxon display towers.

What makes this castle so interesting is the form of the gate tower (Figure 10). This was originally entered via a large ground-floor entrance (subsequently blocked) over which was an upper-storey chamber with two large triangular-headed windows of Anglo-Saxon design. By any stretch of the imagination, the form of the tower severely restricts its defensive capability. In fact, it can hardly be rated a 'defensive' structure at all. However, its form is significant in that at least parts of this 'Norman' structure would have been familiar to a native audience. Despite its continental patron the design of the tower can be related to a pre-Conquest *burh-geat* and, as has been seen, on the eve of the Conquest these display towers served as a marker of lordly rank. Thus what

21

we see at Exeter is not perhaps what might be expected in early Norman England but, importantly, it can be related in turn to a series of later Norman gallery-style gatehouses, such as Sherborne (Dorset) and Ludlow (Shropshire) (Figure 2).

Exeter stands out as an example of how subtle and expressive Norman 'militarism' could be only eighteen months after the battle of Hastings, although it was to all intents and purposes *militarily* ineffectual. Far from being the type of castle we might associate with a hard-nosed military campaign, instead it echoes *English* models of lordly expression and must have been intended to resonate with a native audience; it monumentalised in stone William the Conqueror's claim to be the legitimate heir of Edward the Confessor. As with many urban castles, the tower faces inwards, *towards* the urban population, implying that they were the intended audience.[33] By the twelfth century the castle was described as 'fortified with towers of hewn limestone constructed by the *emperors* [my italics]' and it may not be without significance that the tower resembles the west front of the great medieval emperor Charlemagne's imperial palace at Aachen in Germany.[34] The surviving Roman walls ensured that Exeter might be associated with notions of Empire and *Romanitas*, but there seems to be an additional layer of meaning inherent in the construction of this particular gatehouse. Thus at Exeter we see a curious blend of continuity and change: a dramatic assertion of authority, but what might be termed, in Charles Coulson's phrase, 'peaceable power'.[35]

Castles in the countryside
The extent of castle-building in the countryside in the initial phases of the Norman settlement is extremely difficult to assess. The earliest hint of widespread construction comes from an entry in the *Anglo-Saxon Chronicle* for 1067 when it is recorded that while the king was back in Normandy his lieutenants in England, William Fitz Osbern and Odo of Bayeux, 'built castles far and wide across the country and distressed the wretched folk'.[36] This may be hyperbole on the part of the chronicler, however, as at this time Norman settlement had probably not extended much beyond Wessex and the southern Midlands.[37] As with their urban counterparts, the form taken by early castles in the countryside is a matter of debate, but it is possible that ringworks predominated.[38] This observation stems from the fact that in the areas that first came under Norman influence ringworks apparently outnumber mottes. Examples include Caesar's Camp in Kent, a powerful ringwork sited high on a bluff and dominating the area around Folkestone (Figure 11). In other cases where a motte and bailey castle now stands it can be demonstrated that the motte was a later addition to an earlier enclosure. At Castle Neroche in Somerset (a castle presumed to have been raised in the spring of 1068) the motte was clearly inserted into an existing ringwork.[39] At Goltho in Lincolnshire the existing ringwork was enlarged during the Conquest period and the motte was added later.[40]

Contrary to the idea that the Normans began building motte and bailey castles across the country soon after their arrival, there is the strong likelihood that the construction of mottes (and of castles in general) only took place on a wide scale on both sides of channel in the late eleventh and the twelfth centuries, rather than what we might call the 'Conquest period'. In England, the archaeological evidence suggests a broad chronology of motte-raising over the late eleventh and early twelfth centuries, while in Normandy it seems that mottes proliferated in the generations after the conquest of England.[41] This would seem to suggest that at first there was certainly some degree of continuity of form (if perhaps not of scale) between some castles and thegnly *burhs* during the initial period of the Norman settlement. This did not last, however, and to date, the earliest firm example of the raising of a motte in England is at Winchester. In this case there is good archaeological evidence to suggest that this took place in 1071–72, with the mound an addition to the ringwork castle founded four years earlier.[42] A date in the early 1070s is of some significance since, as explained above, it was at this time that William began the general dispossession of English magnates. Moreover, the king had celebrated Easter at Winchester in the spring of 1070, where he presided over the removal of senior English ecclesiastics and, interestingly, he held a crown wearing.[43] If, as seems likely, the raising of the motte was at least planned at around this time, it could be interpreted as signalling a new drive by William to assert his power by great building rather than direct military effort.

It is also tempting to see the 1070s as the time when castle-building more generally increased in intensity. It was only at this time that the Earldoms of Mercia, Northumbria and East Anglia were opened up to a major influx of Norman nobles as their English earls were removed from power. This suggestion gains some support from the fact that it is also in the 1070s that some monastic houses attempted to gain exemption for their lands from labour services, suggesting that substantial building was taking place.[44] When this castle-building in the countryside is examined, the picture is one of Norman building taking place on a wide scale, but firmly linked to the existing tenurial geography and often related to power structures that were already in place.

Castle siting and distribution

Across the country there are wide variations in both the density and distribution of castles. Some areas were relatively unaffected by castle-building whereas there are marked concentrations in border areas such as the Welsh Marches.[45] The overall distribution of castles has sometimes been explained by reference to strategic military planning, with historians in the immediate post-war period seeking the permanence of Norman victory in networks of castles raised in strategic locations.[46] Such ideas do not bear close examination. Across England and Wales, castles were raised for a variety of social and economic reasons, rather than as a response to one immediate threat that might necessitate a programme of defensive works. Even where high densities exist, for example in the Welsh borders, the evidence points to successive waves of castle

Castles in Context: Power, Symbolism and Landscape, 1066–1500

FIGURE 11. Caesar's Camp, Folkestone, Kent. This castle probably dates from soon after the Conquest and, perhaps like many castles raised at this time, takes the form of a ringwork, rather than a motte and bailey.

construction rather than an organised system of border defence. Thus the neat patterns on distribution maps that seem on first inspection to equate with military planning in fact mask a whole series of decisions and processes.

It is a popular misconception that castles, especially those dating to the Anglo-Norman period, were sited on the highest points of their immediate landscapes. This idea is partly due to an assumption that hill-tops are the 'obvious' place to build fortifications, and also to the fact that the small number that do lie in dramatic locations invite photography and thus appear typical; Beeston in Cheshire (Figure 12) and Corfe in Dorset (Figure 40) are good examples. It should not be thought that the siting of fortifications such as Beeston or Corfe is representative of the majority of castles or necessarily commonplace. Rather, the majority of castles in England and Wales were raised in river valleys and are consequently overlooked by higher ground. While there may be some doubt over whether, in shallow valleys, this seriously inhibited a castle's defensive capacity, in other cases there is little argument that any potential archers would have been presented with a tempting target by virtue of a building's location within the landscape. Furthermore, the Roman treatise on war, *Epitome Rei Militaris* – the most widely read military manual in the medieval period – explicitly states that fortifications should be raised on the highest available ground.[47] The fact that so many castle-builders seem to have ignored this advice suggests that a military rationale for castle siting is misplaced.

The siting of castles makes more sense when viewed within the context of the wider medieval economy and landscape.[48] The castle site represented some level of compromise between the needs to protect property, administer estates and generate revenue. It is for this reason that so many castles lie adjacent to major roads or river crossings. When we are told that a castle 'commands' or 'overlooks' its landscape this should probably be viewed in a social sense rather

Castles, Conquest and Authority

than in the terms of the armchair strategist. When patterns of castles are examined in a local or regional context a number of social and economic factors appear to have had a major impact on siting and distribution, pointing up the inadequacies of reading castle-building after 1066 in terms of military occupation.

Moreover, there is no straightforward correlation between castle-building and population density. Although the raising of castles in towns was intended to guarantee control over regional power centres with local concentrations of population, the majority of people lived in the countryside. In 1086 the most heavily populated region of England was East Anglia and here, somewhat paradoxically, we find the lowest density of castles in the country. In this instance, it is possible that high levels of population, and especially a population characterised by large numbers of freeholders, actually discouraged castle-building.[49] Other factors might influence the distribution of castles; for example, in some shires the landholdings of large ecclesiastical estates seems to have deterred the building of castles. In Hertfordshire, for example, castles cluster in the north-east of the county, away from the area dominated by the holdings of St Albans Abbey. A similar situation seems to have occurred in Suffolk, where the Liberty of Bury St Edmunds restricted the manors available

FIGURE 12.
Beeston Castle, Cheshire. Dramatically sited above the Cheshire Plain, Beeston meets all our preconceptions of what a real castle should look like.

RICHARD PURSLOW

for castle-building in the west of the county.[50] As is only to be expected, castle-building also reflected the distribution of landed estates available to the individual builder. Where magnates had a concentration of manors in a particular county, this would often form the focus for building operations: Ivo Tallibois, for example, held most of his land in Lincolnshire and it was here that he raised a castle at Bolingbroke and founded a priory at Spalding. When spatial distributions of landholding are broken down on a county basis it often reveals why a county possesses a particular number of castles. Thus in Hertfordshire it can be shown that those Normans of the castle-building class who also held significant quantities of land in the county usually built residences on one of their manors, and therefore the number and distribution of castles reflects the tenurial structure of the shire.[51] It is also possible in many cases to demonstrate that the holdings of Norman lords were made up of a core of manors that were themselves part of a pre-Conquest estate. It is thus antecedent structures that go some way to explaining the location of castles raised at this time, rather than the necessities of military strategy.

Benington

The case of Benington in Hertfordshire illustrates many of the wider issues surrounding the building of castles during the Norman settlement. In 1086 Benington was the head of an important barony of 30 knights' fees held by the sheriff of Hertfordshire, Peter of Valognes.[52] The site now consists of a square mound with traces of a bailey to the north-east. A Georgian house and nineteenth-century folly occupy the site, but there are the remains of a flint

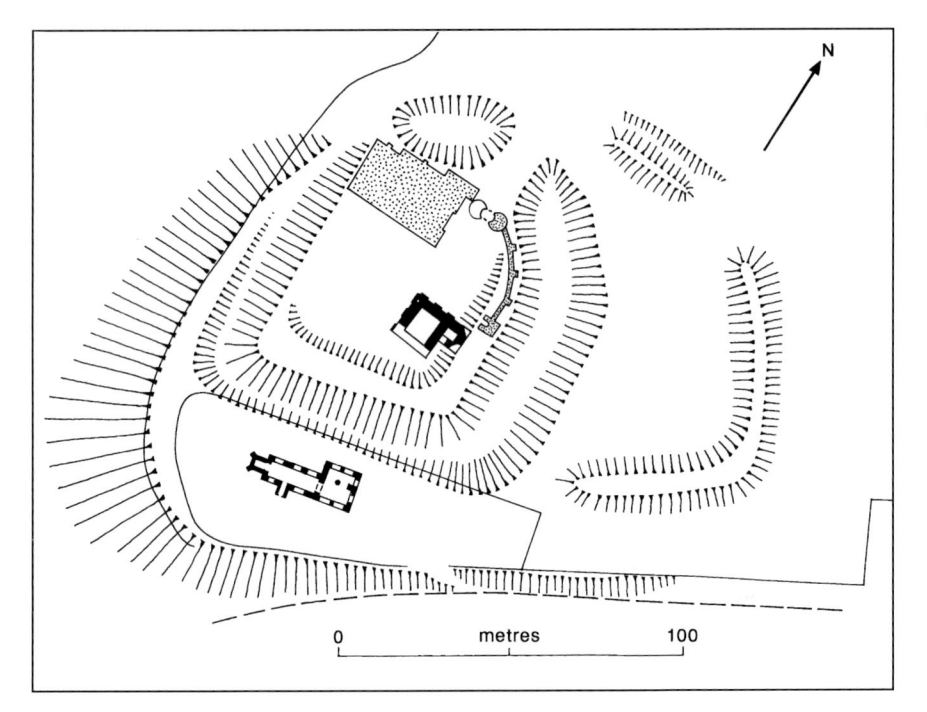

FIGURE 13.
Benington Castle, Hertfordshire. Plan of castle earthworks. After Renn.

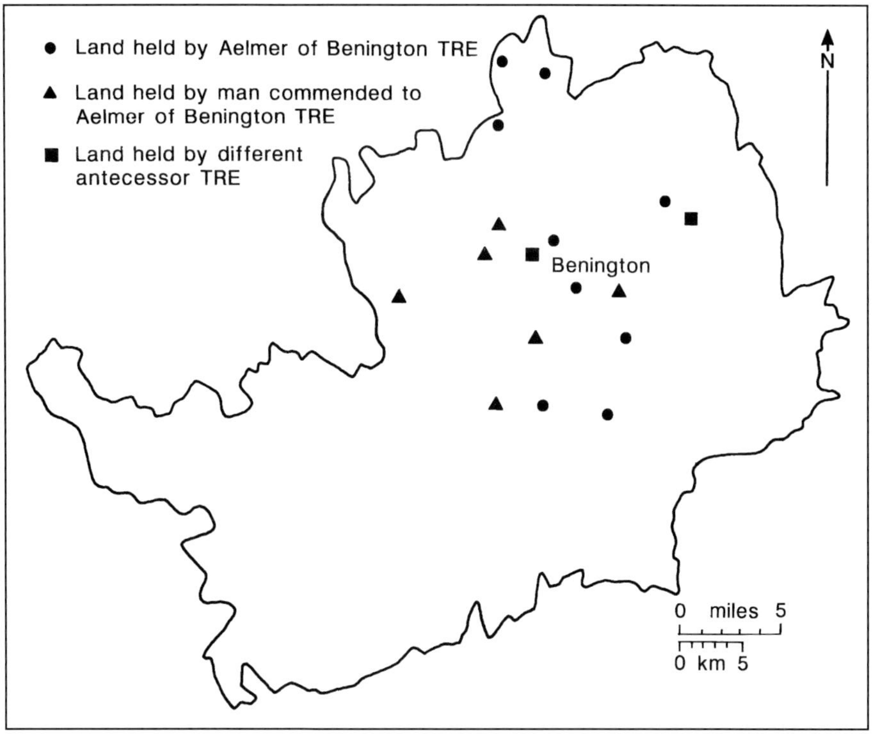

Castles, Conquest and Authority

FIGURE 14. Distribution map of holdings of Peter of Valognes in 1086. The majority of his lands in Hertfordshire had originally formed part of the pre-Conquest estate of Aelmer of Benington.

rubble keep with characteristically Norman 'herringbone' stonework and some ashlar quoins (Figure 13). Although we can be fairly sure that the castle was in place in 1086 it is impossible to know what form it took and how it may have developed over time. The castle clearly had some kind of major stone structure, as in 1177, in the aftermath of rebellion, Henry II ordered '100 picks to cast down the tower at Benington'.[53] The castle was involved in the civil war of John's reign but after this date it ceases to appear in the historical record and was presumably abandoned. Immediately to the south lies the parish church, which was almost certainly in place by 1086, as a priest is mentioned in Domesday Book. Unusually, Domesday Book also records a deer park, and this, together with the high value of the manor (£12) in 1086, clearly indicates Benington's status as an estate centre.[54]

The lands that Peter of Valognes held in the county were themselves formed from an earlier, pre-Conquest estate belonging to a certain Aelmer (Figure 14). Domesday Book reveals that Aelmer himself was of some status. He is explicitly called a 'thane of King Edward's', and was, no doubt, the owner of an aristocratic *burh*. He is also on a number of occasions referred to as 'Aelmer of Benington', a fact of some significance as toponymic names (appellations derived from a place name) were rare in pre-Conquest England, most individuals simply being known by an idionym.[55] That he is found holding in demesne the manor from which he took his name is strong evidence that Benington was indeed the head of the estate and the site of his residence. The

27

Hertfordshire connection for this man is also suggested by the fact that Domesday tells us that his brother (who was also commended to him) held land at nearby Radwell, possibly indicating that the family had their roots in the county. What happened to Aelmer after the Conquest is unknown; he may have been killed in the campaigns of 1066, exiled after the Conquest, or been dispossessed after the English revolt in the 1070s. Either way, the fact that Peter of Valognes held all of Aelmer's land in 1086 and that Benington was chosen as the site of his castle is suggestive of a straightforward take-over of a seigneurial site.

Although the lands that made up the honour of Benington reflected the holding of Peter's *antecessor* (literally, predecessor) it was not simply a case of a neat and tidy exchange of land. In addition to the manors that Aelmer had held himself, a significant number of Peter's holdings had in fact come from men who had been commended to Aelmer of Benington. Thus the manor of Digswell had been held by one Topi, who was Aelmer's man but who, according to Domesday, 'could sell' his land. In pre-Conquest England the bond between lord and man could be, and frequently was, totally separate from land tenure. This was different from Norman practice, in which there was a much closer bond between personal homage to one's lord and land tenure. In the years of the Norman settlement this led to much confusion, as incoming lords took the land of men who had been commended to their *antecessor* by mistake, or disregarded the nuances of English legal practice and took what land they felt they could in the circumstances. Of relevance here is that the honour of Benington reflected an earlier pattern of seigneurial significance: the estate of Aelmer of Benington. Aelmer's status as a King's thegn, his toponym and the close proximity of the castle to the church make it highly likely that Benington was the *caput* of Aelmer's estate and that Peter of Valognes raised his castle over his thegnly predecessor's pre-Conquest manor house.

Antecedent structures

The contention (on the basis of the tenurial geography) that the castle at Benington was raised over a late Saxon defended residence is one which ultimately could only be proved by archaeological excavation. In this respect it is typical of a substantial number of castles that lie scattered across the countryside. This said, there is a limited, but significant, number of early Norman castles where it has been demonstrated by archaeological excavation that they overlie (or in all probability overlie) Late Saxon defended residences. These are distributed across lowland England and their names are familiar to castleologists (mainly because their importance in the present sometimes outweighs their probable significance in the past): Goltho (Lincolnshire), Portchester (Hampshire), Middleton Stoney (Oxfordshire), Sulgrave (Northamptonshire), Trowbridge (Wiltshire), Eynesford (Kent), Castle Neroche (Somerset), Castle Bromwich (Warwickshire) and Castle Acre (Norfolk) all fall into this group.[56] If we take the estimate of *c.* 500 castles in residential occupation around the

FIGURE 15. Castle Camps, Cambridgeshire. The close connection between castles and parish churches probably reflects pre-Conquest arrangements. At Camps, the church stands within the castle bailey.

MICK SHARP

Castles, Conquest and Authority

year 1100 then the number of sites that have been investigated archaeologically is pitifully small. Yet if these sites do represent a typical pattern it would mean that incoming Norman lords actively chose to build their castles in places that were already of some importance, rather than in what we might think of as the best 'tactical' location.

There is also a good deal of circumstantial evidence that this kind of situation was common. At a national level the association between castles and churches is commonplace (Figure 15) and there are hundreds of examples where a parish church lies immediately adjacent to, or has a close spatial relationship with, a manor house, hall or castle. In counties such as Herefordshire, where a large number of churches lie adjacent to castle mottes, it can be assumed that this relationship is at least as old as the twelfth century.[57] In many cases this relationship may well be much earlier, even reflecting a pre-Conquest arrangement. The two centuries before 1066 saw marked changes in ecclesiastical organisation during which large territories served by mother churches or 'minsters' broke down into smaller units served by individual estate churches.[58] In due course these smaller units of ecclesiastical jurisdiction became parishes with the attendant parish church serving the spiritual needs of the local community. Although the precise chronology and nature of this re-organisation is unclear it is beyond dispute that local lords played a significant role in church foundation in the tenth and eleventh centuries. These private or lordly churches – eigenkirke – were invariably situated in close proximity to the seigneurial hall or thegnly *burh*. In most cases the manorial buildings have long since disappeared but where a castle lies next to a church it is highly likely that this signifies an incoming Norman lord raising his castle over an existing *burh* or thegnly residence. If the close relationship between castles and churches represents even a general guide to the level of take-over of existing sites then this would imply two things: firstly, late Saxon lordly residences were already thick on the ground in 1066, and secondly, castle-building after the Conquest represented a massive *replacement* of existing sites.

Building on the past

If this idea of a seigneurial take-over is accurate then the rebuilding of secular residences can be placed in the context of the Norman rebuilding of cathedrals and monastic and parish churches. Whether a fortification or an ecclesiastical structure, the act of building clearly demonstrated to the native English that a new elite had arrived. This was as true for ringworks as for mottes but given the length of time needed to raise a mound (it has been estimated that it could take as much as two years to build a motte and bailey castle) the *continual* demands of labour services must have served to ram the point home.[59] Early examples of monastic houses attempting to gain exemptions from labour services, such as at Battle Abbey in 1070, certainly suggest widespread enforcement.[60] This does mark out the post-Conquest period as unusual: the sheer *scale* of building at this time was unprecedented. In particular, the building of castles by relatively minor tenants pushed up numbers of castles in the post-Conquest decades, something which can be seen very clearly at the Honour of Richmond in Yorkshire. Castle-building across the honour can, like castle-building generally, be broken down into the three stages described above. The central castle was at Richmond itself, but three others (Catterick, Pickhill and Topcliffe) were raised on large demesne manors in each Hundred thus securing an administrative link with existing tenurial arrangements. A further five castles were then built by important knightly tenants.[61] This example can be multiplied across the country, so it is little wonder that English contemporaries complained about the evils of castle-building.

In cultural terms, the rebuilding of an existing centre of authority or social importance was a deeply political act. When a Norman succeeded an English thegn, building on his predecessor's residence was not only an attempt to promote his authority but also to emphasise his legal right to claim the rents and services that tenants now owed to him.[62] This continuity of place was

Castles, Conquest and Authority

clearly extremely important, as in many ways it is impractical to physically destroy existing buildings and construct new ones over their remains. In the pre-Conquest period obligations to upkeep defences ultimately derived from royal rights to labour services. When bookland (a heritable grant guaranteed by written charter) was granted by the crown to individual magnates, the recipient then had the right to appropriate such services for himself. Such duties were rendered at the hall of a thegn concerned and this goes some way to explaining the mechanism by which the ringworks surrounding thegnly *burhs* were constructed. There is the strong suspicion that these Old English obligations for *burh*-work were translated into obligations to work on castles. By discharging their obligations to upkeep earthworks on a new lord's castle the populace were implicitly acknowledging the new incumbent's legal right to the renders concerned, an important aspect of the legitimation process. The fact that lords seem frequently to have eschewed the benefits of a new site in favour of existing centres of local power hints at their anxiety to demonstrate lordly authority in a physical form.

There are also indications from the buildings themselves that castle construction in this period was partly concerned to invoke, or at least provide a link with, the Anglo-Saxon past. On a general level, the idea that castles reflected the (alleged) broader course of the Conquest – that is, an initial 'military' phase, subsequently evolving into a more peaceful state of co-existence and settlement – is not suggested by the architectural evidence. Rather, the opposite seems to be true: castles seem to become *more* military in style the further one moves away from the Conquest.[63] The highest priority for builders in the early post-Conquest years seems to have been the desire to actively and formidably display seigneurial power to a wide audience rather than a concern to pacify and subjugate a potentially hostile population. This demonstration of lordly authority was not so much a simple statement of *military* power, but rather seem to be an assertion of authority using a mixture of traditional and new lordly motifs.

Although the ringwork existed in England prior to 1066 as a form of fortification, the greatest English contribution to the form of early Norman masonry castles was the gate tower. As we have seen, one of the markers of thegnly rank was the entrance tower to the *burh*, the borough gate or *burh-geat*, structures that appear to have been intended for display purposes rather than for military defence. It is significant that elements of the *burh-geat* idea are also found on some early Norman castle entrance towers. This has already been seen in the case of Exeter but similar examples are found at Ludlow (Shropshire) (Figure 2), Richmond (Yorkshire) and Bramber (Sussex). At Ludlow the original gate tower was furnished with a large ground floor entrance and a row of windows, all subsequently blocked (Figure 16). There can be no doubt over the implications of this for any defensive function. As Derek Renn has said, 'the row of windows facing south above the (now blocked) entrance passage may not have been very warlike, and showed an attacker that the wall was weak here, but they did add an impressive feature

Castles in Context: Power, Symbolism and Landscape, 1066–1500

FIGURE 16. Despite its apparently military purpose, the original form of the castle gatehouse at Ludlow can be linked to an Anglo-Saxon tradition of lordly display. The tower was altered later, blocking the ground-floor entrance (the outline of which is still visible).

Castles, Conquest and Authority

to the façade'.⁶⁴ He uses the term 'parade front' for the southern exterior of the structure: a strong martial image, but clearly a long way from any military reality. When we consider that this building is of the late 1080s (the exact date of construction is not clear) and is situated in the border region of Shropshire then a far more complicated picture of the military character of the Norman settlement begins to appear. Much the same can be said for Richmond, where the original entrance tower of *burh-geat* type was later incorporated into a twelfth-century keep. At Bramber a motte was originally raised at the centre of this 'military district' but within a generation the focus of the castle was shifted to an entrance tower of burh-geat character. Within a short space of time, it would seem, the priority of castle-builders had changed from enforcing labour services to displaying lordship.⁶⁵ At Castle Acre in Norfolk a low ringwork bank surrounded the stone residence of William de Warenne and the building itself was so devoid of fortification that the excavator dubbed it a 'country house'.⁶⁶ Clearly we are a long way here from Norman lords resisting the passive hostility of the native English from their fortifications.

Cultural appropriation

Together with the motte itself, the stone keep or *donjon* was also a Norman introduction and formed the centrepiece of William the Conqueror's two largest secular building projects: the White Tower in London and Colchester castle.

FIGURE 17. Colchester, Essex. Colchester was probably the first *donjon* in England and the site of the castle lay on that of the former Roman temple dedicated to the Emperor Claudius. In the design of their most important buildings the Normans readily appropriated images of Imperial authority.

At Colchester the *donjon* was raised directly on the site of a former Roman temple dedicated to the Emperor/God Claudius (Figure 17). The location was probably also the centre of the pre-Conquest royal manor and the decision to build c. 1076 what was to be the largest *donjon* in England was a clear symbolic act of colonisation.[67] Of greater interest is the fact that one of the two pre-Conquest chapels adjacent to the castle was retained. This was dedicated to St Helena and appears to have been the centre of a creation myth linking Colchester with the Iron Age king Cunobelin.[68] Although Colchester was the county town of Essex, why exactly it was singled out for such a huge building project has always been something of a puzzle, but the answer may lie in the idea that this was a dramatic appropriation of cultural authority by the Normans. If 1076 was the date of building then it may also be significant that construction began less than a year after a major rebellion in the region. The fusion of political authority, a Roman past and a mythical founder may have been too irresistible for the Conqueror to pass by without comment.

At the White Tower in London (probably started in 1078) the *donjon* was placed within the earlier ringwork founded in 1066 in the angle of the Roman city wall. The structure appears to have consisted of a basement, an entrance floor, a further floor and a dummy story above giving the appearance from outside of a three-storeyed building.[69] The internal arrangements suggest that the White Tower was effectively a giant ceremonial building containing a series of reception rooms. Rather than being intended to frustrate an intruder, the entry to the building instead appears concerned with creating a grand approach. Access to the building was via an external wooden staircase and the entrance itself comprised an ashlar-built vestibule with wide steps. The whole *ensemble* is reminiscent of entrances to Classical buildings.

The Normans also cultivated the theme of *Romanitas* in other buildings. At Chepstow (Cas-Gwent) in Monmouthshire, similar concerns to those demonstrated at the White Tower seem to structure the arrangement of the early Norman building.[70] Here the great tower was entered via a wooden staircase and passage to the first floor was via a stairway in the wall. The external entrance again seemed to play upon images from Antiquity, with mortar of crushed Roman tile setting off the elaborate gateway. The first floor was made up of a single long room decorated with an arcade of stone niches. The absence of fireplaces or latrines suggests a non-domestic function, but a military interpretation does not seem appropriate either: the entrance is weak and there is no provision for protective archery. Rather, the Great Tower at Chepstow again appears to be connected with some kind of ceremonial function, perhaps as a grand reception room.

Colchester and the White Tower represented building at the highest social level. However, despite the widespread building after 1066, not all Norman settlers raised castles and so we must assume that many of the humblest followers of a lord moved into existing manorial buildings. We must also assume that existing lordly seats and their *burh-geats* continued in use and retained their meaning. One such example was at Cockfield in Suffolk; it was recorded in the twelfth century that there had been a 'wooden belfrey 140 feet high' built by a certain Adam, whose grandfather was an Englishman.[71] At both Sulgrave and Eynesford, archaeological evidence suggests that the stone towers continued in use after the Conquest. Although discussions of the Conquest tend naturally to focus on Norman 'imports' at the highest social level, such as the great tower and the motte, it should be remembered that Anglo-Saxon England had a long traditional of building, especially in wood. It is interesting to note in this context the evidence from twelfth-century stone halls in Normandy which suggests that English styles may have directly influenced styles of hall in the conquerors' homeland.[72]

Conquerors and conquered

While it may be possible to question some of the more overt 'military' explanations of castle-building at this time, the sense of grievance and bitterness on the part of the conquered English should not be underestimated. The case of one Alric at Marsh Gibbon in Buckinghamshire who, it was recorded in Domesday Book, now rented his own land from a Norman, 'wretchedly and with a heavy heart', could doubtless be repeated across the kingdom.[73] Our sources in all likelihood conceal thousands of personal tragedies as individuals were dispossessed of their land and impoverished. At a local level, tensions between Englishman and newcomer in the early years of the settlement found legal expression in the *murdrum* fine, which imposed an amercement on a community when a Norman was found murdered. The stress caused by incomers wishing to secure their title to land by marrying native brides (another legitimisation strategy) is also hinted at on some scale by Archbishop Lanfranc who complained that English women were entering nunneries 'not for love of religious life but from fear of the French'.[74]

A curiously under-exploited source, the *Gesta Herwardi* – 'The Deeds of Hereward' – gives us a vivid picture of the kinds of tensions at a local level at this time.[75] The *Gesta* is an early twelfth-century source that tells the story of the English rebel Hereward, the romantic figure beloved by the Victorians. When Hereward returns to England in the aftermath of the Conquest (conveniently, he was overseas during the events of 1066) and travels to his familial home he finds that his father has been dispossessed, his younger brother killed and there are now Normans living in his familial hall. The local English population are obviously unhappy at the situation but are powerless as the newcomers are there because the 'king has commanded'; presumably the Normans had a writ from the shire court giving them legal title to the land. We can surmise that there must have been many native Englishmen across the kingdom that found themselves in the same situation.

In this context it is worth assessing the levels of lawlessness or violence castles were expected to encounter during the period of the Norman settlement. Major attacks, such as those on York and Montecute in 1069, were rare, and as a deterrent against local violence and a volatile land market the substantial earthworks of a site such as Norman Sulgrave were probably sufficient. Highly instructive here is a document concerning the estates of the Abbey of Ely known as the 'Ely plea', dated to 1071–75 – that is, precisely at the time when castle-building was taking place.[76] Here the Abbot complains that dozens of his manors across four counties had been illegally removed from his jurisdiction. Neighbouring lords had taken timber, crops, livestock and tenurial services – in a general state of upheaval even major barons were taking the opportunity to acquire more than that to which they were perhaps entitled. There is no hint of 'English versus Norman' here; rather this is the kind of situation where strong lordship guaranteed rights regardless of origin. And when it came to signalling the lordly presence in a locality the building of a castle was a potent symbol of occupation.

Other pieces of information can balance the picture of the 'Norman Yoke'. Although sources such as the *Anglo-Saxon Chronicle* greeted castle-building with howls of protest there was no outcry about the Norman policy of rebuilding cathedrals and monastic churches. The only hint of objection in written sources comes from bishop Wulfstan of Worcester who, looking on the new building project at Worcester in the 1080s, commentated that 'we miserable people have destroyed the work of saints, that we may provide praise for ourselves. The age of that most happy man (St Oswald) did not know how to build pompous buildings, but knew how to offer themselves to God under any sort of roof, and to attract to their example their subordinates. We on the contrary strive that, neglecting our souls, we may pile up stones'.[77] It is also the case that once William the Conqueror was crowned he was assured of a degree of loyalty from his subjects. The loyalty of Englishmen to their king was something that provoked comment: the English, it was said, 'were accustomed to obey a king, and wished to have a king as their lord'.[78] Additionally, it should be remembered that there must have been many native English who prospered because of the massive building projects instigated by the Normans. Anglo-Saxon architectural details found on parish churches, castles and cathedrals all suggest the employment of English masons. Examples of Englishmen benefiting from the Conquest need to be placed alongside things like the *murdrum* fine; and indeed, in the case of the latter it is remarkable how soon this lost its original purpose and became a form of tax on the Hundred.[79]

A Norman import?

To some readers, this chapter may have taken an unusual approach to explaining castle-building after the Norman Conquest. It should be stated that some of the arguments expressed here are, to many, very new and controversial. Critics of this approach often say that, taken to its logical conclusion, it would suggest that the Conquest never happened. It would, of course, be folly to even attempt such an argument. Even today, to glance at the urban landscape of Norwich, Durham or Lincoln is to be forcibly reminded of the impact of the Norman invasion. What this chapter has tried to show, however, is that

Castles, Conquest and Authority

the status of the castle and its *raison d'être* during this time are uncertain and complex. When looked at over the course of castle development as a whole, there are some important aspects of continuity. Comments on the debate in the late 1960s over whether the castle was a 'Norman import' have been deliberately omitted until this point, as it is implicit in the argument above that the idea of 'import' is simply a matter of definition. Two pieces of evidence stand in the way of asserting that castles in all but name existed in pre-Conquest England: the *Anglo-Saxon Chronicle* and the *Ecclesiastical History* of Orderic Vitalis.

The first Norman 'castles' in England were those raised by Norman followers of Edward the Confessor during the 1050s and are referred to in the *Anglo-Saxon Chronicle*. Very little is known about these sites; there appear to have been five in total which have been tentatively identified with Clavering in Essex and four sites in Herefordshire: Hereford, Richard's Castle, Ewyas Harold and another as yet unknown site. None of these identifications is secure, and in the case of Ewyas Harold it is unlikely to be correct as it has recently been shown that the land on which the castle was situated was in Wales at this time and it therefore cannot be the castle mentioned in the *Chronicle*.[80] When the English chronicler came to record the construction of a castle in Herefordshire (probably at Hereford) in 1051 he used the foreign word 'castel' to describe the structure with the clear intention of highlighting its alien character: 'The foreigners then had built a castle in Herefordshire in Earl Swein's province, and had inflicted every possible injury and insult upon the king's men in those parts'.[81] If a motte had been raised at Hereford (and it is impossible to know this) this might explain the specific language of the chronicler. Yet this account is more ambiguous that meets the eye. While the chronicler does use a particular word to describe the castle his main concern was to point up the fact that the Normans who built it were in conflict with the king's men in the shire. It was the foreigners who were creating the problem, rather than the structure itself.[82] What may be significant here is that the castle-men were probably interfering with the public administration of the shire from their fortified base – something common on the Continent where aspects of 'public' government were conducted from the seigneurial seat – hence the reference to the insults to the king's representatives. Since the administration of public justice from the seigneurial seat appears to have been extremely rare in Anglo-Saxon England it is perhaps not surprising that we get the *castel* singled out for attention.[83] Indeed, the arrival of the honour court can be seen as a tenurial innovation of the Conquest which meant that some baronial castles did fulfil a different role to their English counterparts.[84]

In his *Ecclesiastical History* of *c.*1125, Orderic Vitalis famously remarked that 'the fortifications called castles by the Normans were scarcely known in the English provinces, and so the English – in spite of their courage and love of fighting – could only put up a weak resistance to their enemies'. Orderic's apparently clear statement is not without its ambiguities. His comments on the almost complete absence of castles appear in a part of his narrative specifically concerning William the Conqueror's campaign through the Midlands in 1068 and applying his reasoning to the national situation in 1066–86 is problematic. It is also possible that Orderic was simply following an earlier account of events given by William of Poitiers in the *Gesta Guillelmi* in which case these remarks should be treated within the context of a piece of writing intended to praise the martial virtues of William the Conqueror. Orderic himself was of mixed Anglo-Norman parentage and familial connections with Shropshire (a shire ravaged by William in 1069) may have led him to offer a simplistic explanation for the events of these years. Moreover, as has been seen, by the time Orderic was writing (*c.* 1125) there had been a rapid increase in the numbers of castles built on both sides of the channel. From the standpoint of the twelfth century when, indeed, large masonry castles were more common features in the landscape, it may well have been reasonable to assume that an absence of castles had been a major factor in the English defeat.

As has been shown here, there is a good deal of evidence to suggest that the Normans, although they might have done things on a grander scale, utilised existing models of lordly expression to legitimise their succession. It might also be useful to apply to England a comment made about another 'military' conquest by the Normans, that of Ireland. Of the Norman settlement there, following 1166, it has been said that 'the men who built castles were primarily showing off the fact that they had the wealth and status that permitted them to build a castle, rather than providing themselves with refuges to he held against local rebellions ... castles ... were the product of lordship, not the means of establishing it because that lordship was not opposed by the whole population.'[85] Such ideas may also be directly relevant to the Norman Conquest of England.

Castles in Context: Power, Symbolism and Landscape, 1066–1500

CHAPTER THREE

Architecture and Power

Introduction

The previous chapter sought to demonstrate that there is not necessarily a straightforward equation between the building of castles and military strategy during the period of the Norman Conquest. In this chapter we will examine aspects of the architectural development of castles and evaluate the motives which led aristocrats to raise fortified residences during the Middle Ages. Here we return to the problem outlined in the introduction to this book and encapsulated by the arguments over Bodiam: are the military features of castles utilitarian in function (i.e. they were intended to facilitate the defence of a castle in the event of a siege), or were they part of an architectural style through which aristocrats attempted to demonstrate their position within society (Figure 18)? To some extent an unnecessary dichotomy has arisen within castle studies on this point, with (to characterise both unfairly) 'militarist' and 'revisionist' schools in disagreement over this issue. To many militarists, the new thinking on castles seemingly neglects the fact that it has always been known and appreciated that castles had a residential purpose, reflected the status of the owner and were capable of sustaining a range of symbolic meanings. To revisionists, the central tenets of the older military tradition seem to persist when what is required is a complete reappraisal of the subject.[1] The argument over this point has led to a highly misleading situation where castles apparently have to belong to one category – 'war' – or the other – 'status'. Discussion of this issue throws into sharp relief a fundamental problem, one that has taxed scholars for the past century: how should a castle be defined? As we saw in the Introduction, in the nineteenth century castles were deemed to belong to the category of 'Military Architecture'. This led them to being defined as 'fortified residences', by default placing an emphasis on the fortification. Not only does this imply a utilitarian purpose for the battlements, murder holes, arrow slits and other 'military' features but it also leads to the judgment that it is possible to separate out those buildings where the fortifications are 'serious' – here we meet the 'Real Castle' – from those where they might be for 'display' – the 'Phoney' or 'Sham Castle'. To attempt such an exercise is ultimately fruitless for a number of reasons. To begin with, it is self-evident that the building of a crenellated wall was obviously concerned with war on some level: its meaning was inherently military, whatever else it could stand for. Moreover, if a battlemented wall was constructed with the aim of advertising social rank, it is still 'functional', regardless of its military potential. For this reason it is confusing to label fortifications where crenellation is obviously decorative as 'sham' or 'false'. What must be emphasised, rather, is the fact that in the medieval period the distinction between 'Real' and 'Phoney' castles *never* existed. In modern English the word 'castle' has become prescriptive and lost the more flexible meaning of the medieval word *castrum* which, to some extent, is retained by the French word *château*. In the Middle Ages the word *castrum* not only applied to those buildings that we might wish to call a castle, but also extended to churches, monasteries, town houses, city walls (Roman and medieval), campaign forts, warships and sixteenth-century artillery forts – a vast array of structures many of which were certainly never intended to be militarily functional.[2] Attempting to separate those castles that are 'Real' from those that are not seriously distorts the ways in which medieval people viewed these buildings and in turn takes us further away from an understanding of what castles might have meant to those who experienced them.

FIGURE 18. Scarborough Castle, Yorkshire. The *donjon* of Henry II overlooking the east coast. Such buildings are now being interpreted as palatial symbols of power rather than military strongholds. The ruined state of the great tower is a result of shelling by German warships during the First World War.

MICK SHARP

Architecture and Power

This chapter will not attempt to narrate in great detail the architectural development of the castle – this would take a book in itself – but instead will aim to show how scholars have readdressed key elements in the 'castle story'. Three elements will be discussed: the changing nature of the Anglo-Norman keep (a time when military castles were on the 'rise'); the Edwardian castles of North Wales (the apogee of castle-building); and the fourteenth and fifteenth centuries (a time when castles were in 'decline').

Noble building

At this point it is worth considering why medieval aristocrats built castles at all. Most obviously, nobles needed somewhere to live and the overwhelming majority of castles were, first and foremost, residences. Aristocratic homes also needed to afford some degree of personal security and this necessitated some kind of defensive circuit, ditch or moat. Both of these requirements could, however, be fulfilled by the construction of a manor house. A castle was something different and the decision to build was a result of a combination of other factors. Castle construction was expensive, and a lord needed a certain level of wealth before he could realistically decide to build. The ability to sustain an aristocratic lifestyle ultimately came from landed resources and lords needed some chief place from which these holdings could be managed. They also needed a place from where the judicial demands of their rank could be exercised. It was perhaps inevitable that one manor (or in the case of the wealthiest more than one manor) would be singled out for importance and would form the focus for a variety of lordly interests, of which great building was only a part. For the wealthiest magnates, the castle was situated at the *caput* or 'head' of a collection of scattered holdings significantly known as the baronial 'honour'. From the eleventh century the highest members of the aristocracy identified themselves very much with particular locations and this often manifested itself in the use of a toponym. Gilbert, son of Richard of Brionne, for example, came to be known as Gilbert de Tonbridge and Gilbert de Clare, where, unsurprisingly, are to be found two of his castles – the first in Kent, the second in Suffolk. To the medieval mind, the castle was therefore far more than a place to live or an administrative centre: it represented and reflected the rank and dignity of the lord.

Although the medieval word *castrum* could be applied to a wide range of buildings, it was ultimately the presence of fortifications that marked out a nobleman's home from other forms of residence. This does not mean, however, that levels of fortification are in any straightforward way 'functional', able to be 'measured', and that the building can thus be ascribed the status of a 'castle'; rather, it needs to be remembered that castles were only *one* form of noble castellated architecture. While most, perhaps all, medieval residences exhibited some form of security against intruders, at some places aristocrats chose to build residences that were effectively unfortified. Royal palaces such as Clarendon or Woodstock lacked substantial defences, as did the residences of the knightly tenantry, such as at Weeting in Norfolk.[3] Had there been any overriding military imperative in medieval England that necessitated the building of fortifications we should expect to see nobles living exclusively in heavily fortified houses and also to see more evidence of defended villages.[4] The fact that we do not demonstrates that when medieval nobles built in a military style they had *chosen* to do so and were doing so, at least in part, for social or ideological reasons.

Whether medieval aristocrats ever drew their swords in anger or not, they believed that it was their God-given duty to fight to defend society.[5] A military ethos permeated secular elite culture throughout the Middle Ages and beyond. It is no surprise, then, that a fitting home for a member of the aristocracy was one which carried the trappings of fortification. Indeed, aristocratic society *demanded* that men of such status owned appropriate residences. In 1150 Cadell ap Gruffudd, prince of Deheubarth, repaired Carmarthen (Caerfyrddin) Castle 'for the strength and splendour of his kingdom'.[6] In the 1130s Bishop Roger of Salisbury instigated a major construction programme of castles because he 'wished to be thought of as a great builder'.[7] It could therefore be contended that men of rank built castles simply because they were expected to do so, or, given the intense competition between lords at this time, because their neighbours did so.

Style and design

Every castle is unique and a host of factors could influence the ultimate design of a building. This is neatly illustrated by the 'Three Castles' in the modern county of Gwent – White Castle, Grosmont (Figure 38) and Skenfrith – all built or rebuilt by the royal justiciar Hubert de Burgh in the early thirteenth century. The motte and bailey at Grosmont was substantially upgraded and provided with an elaborate domestic chamber; at White Castle an existing *donjon* was demolished and the castle rebuilt on a rectangular plan; while Skenfrith was built on a new site and comprised a round *donjon* with a rectangular curtain wall.[8] Each castle took a different form, with the local topography, antecedent structures and no doubt the personal wishes of Hubert all dictating the nature of the new buildings.

One of the most important factors that influenced the final form of a castle was the wishes of the patron. Manuscript illustrations often show kings taking a keen interest in the raising of their castles, and the visits made by monarchs such as Henry II and Edward I to royal building sites attest to the direct supervision of their projects. The pride that such operations could engender is amply demonstrated by Richard I, who was so pleased with the speed with which he was building Château-Gaillard in Normandy that he gathered his entourage on site and harangued them: 'how fair a child was his, this child but a twelve month old!'. The chronicler William of Newburgh was more scornful of the king's attitude to his grand building. He relates how a shower of blood-red rain drenched Richard and his labourers on site but such was the

Architecture and Power

king's desire to see the project to completion 'if an angel had come down out of the sky to bid him stay his hand, he would have got no answer but a curse'.[9] Although the patron probably had the final say in what was, or was not, built, there would have been considerable dialogue with the architect or master builder, and the lord in question probably made the major decisions in consultation with his senior household and counsellors. This element of collective decision-making can be seen in the foundation of Montgomery castle (Figure 19). During the royal expedition against the Welsh in 1223 it was decided that a new castle was to be built at Montgomery to replace the existing motte and bailey (now known as Hen Domen) that had been destroyed by Llywelyn the Great earlier in the year. The royal advisors toured the vicinity and it was suggested to Henry III that 'a suitable spot for the erection of an impregnable castle' was to be found on an outcrop of rock nearly one mile to the southeast. The young king (it was the day before his sixteenth birthday) agreed and the castle of (New) Montgomery was raised on the elevated site.[10] Such an interest in building operations could have its drawbacks, however: in 1085 Walter de Lacy was killed when he fell from the scaffolding while inspecting the building of a new church at Hereford.[11] The keen interest aristocrats undoubtedly had in the appearance of their buildings does also serve to illustrate an important wider issue. Nobles had far too much invested and took too much interest in their castles to make mistakes. They may have encountered structural problems whilst building (as happened at Norwich when the *donjon* started to collapse when the motte subsided) but any major military deficiencies we might find in castles are highly unlikely to be the result of casual errors.

It should also not be thought that nobles necessarily needed permission from the king in order to build a castle. This idea does have a long pedigree in castle-studies, where it has been supposed that, since castles were dangerous instruments in the hands of robber barons, monarchs must have taken steps to limit their construction.[12] This was seemingly evidenced by 'licences to crenellate', documents issued by the crown that appear to dispense the right to fortify. For example, at Moccas in Herefordshire the king granted licence in 1293 to Hugh de Frene to: 'strengthen his house of Mockes, co. Hereford, with a wall of stone and lime, without tower or turret and to crenellate it so that the wall below the crenellation be ten feet high'.[13] While the control monarchs retained over castle-building in the Anglo-Norman period is still open to debate, detailed work on licences to crenellate has undermined the idea that they represented a policy on the part of monarchs to restrict the building of fortifications.[14] To begin with, there were very few refusals by the crown to those who sought such licences; indeed, they seem to have been relatively easy to obtain, hardly suggesting that the crown was actively policing the spread of baronial fortification. Alongside secular magnates, urban corporations and religious establishments also received licences for town walls and monastic precincts – scarcely dangerous structures that needed restriction. Licences granted rights other than fortification: to markets, fairs and mills,

FIGURE 19 (*left*). Montgomery castle, Montgomeryshire. Montgomery offers a rare insight into the planning that took place before commencing a large building project. In this case, the king's chief officials toured the local countryside seeking out a suitable location for the new castle before making their recommendation to the young Henry III.
© CLWYD-POWYS ARCHAEOLOGICAL TRUST

FIGURE 20 (*right top*). Stokesay castle, Shropshire. Raised by wool merchant Lawrence de Ludlow at the end of the thirteenth century, Stokesay was carefully sited in its landscape in order to maximise its visual impact.
MICK SHARP

none of which was prescribed by the crown. Moreover, important baronial castles such as Beeston (Figure 12) or Bolingbroke (Lincolnshire) never received licences and on other occasions the recipient of a grant seems never to have built at all. When it is considered that the bulk of recipients were aspiring gentry the purpose of licences as emblems of aristocratic status, indicative of an affinity with the king, becomes clear. Once issued, such licences were read aloud at public venues such as the shire court where the assembled county community could thus contemplate the rise of one of their neighbours. The actual licence would then no doubt be given pride of place at the recipient's new building. At Cooling castle in Kent this proclamation was physically manifested on the castle itself, where a copper impression of the licence was built into the outer face of the gatehouse declaring that 'I am made in help of the country'.[15] A licence to crenellate was thus a result of a successful petition by individual wishing not only to monumentalise their achievements in architectural form, but who also desired the extra cachet of an affinity with the king couched in the language of royal permission to build. The decision to build, the style in which to build and the site that was chosen were all bound up with the identity of the lord in question.

Stokesay

A site that brings these general issues into focus is Stokesay castle in Shropshire.[16] Stokesay was largely rebuilt at the end of the thirteenth century by the successful wool merchant Lawrence de Ludlow who, in 1291, obtained

FIGURE 21 (*right*). The South Tower, Stokesay castle, Shropshire. The tower took its inspiration from larger castle gatehouses such as those raised by Edward I in Wales in the previous decade.

a licence to 'build and crenellate his manor of Stokesay with a wall of stone and lime'. The resultant building was originally surrounded by a water-filled moat and the subsequent lowering of the curtain wall has meant that it has lost some of its martial appearance (Figure 20). The defining architectural feature of the castle is the south tower, which is based on a complex geometric pattern of an octagon and two dodecagons. The tower is crenellated and there are arrow slits between the merlons (at this date these would have represented the most modern military technology), but this belligerent image is partially offset by the large symmetrically arranged windows, the significance of which is only fully apparent from the outside.

The arrangement of the castle, and the south tower in particular, makes a good deal of sense when viewed from the original approach route to the castle from nearby Ludlow, from where Lawrence took his name. Stokesay castle occupies a prominent location alongside the main Ludlow to Shrewsbury road, ensuring that the tower stood out as a landmark. The main approach would have taken the visitor along a raised causeway flanked on either side by a series of fishponds. When the south tower is viewed from this direction the symmetrical plac-

45

ing of windows makes perfect visual sense and it would have appeared as a smaller version of a much larger castle gatehouse, specifically those of the royal castles such as Caernarvon (Caernarfon) or Denbigh (Denbych) in North Wales built by Edward I a decade earlier (Figure 21). There is also some indication that the stones were originally banded in order to heighten the visual effect, again something seen at Edwardian castles in Wales. The provision of a wet moat could only heighten this dramatic image further, as the reflection of the gatehouse in the water would have given the impression of greater strength. From here the visitor would pass the main hall block, again with symmetrically arranged windows. They would have then passed, via the parish church, round to the gatehouse before being granted entry. On arrival, the most striking feature is not a formal courtyard with ranges of buildings but rather a classic medieval manor house. Whether this was an anticlimax from the point of view of the medieval visitor is difficult to say, but it is clear that more effort seems to have gone into how the building looked from outside. It is sometimes thought that the idea of a 'show front' or 'entrance façade' was only invented during the sixteenth century. Stokesay demonstrates that this is not the case, and that such architectural design existed centuries before the Renaissance.

The domestic character of Stokesay has been explained in the past with reference to a decrease in the levels of military tension in the borders following the Edwardian conquest of North Wales. The fact that Lawrence chose to build in a military *style* seems to be a particularly clear example of a man wishing to project his credentials as one of 'those who fought' (that is, a true aristocrat). Of most interest, however, is the fact that he chose to build a tower whose closest affinities were at Caernarvon and Denbigh; of all the possible designs he could have chosen Lawrence actively chose to associate himself with Edward I and the royal dignity. This discussion of Stokesay does point up the problems in trying to fit a castle's architectural form into the artificial categories of 'war' or 'status'. The building was clearly intended to serve as a residence, yet its tower also exhibited some of the most sophisticated military technology of the age. There was clearly nothing incongruous about placing such a tower alongside a conventional domestic hall. Despite some of the architecture, there is no reason, then, to interpret Stokesay as a military building.

However, it could be contended that Stokesay is a bad example with which to illustrate the revisionist case: it is a relatively minor site and was only referred to as a castle in the sixteenth century. A more interesting issue is raised by the application of the same logic to other castles which were indeed raised by great lords with massive disposable wealth, who certainly did take their military role in society seriously. The great stone towers of the Anglo-Norman aristocracy – keeps – are a case in point.

The debate over keeps

The idea that the word 'keep' is in some way associated with keeping people out (or locked in) is a relatively modern innovation. The word was coined only

Architecture and Power

towards the end of the Middle Ages and is probably derived from the Middle English word *kipe* or 'coup': English troops in France during the Hundred Years war apparently likened the shape of the round tower at Guines near Calais to that of a wooden barrel.[17] Prior to the use of the word keep, such buildings were commonly referred to simply as 'towers', more specifically the 'great tower' or *donjon*. Our modern word 'dungeon' is a corruption from the medieval *donjon* and the unpleasant connotations that the word conjures up today were not present in the Middle Ages. Rather, *donjon* was derived from the Latin *dominarium*, meaning 'lordship', which explicitly linked the structure with the authority of the builder. When we apply the words 'dungeon' and 'keep' to the great towers of castles we are inevitably placing our own preconceptions onto buildings of a very different age.

It is easy to see why keeps have acquired the status of 'places of last resort'.[18] Even today, many are impressive buildings that frequently retain an intimidating atmosphere. Now devoid of their external decoration, and with their grim battlements and thick walls, keeps often have a blunt, austere edge. The medieval castle keep seems to belong to the period when castles really were military buildings and they have, historically, come to epitomize the 'real' castle (Figure 18). Indeed, the development of the keep in the twelfth century is a central part of the castle 'story' outlined in the Introduction. At the risk of neglecting some of the nuances, the long-established story of the keep in England and Wales has been written in the following way.

The earliest keeps in England, such as Colchester, the White Tower and Norwich, were essentially tools of occupation. They were solid, square, stone-built edifices, difficult to capture and owing their existence to the need of the Norman kings to pacify the kingdom in the wake of their successful conquest. The square design had one main weakness, however: the corners. These were vulnerable to mining, picking and boring and a square design also restricted the visibility of any defending force attempting to drop missiles or shoot arrows at an attacker. From about the middle of the twelfth century experiments were made in order to correct this problem. There was therefore a 'transitional' phase where new ideas on defence developed alongside older traditions. One of the most celebrated transitional buildings is Orford castle in Suffolk, built in 1165 by Henry II (Figure 22). Here, the great tower incorporated an innovative polygonal core, which ameliorated some of the problems of square corners, but retained older features such as the three square buttresses that clasp against the central polygon. After some time, the problem of square corners was resolved and from about the year 1200 circular towers, such as Pembroke (Penfro), became the norm. However, by this date the Anglo-Norman keep had already gone into decline; defensive apparatus and domestic accommodation began to move out towards the gatehouse and the outer curtain, and as early as the late twelfth century a major castle such as Framlingham in Suffolk could be built without a tower to advertise the lord's status. The thirteenth century saw the development of elaborate gatehouses and concentric defences, trends that eventually reached a high point with the

Castles in Context: Power, Symbolism and Landscape, 1066–1500

FIGURE 22. Orford castle, Suffolk. Henry II's great tower has been interpreted in the past as a 'transitional' keep, marking the shift from square to rounded military designs. The unique form of the tower is more likely to stem from the desire of Henry to express his kingship: the building takes its inspiration from Byzantine palaces.

castles of Edward I. The place of the keep in the 'castle story' was well and truly over.

The sea-change in approaches to the castle in general, together with reappraisals of some key buildings, means that this argument is no longer tenable. Quite *why* this is the case is of some importance and the revisionist arguments over the keep are critical to our understanding of castle development across the whole medieval period, since if it can be shown that keeps were emphatically *not* raised for utilitarian military purposes (and it should be said that this is still contested) then a central – and arguably the most important – plank of the traditional military interpretation of castles is removed. However, despite the work of scholars in this particular field, the idea that the castles of the Anglo-Norman period were primarily military in purpose is still deeply rooted

Architecture and Power

FIGURE 23.
The fourteenth-century keep at Clun, Shropshire.

in historiography and the idea of a 'military' phase of castle-building up to the year 1300, followed by decline thereafter, retains its potency.

The most serious problem with the scheme of *donjon* development outlined above is that the proposed change from square to round designs over the course of the twelfth century due to the demands of siege warfare simply does not fit the known chronology of building. The first rounded *donjon* in England was raised *c.*1146 at New Buckenham in Norfolk. While new to England, such as a design was not quite so innovative in a European context, as experiments with cylindrical designs and their variants were being made in the 1120s and 1130s, most notably at castles such as Gisors in the Vexin in France. We might therefore expect square towers to fall out of favour at about this time. Additionally, if magnates were capable of building fully-fledged rounded towers from the first quarter of the twelfth century, there is seemingly no need for a 'transitional' style: the 'improved' design was already available. If we examine the form of *donjons* from the mid twelfth century onwards a clear change from square to round is precisely what we do not see, even at the highest social level. Square *donjons* continued to be constructed after this date and can be found at, amongst other places, the royal castles of Newcastle, Scarborough and Dover. The 'transitional' tower at Orford, therefore, cannot be anything of the kind. Henry II was already aware of rounded keeps prior to 1165, when he raised Orford, and he continued to build square towers for a further ten years after this date. Furthermore, the construction of four-cornered towers continued for centuries after the Anglo-Norman period, as fourteenth-century castles such as Clun (Shropshire) clearly attest (Figure 23).

A further problem over the military function of *donjons* comes from analysis of the buildings themselves, which reveals some alarming deficiencies. To begin with, even when allowing for the reduced defensibility of square towers, some were built to extremely poor military designs. The inclusion of the three clasped buttresses on the *donjon* at Orford in fact multiplies the number of corners. This is compounded by their location in relation to the rest of the building, which results in several blind spots that would have compromised an effective defence. Any defending archer would have had to lean right out over the battlements in order to attempt a shot. The dangers of such acrobatics aside, this would have left him highly vulnerable to enemy fire. Moreover, the buttresses themselves contain chambers that reduce the thickness of the walls and leave them susceptible to bombardment. The problems caused by a multiplicity of corners are not confined to Orford. Conisborough in Yorkshire is a remarkably elegant *donjon* of *c.* 1190 but its design incorporates no fewer than twelve corners on its exterior buttresses and there is no provision for archery. At Trim castle in Ireland, the magnificent great tower of Hugh de Lacy (probably started *c.* 1175) has a multiplicity of square corners and an entrance on the ground floor. While there are arrow loops they offer no co-ordinated flanking fire and their design actually appears to *invite* attack at that point.[19]

The catalogue of the military deficiencies of the Anglo-Norman *donjon* could be extended at tedious length. Put simply, while some aristocrats may have favoured rounded keeps over the course of the twelfth and thirteenth centuries this was certainly not due to the fact that builders had finally realised the best 'military' form for their great towers. In addition, it should be noted that listing the perceived deficiencies of great towers in this way cannot be considered academic nit-picking: designing a building with the features outlined here could, and did, compromise a defence. This can be illustrated by examples from the period itself. In 1139 at Torrington in Devon, intruders captured William Fitz Odo after throwing flaming torches through the windows of a tower.[20] At Norwich, there is evidence for fire damage on the keep, best interpreted as the result of action either in 1173 or 1216; in either case, it cannot be accidental that this is only found on one of the weakest sections of the wall and where the design of the building shielded an attacker

Castles in Context: Power, Symbolism and Landscape, 1066–1500

Architecture and Power

from view. Modern experiments on the effectiveness of the arrowloops at White Castle in Monmouthshire have also demonstrated that even an inexperienced archer could shoot arrows through the loops to the defender behind.[21] If this were the case with specially designed arrowloops then the presence of large windows on buildings such as Castle Hedingham (Essex), Castle Rising (Norfolk) or Restormel (Cornwall) would have represented potentially serious weaknesses. There is no doubting the fact that immense resources went into the building of *donjons* in this period, or that the problems identified by castle scholars are real, not imaginary.[22] If not for primarily for defence, what was the purpose of the *donjon*?

Courtly choreography

The *donjons* of the eleventh and twelfth centuries are an eclectic collection of buildings and it is unhelpful to view them as a coherent body of structures that all shared a similar purpose.[23] However, despite the obvious differences between them it is possible to discern some common themes that appear to have been of importance to those in a position to build stone towers over this period. Much recent work has sought to illuminate the ways in which *donjons* were accessed by visitors and how their internal spatial arrangements reflected the concerns of the builder and the hierarchy of medieval lordship. It is now possible to see an element of theatricality or 'choreography' in the ways in which some *donjons* served to reinforce the power of their owners.

It was demonstrated in the previous chapter that the design of the great towers at White Tower and Chepstow seemed to be part of an attempt to create a particular impression to anybody entering the building. This can also be seen at a number of other castles dating to the eleventh and twelfth centuries. The exterior of the great tower at Norwich (*c.* 1090) comprised a highly complicated arrangement of blind arcading that served no military purpose but which help make the building one of the most ambitious secular architectural projects in western Europe.[24] Particularly innovative was the construction of the 'forebuilding', a stone stairway and entrance tower that led up to the first floor. The forebuilding has often been seen as a defensive feature that provided an opportunity for defenders to kill any intruder before they could gain access to the main building. At Norwich, due to the elaborate architectural decoration, some kind of a ceremonial entrance-way seems a more likely explanation. The route into the keep took the visitor up the forebuilding stairs, after which entry to the great hall was marked by a heavily decorated and geometrically complex arch and doorway. Marking the entrance arch are decorated capitals and voussoirs representing various scenes and motifs including hunting, mythical beasts and fighting men. A further arch frames this Romanesque riot, but unusually, adjacent to the main door is a smaller blind arch that is simply left plain. Although it is impossible to be sure, it has been suggested that this is intended to evoke the image of Roman city gateways. When it is remembered that the patron of Norwich keep was William

Rufus, a monarch noted for the largesse and splendour of his court, the Classical image presented to guests entering the building is clearly intended to make a political statement. The most sophisticated design faced the main approach road from London.

At other places a more intimidating approach to the lordly presence appears to have been specifically engineered. This was certainly the case at Castle Hedingham in Essex (Figure 24). Hedingham was the seat of the de Vere family and the *donjon* was raised *c.*1142, probably in celebration of the

Castles in Context: Power, Symbolism and Landscape, 1066–1500

FIGURE 24. Castle Hedingham, Essex. The great tower raised *c.*1142 for Aubrey III de Vere. Recent work on the building has suggested that it served primarily a ceremonial purpose, a magnificent and intimidating setting for seigneurial ritual.

elevation of Aubrey III de Vere to the earldom of Oxford.[25] The tower itself is a beautifully-preserved structure of high quality ashlar and comprises a basement, a hall at first floor level and a main hall at second floor level that rose through two storeys, allowing a gallery. A further dummy storey hid the roof and gave greater visual impact when the *donjon* was viewed from outside, as this level exhibited the most elaborate fenestration. Entrance was at first floor level (the forebuilding was added later; as originally executed the entrance was entirely undefended) into the lower hall. Those inside could restrict access to the upper hall and anybody wishing to gain access would have to climb another staircase. They would have entered the upper hall via a straight wooden stair, an approach that ensured that they encountered the lord at a social disadvantage: while entering, the visitor was physically below him and, one they were in the hall, they would have been confronted by the host on his throne and silhouetted against a fireplace. The gallery above this room could also be reached via the main staircase, allowing visitors to gaze down on whatever activity was going on in the main hall below. The architectural decoration of the doorways suggests that guests were intended to circulate along a specific route and were thus permitted to appreciate what was going on below, while at the same time being denied participation. It is instructive here to think of the supposed military purpose of the *donjon*: at Hedingham anybody breaking in would have been able to move up into the upper levels and then pour fire down onto the defenders in the upper hall. The *donjon* at Hedingham therefore seems to have been a giant ceremonial building comprising two sets of reception rooms. As intimated above, the key ceremony for which it may have been built was the reception of the new Earl of Oxford.[26] By building such a structure at the old family *caput*, Aubrey de Vere was not only demonstrating his elevation to the peerage, but was marking out his rise with reference to a long established tradition of noble building.

Recent work on castles such as Orford and Hedingham has completely demolished the idea that the *donjon* was primarily designed for defensive purposes. To affirm that they were would be to suggest that kings and magnates made colossal military mistakes time and time again. Given the importance of these structures, this is pushing credence too far: their design was too important and their construction too expensive to be left to chance. In the case of towers such as Hedingham, the absence of domestic accommodation or services suggests that a ceremonial function was uppermost in the mind of the builder. In others, such as Castle Rising, the presence of a kitchen within the tower suggests a more residential role. It would be unwise, however, to apply too dogmatically modern notions of 'residence' and 'ceremony' to these buildings.[27] The exact domestic habits of the households of eleventh and twelfth century nobles are not entirely clear and in practice medieval men and women may not have drawn so sharp a distinction between the two as we might think. There is little doubt, however, that only a small proportion of people could even contemplate building a great tower. The *donjon* was an important marker of noble dignity and this may be why social climbers built some of the finest examples. It is probably not accidental that towers such as Hedingham, Rising and Conisborough appear to have been constructed immediately, or soon after, their *arriviste* patrons acquired earldoms or had made favourable marriages. If we extend this logic, it might help explain the thinking of the patron of Colchester and the White Tower: Duke William of Normandy was perhaps the greatest *arriviste* of his generation.

If the *donjon* is considered a badge of arrival then it becomes possible to consider the probable motives of the builder. The apparently militarily-outdated design of the towers at Dover, Newcastle or Scarborough is rendered intelligible when it is thought that Henry II may have been appropriating the image of his Norman ancestors when he chose to construct *donjons* reminiscent of the White Tower. This seems very different to his thinking at Orford (Figure 22). Here the design of the tower embodies a range of sophisticated cultural meanings articulated through classically-inspired entrances and windows, with the whole ensemble intended to invoke an eastern tradition of palace building with associations of cosmic kingship and spiritual authority. When construction began in 1165, Henry II was embroiled in his struggle with Thomas Becket, and such imagery on a royal castle must have been particularly potent. This is different again to the image his son Richard I wished to project at Château-Gaillard in Normandy. This is of some interest as the castle is often (due to aspects of its design and the famous siege of 1204) characterised as a military stronghold. In fact, the *donjon* comprised two rooms, an anteroom and an audience chamber, the window in the latter seemingly intended to frame a throne. As at Hedingham, the approach and entrance to the audience chamber left Richard Coeur de Lion's visitors at a distinct social disadvantage.[28] Explaining some alarming military defects at Château-Gaillard (the castle is built on soft chalk and there does not appear to have been a well) is rendered unnecessary when it is considered as a visible statement of Angevin intent to reassert lordship over lost territories. The provision for the probable throne room underlines the castle's political purpose and its name – 'saucy castle' – needs little refinement.[29]

Castles of chivalry

A discussion of the purpose of the *donjon* illustrates the close link between the building of castles and the wider political ambitions and standing of individual medieval aristocrats. The desire to create magnificent edifices that embodied a range of cultural aspirations did not diminish after 'the age of the keep' and is apparent in the castles raised by Edward I during his conquest of Wales in the late thirteenth century.

This group of castles, forming a so-called 'ring of stone' around the kingdom of Gwynedd, have rightly been held up as some of the finest ever built in the British Isles during the Middle Ages. Caernarvon castle boasts some of the most complex arrow loops to be found anywhere and Harlech and Beaumaris are both concentric fortifications, the latter with near perfect

Architecture and Power

symmetry. All these features are suitable architectural attributes for castles raised by one of England's greatest warrior kings for the purposes of subduing a hostile and foreign population. Many of the assumptions about Edward's building programme can be summed up by Richard Morris's apt comment that 'the impression is firmly given of an elite group of men-of-war, long-standing comrades in arms of the king, indulging in an orgy of military architectural expression on an almost unlimited budget'.[30] There is surely not much room for reinterpretation or revisionism here, despite the concessions made to domestic comfort (Figure 25).

The way in which Edward set about imposing his authority on North Wales by great building bears some comparison with the themes surrounding the Norman Conquest discussed in the previous chapter. The boroughs established at Flint (Fflint), Rhuddlan, Aberystwyth, Conway (Conwy), Caernarvon, Criccieth (Cricieth), Harlech and Beaumaris illustrate that the economic role of the castle was still of importance at the end of the thirteenth century. The appropriation of existing administrative or culturally-significant sites again appears central to the mechanism of settlement. Edward's determination to stamp his mark on the landscape was signalled by his attempt in 1281 to transfer the bishopric of St Asaph to his new castle and town at Rhuddlan. Although ultimately unsuccessful, Edward was prepared to spend whatever was required to move the entire ecclesiastical establishment to a new location, and he offered one thousand marks towards the building of a new cathedral.[31] Conway (Figure 42) witnessed a more aggressive act of cultural requisition. The abbey of Aberconwy, not only the largest Cistercian house in North Wales but also the burial place of the Welsh hero Llywelyn the Great, occupied the chosen site for the castle and town. The monks were evicted and their house moved some eight miles up the valley towards Snowdonia. Their abbey church was retained, however, and became the parish church for Edward's new borough. A preliminary draft of the Statute of Rhuddlan (a royal declaration that extended English law to Wales and effectively proclaimed Wales' annexation) indicates that originally Conway was to be the centre of Edwardian government in North Wales; the occupation of the resting place of one of the most famous Welsh princes was surely intended as a symbolic act of colonisation.[32] Similar thinking lay behind the decision to take timbers from the native Welsh castles in the region for use in the construction of Caernarvon. As mechanisms of settlement (rather than tools of conquest) the Edwardian castles were just as effective as their Norman counterparts two centuries earlier. When it comes to evaluating the status of these buildings it would be foolish to deny that they were raised as part of a determined, and ultimately successful, military effort by Edward I to bring to an end the independence of the Princes of Gwynedd, the last native Welsh dynasty. However, it is far too simplistic to see Edward's 'ring of stone' in straightforward military terms.

The influence of Edward's master builder, the Savoyard Master James of St George, has often been seen as being responsible for the distinctive architectural design of the royal castles. While there are undoubtedly some common

FIGURE 25.
Rhuddlan, Flintshire: Edward I's magnificent concentric castle raised after the first Welsh war in 1277. The castle was furnished with a large garden for Queen Eleanor of Castille, consisting of 6,000 blocks of turf and enclosed with staves from barrels.

elements between the castles in North Wales and those in Savoy, as Nicola Coldstream has recently pointed out, in other respects these buildings are very *English* in design.[33] When it comes to the some of the most characteristic elements, such as the twin towered gatehouses, there are greater stylistic parallels with castles such as Tonbridge in Kent or Caerphilly (Caerffili) in Glamorgan. Master James may have been employed more for his skills in organising the domestic ranges than for the provision of the most up-to-date military technology. This suggestion is certainly supported by the spatial arrangements of the domestic ranges. At Beaumaris, for example, the most 'perfect' example of medieval military science, there was provision for a maximum of eleven separate households; to contemporaries it may have appeared more like a palace, rather than a tool of war.[34] Furthermore, when compared to the castles built by native Welsh lords, such as Dolwyddelan (Figure 26) or Dolbadarn, those of the English king are in a totally different league. The Kingdom of Gwynedd may have been a hard nut to crack, but fortresses of lesser status could have enforced the English conquest. Edward's castles represented such extreme measures that further explanation is required.

It has long been known that there was an additional layer of symbolism to Edward's castle-building, especially at Caernarvon (Figure 27). In the 1960s, Arnold Taylor drew attention to the eagles that adorn the merlons on the principal tower and the banding of coloured stones on the southern exterior walls.[35] These are without doubt related to Imperial imagery: the eagles a symbol of the Roman Empire and the banded stones and polygonal towers imitating the walls of Constantinople. Caernarvon was also the site of the

FIGURE 26. Dolwyddelan, Caernarvonshire. Built by the Princes of Gwynedd, Dolwyddelan was captured by English forces in 1283 during the Edwardian Conquest. The castles built by Edward I dwarfed those of the native Welsh aristocracy.

MICK SHARP

FIGURE 27. Caernarvon castle, Caernarvonshire. The banded masonry and polygonal towers were intended to invoke images of an Imperial past. For Edward I, the castle was also an expression of his interest in Arthurian legend and his chivalric ambition.

Roman fort of Segontium, which appeared in the Welsh saga the *Mabinogion*, and so the construction of a castle actively linked Edward with native Welsh mythology. More recently Richard Morris has taken this analysis further and examined Caernarvon as a work of art, along with the ideals that may have influenced its form.

Specifically, Caernarvon can be related to the chivalric culture of Edward I's court, particularly the well-known interest that the king had in Arthurian Romance. From the twelfth century it was believed that King Arthur was the grandson of the Roman Emperor Constantine and Caernarvon's link with Constantinople was strengthened when the body of Magnus Maximus (in legend Constantine's father) was found when work began on the castle. Edward also received the mythical crown of Arthur from the Welsh and in 1284 he held an Arthurian court at Nefyn on the Lleyn peninsular, where the king played Arthur and his household dressed up as knights of the Round Table. Such concerns seem to have played a key role in determining the eventual form of Caernarvon.

This is certainly suggested by the gatehouse, the design of which is based on three octagons placed in a triangle. Above the exterior gate a statue of the king looks out over the town and any visitor wishing to enter the castle would need to negotiate five sets of doors and pass under six portcullises. Such an arrangement far surpasses military necessity and instead seems to come straight from Arthurian literature. The gatehouse is different from the eagle tower, where the design was based on a decagon with hexagons and octagons for the smaller chambers. The complexities of the geometry, together with the decorative elements, suggest a strong concern with how the castle was experienced; it is a building that is intended to surprise and delight. Caernarvon might well be a supreme example of medieval military architecture, but it is also 'an Arthurian castle in all but name'.[36]

The later medieval castle – an age of decline?

The two centuries following the Edwardian building in Wales have often been characterised as a period when the castle went into decline. Of course, this is decline in martial terms: it was supposedly during this time that castles finally gave up any meaningful military role and eventually evolved into the country house. By the sixteenth century noblemen lived in mansions that carried decorative, rather than 'functional', crenellations. As has been demonstrated in this chapter, there is now good evidence for questioning the military rationale of castles up to the year 1300, which renders this concept of military decline thereafter somewhat redundant. Scholars are now inclined to see the fourteenth and fifteenth centuries as a time of continued development, with architectural elements being refashioned and reinterpreted for contemporary purposes.[37] Certainly the striking visual appeal of castles such as Warwick (Warwickshire), Bolton (Yorkshire), Nunney (Somerset), Saltwood (Kent) or Herstmonceux (Sussex) does not leave the impression of a form of noble

Architecture and Power

building that was slowly becoming outdated or losing its social meaning. Although their outward appearance sometimes may suggest a clear residential purpose, the castles of the fourteenth and fifteenth centuries are just as much 'real castles' as their twelfth- and thirteenth-century counterparts.

In terms of architectural form, many of the distinctive elements of the later medieval castle represented variations on traditional themes. This is perhaps most obvious in the case of the great tower. The 'age of the keep' did not end in the early thirteenth century; rather, the construction of great towers carried through to the fourteenth and fifteenth centuries, as at Flint (Fflint) in Flintshire, Knaresborough (Yorkshire), Clun (Shropshire), Southampton and Tattershall (Lincolnshire). The last is a four-storeyed brick-built tower raised by the royal treasurer Ralph, Lord Cromwell, and probably comprised an lower reception hall and an upper private hall, an arrangement little different from some Anglo-Norman towers (Figure 4).[38]

Although the fourteenth and fifteenth centuries saw a continuation of the idea that a tower was a fitting visual focus for the noble residence, this period also saw some important changes in design. Perhaps the most obvious is the development of what is often termed the 'courtyard' or 'quadrangular castle'. This comprised a courtyard around which were ranged the great hall and ancillary buildings such as kitchens, chambers and lodgings. While similar arrangements can be found at some late twelfth- and thirteenth-century castles, it was only in later centuries that the provision for the domestic ranges became fully integrated into the main design. These developments obviously reflected wider changes in medieval society and part of the explanation lies not in the changing demands of warfare, but in the nature of aristocratic society. In particular, it is possible to detect, from the late thirteenth century onwards, some major castles undergoing substantial redevelopment, with particular emphasis on new suites of accommodation.

At Chepstow (Monmouthshire), the castle was transformed in the 1280s–90s as the Norman great tower was heightened and a new accommodation block for the lord, Roger Bigod III, was constructed in the lower bailey.[39] Berkeley castle (Gloucestershire) was also rebuilt at about the same time with lodgings, offices, kitchen, hall, chapel and private apartments all added to the Norman structure.[40] This trend for new suites of accommodation continued into the fourteenth century. At Richmond (Yorkshire), in the 1330s, John, Duke of Brittany, added a new hall and chapel to the Norman castle and raised the height of the castle towers in order to provide additional chambers. The rebuilding of Warwick by the Beauchamps (1330–60) saw the construction of a new hall and range of apartments together with the magnificent Caesar's and Guy's Towers, both of which comprised high-quality stacked accommodation. These examples could be repeated at some length and all attest to some need to redesign existing buildings to meet new circumstances.

Goodrich castle, in Herefordshire, illustrates many of these wider trends. Goodrich was the chief residence of the Valence family and during the 1290s

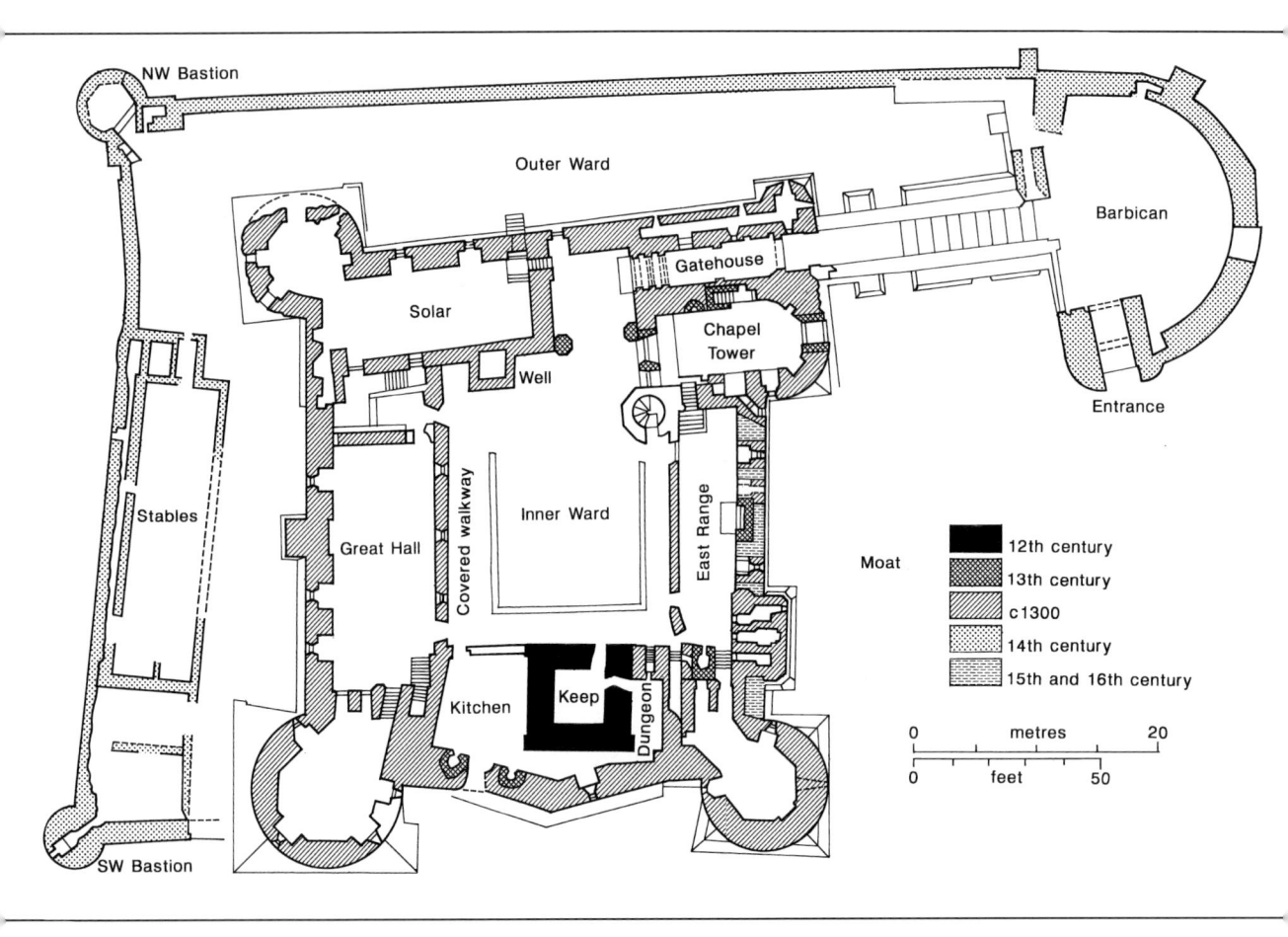

William de Valence presided over major works, with the castle being almost entirely rebuilt (Figure 28). The new structure comprised a series of rooms with a clear emphasis on providing high-quality accommodation. The principal lodging was situated in the north-west tower and was linked to a private solar. To the south was the great hall that was linked to a kitchen and to the south-west tower which itself contained chambers with garderobes. The southeast tower contained more chambers that in turn had access to a second hall and the castle chapel. In the north-east corner was the smaller gatehouse tower that in turn contained more chambers. Clearly there was some pressing need at this time that demanded an increase in the domestic provision at the site.

What makes Goodrich so interesting is the existence of historical work on the Valence family that sheds light on how the castle actually functioned at this time.[41] The head of the household in the absence of a male family member (this was a common situation in the Middle Ages) was Joan de Valence and, along with her, there were approximately 130 individuals residing at the castle. This number rose during periodic visits from family members who brought with them their attendant households. Other noble guests

FIGURE 28. Goodrich castle, Herefordshire. Plan showing phases of building. The castle was almost completely re-built at the end of the thirteenth century with the new structure providing accommodation for the resident household and guests. After Renn, 1993.

stopped occasionally at the castle for a few nights and took advantage of Valence hospitality. The largesse of Joan also extended to the poor – a minimum of twenty individuals who received alms were also apparently resident at the castle. The new design from Goodrich appears to have been intended to provide a series of rooms in which the family and their guests could be housed and accommodated, something that the older Norman castle could apparently not sustain.

The changing needs of the baronial household provide some explanation as to why castles such as Goodrich or Chepstow altered in this period. In the Middle Ages aristocrats were itinerant; lords moved from manor to manor, collecting rents, conducting their business and consuming the produce from their scattered estates. In the thirteenth century the royal and baronial households began to itinerate less frequently and consequently spent longer periods of time in a smaller number of residences than had hitherto been the case. At the same time, the size of the average household increased, a trend that continued until the early sixteenth century.[42] From about the end of the thirteenth century, then, it seems as if at least some castles were intended to be occupied on a permanent or semi-permanent basis. Longer periods of residency at particular places, along with larger households, necessitated changes in castle design.

The development of the courtyard plan was a response to these changing circumstances. The basic building block of the later medieval residence was the hall, and this would remain the case well into the post-medieval period. Rather than simply adding rooms onto a hall block in a linear manner (which would have resulted in an inconveniently long building), the building might be turned through ninety degrees to the hall range, resulting in a half 'H' or an 'E' shaped plan. At the most important houses this could be extended into a fourth range, resulting in the courtyard plan. Where necessary a further (or lower) courtyard could be added. Courtyard castles usually boasted impressive gatehouses and well-proportioned corner towers, which contained stacking levels of chambers. Again, elements such as gatehouses and mural towers had been familiar at English castles for many generations, but it was their fusion into an overall design scheme that sets the later medieval period apart from what had gone before. It was this sophisticated planning that resulted in castles such as Bodiam, Maxstoke (Warwickshire), Sheriff Hutton (Yorkshire) and the unfinished Kirby Muxloe (Leicestershire).

The need to provide more accommodation was compounded by other social changes. Although it is anachronistic to impose modern ideas of privacy and individualism onto the medieval world, it is the case that lords increasingly desired privacy from their household staff; moreover, the later Middle Ages saw shifts towards specialisation in the household itself and, as a consequence, a more specialised division of space. The desire of lords and their immediate families to separate themselves from the remainder of their households is readily detected in castle buildings. As already mentioned, at Chepstow Roger Bigod III's creation of a private tower in the bailey with rooms, garderobes and a chapel was specifically intended to create space for himself and his immediate family. At Pontefract (Yorkshire) the castle was rebuilt in the fourteenth century and part of this project involved creating separate towered suites for king and queen.

It is important here to bear in mind that castles that were in more or less permanent residential use not only had to accommodate the lord's personal family and his household, but also the households of noble visitors, as evidenced by Goodrich. The numbers of people who could appear at a castle requiring food and lodging should not be underestimated. When the Duke of York appeared, simply for lunch, at Warwick castle in 1458 he brought with him thirty retainers. At Old Wardour (Wiltshire) *c.* 1393 the new castle, which was intended to serve primarily as a hunting lodge, contained over twenty rooms for guests.[43] The largest social events could attract huge numbers. Some 2000 people attended the feast at Cawood castle in January 1466 to celebrate the enthronement of George Neville as archbishop of York.[44] It is hardly surprising, then, that the fourteenth century saw some major changes in castle design.

The desire for high-quality accommodation accelerated during the fourteenth century and pioneering work in the 1950s on the domestic arrangements of castles by Patrick Faulkner first drew attention to the sophistication of planning in this period.[45] Faulkner analysed castles in terms of the function of rooms and how access to each was negotiated. He demonstrated that the needs of domestic planning best explained the spatial organisation of several castles in the north of England, rather than any attempt to disrupt the passage of intruders. At castles such as Bolton (1379) the domestic apartments were fully integrated into the whole quadrangular structure, with suites of rooms in the four massive corner towers. Bodiam has a similar arrangement and it is possible to see these castles as up-to-date exercises in domestic planning.

At castles such as Bolton and Bodiam it is the integration of domestic accommodation into the overall plan of the castle that made them distinct. The courtyard castle also facilitated the development of 'cellular' lodgings: suites of accommodation comprising small rooms with independent access and often their own fireplaces and latrines. The first of their kind at an English castle seems to have been at Windsor, where in the mid fourteenth century a range was constructed in the bailey. By the turn of the fourteenth century it was possible to have an arrangement where the great hall lay opposite the entrance block with ranges of lodgings on either side enclosing the court, as at Dartington (Devon). Over the course of the fifteenth century these arrangements developed so that at the largest sites double courts were divided into upper and lower sections. At sites where there were two courtyards the upper court usually contained the most important accommodation, with the lower reserved for ancillary buildings and servants. This was certainly the case at South Wingfield (Derbyshire), Haddon (Derbyshire) and Caister (Norfolk). At the latter, such was the provision for lodgings practically every servant at the castle had their own room (Figure 29).[46] Again, this can be seen as a

Architecture and Power

FIGURE 29.
Caister Castle, Norfolk. Caister was built for the English captain Sir John Fastolf and is a good example of a late medieval brick-built castle with an upper and lower court.

response to wider changes in society: specifically 'bastard feudalism', a system whereby lords retained men to them by a money payment, a corruption of 'true' feudalism, where the bond between lord and man was based on land. Historians have long argued over the precise nature and evils of such indentures but it is significant that those high-ranking lords who retained men to them by fiscal means are also found building residences with cellular lodgings.[47]

Over the course of the fourteenth and fifteenth centuries, then, the quality of the domestic accommodation in castles generally improved. There was a move towards more, but smaller, rooms that had improved heating and better sanitation. These changes should all be seen within the context of lordly expression and aristocratic competition. If in the twelfth century the design of the *donjon* could mark out social rank, then in the fourteenth and fifteenth centuries it was signalled by other means. Ranges of accommodation that were well-lit and amply provisioned with fireplaces and garderobes now demonstrated a particular – and better – style of living. With perhaps only one residence on which to spend, it is not surprising that the later medieval period sees the use of new materials such as brick, and investment in glass, tapestries and furniture.

Although it is possible to explain the development of castle plans in the later medieval period as a response to new residential needs, the outward display of military status did not diminish. Rather, aristocrats readily adopted newer trappings of fortification. In the south of England the adoption of gunports is a notable addition to the repertoire of seigneurial display. Experiments with gunpowder weapons seem to have started in the early 1300s but handheld guns and cannon only became effective as the fourteenth century progressed. By the fifteenth century cannon could have a decisive impact on the battlefield, and on the continent changes began to be made in the design of fortifications to resist the impact of shot. In England and Wales, however, there is little evidence, even in the fifteenth century, that castle-builders followed the lead of continental Europe. Castles such as Herstmonceux in Sussex and Baconsthorpe in Norfolk have insubstantial walls less than two metres thick, which could not have resisted any kind of sustained bombardment. While castle owners seem to have been disinterested in making their residences resistant to attack from cannon, they were certainly anxious that they exhibited an awareness of new forms of weaponry. From about the middle of the fourteenth century so-called 'key hole' gunports for the use of guns appeared at castles such as Cooling (Kent) and Bodiam. Their appearance was not confined to castles, however; they are also found in urban walls and gateways such as those at Canterbury and Southampton. There was also a trend for existing castles to have loops added to their defences, as at Dover, Saltwood and Carisbrooke. The lowliest castle could be provisioned for guns; even places such as Oxborough (Norfolk) could boast a few loops. The motivation here had little to do with use; what we see again is the competitive instinct of the medieval aristocracy coupled with developments in military technology. The demands of social rank necessitated at least an awareness of the latest forms of military hardware.

The end of the castle?

When castle-building ceased in England is an intriguing question. For many years the sixteenth century has been seen as the time when the castle finally lost its military role. Its defensive function had been supplanted by new fortifications that were built by the state for national defence.[48] In England this was marked by Henry VIII's chain of artillery forts built along the south coast.

FIGURE 30.
Cromwell's Castle, Isles of Scilly. Built during the Interregnum by the conquering parliamentarian forces, this 'castle' guarded the Tresco Channel with cannon: a building with a purely military function, but which retained the name 'castle'.

RICHARD PURSLOW

There is no doubting the defensive character of these fortifications; places such as Deal, Walmer and Camber were essentially platforms for artillery. There is no sense in which buildings such as these could be described primarily as residences; their accommodation was simply intended for the use of the gunners and garrison troops. Similar buildings were still being built at the time of the Interregnum (Figure 30).

Undoubtedly the sixteenth century did witness great changes. The most recent analysis sees three interlocking processes that together brought about a substantive shift in noble building. Matthew Johnson has written cogently that the sixteenth century witnessed a breakdown in what he terms architectural 'cross-referencing'.[49] Thus in the later medieval period a series of underlying structural principles governed the ordering of space and gender, and the architectural form of great buildings. Over the course of the sixteenth century these broke down. The development of artillery forts divorced ideas of residence and fortification; the Reformation saw the end of a common architectural vocabulary between secular and ecclesiastical structures; the increasing power of the monarchy at the expense of the wider aristocracy meant that royal buildings eclipsed those of secular magnates. The sixteenth century, it is suggested, witnessed a reordering of traditional motifs and the rise of 'domestic architecture', something different to that which had gone before.

As the sixteenth century progressed the use of more overt 'military' display at great houses slowly diminished and was gradually replaced by a concern to

65

incorporate Classical ideas into the form of the noble building. Sixteenth-century noble society was now increasingly focused on the royal court and its Renaissance tastes, rather than on the baronial court of the regional magnate. As a consequence status became linked with an appreciation of Classical knowledge and Renaissance manners rather than simply being concerned with how many retainers a particular lord could put into the field. Thus at great houses we see a concern for symmetry in buildings and the use of Classical forms such as pillars in doors and windows. A growing understanding of Classical architecture together with a general decline in the size of households meant that the days of the courtyard plan were numbered. It now became important to have internal as well as external symmetry, something that could be best appreciated from entering via a porch, rather than a great gatehouse. Associated with these changes in the form of the building was the decline of the wet moat. As we shall see in Chapter 4, the idea that a noble mansion should be surrounded by water had been current for many centuries but this undoubtedly became less important as the sixteenth century progressed. Hardwick Hall in Derbyshire (1591) is an excellent (if rather atypical) example of the newer form of the Tudor house: rather than a single-piled structure ranged around a courtyard, it is double-piled with external symmetry (which betrays its Palladian influence) and elaborate fenestration which led to the epithet 'Hardwick Hall, more glass than wall'. It would be difficult to argue that a building of this nature was a castle.

However, while it is not in doubt that the sixteenth century witnessed dramatic changes, the legacy of castle-building did not disappear overnight and elements of late medieval practice continued into the sixteenth century and beyond. This is perhaps seen most clearly in the longevity of the court-yard plan as the basic form of the noble mansion. As late as 1610 a house as elaborate and expensive as Blickling Hall in Norfolk could comprise of a single-piled structure arranged around a courtyard (Figure 31). As a basic formula this was remarkably enduring and can be found at, among other places, Audley End (Essex) and Hengrave Hall (Suffolk). While often not as prominent as on some later medieval houses, crenellation continued as a noble emblem well into the seventeenth century. At Lulworth in Dorset, the new house for Thomas, Third Lord Bindon (1608–10), was built in a castellated style and was actually referred to without, it seems, any irony, as a 'castle' (Figure 32).[50] It is perhaps too easy to underestimate some of the continuities, not only in form, but also in interpretation, in noble building from the fifteenth to the seventeenth century. Double-piled houses based on true Palladian principles only became widespread in England after the Restoration and it may be that the decisive shift in noble building in fact occurred in the middle of the seventeenth century, rather than at the time of the Reformation. It could be said that castles continued to be built as long as aristocrats believed that the building of crenellations gave the appropriate signal of noble dignity.

Castles in Context: Power, Symbolism and Landscape, 1066–1500

Architecture and Power

FIGURE 31.
Blickling Hall, Norfolk. Although raised in the early seventeenth century, Blickling retains several elements familiar from the Middle Ages, most notably its courtyard plan.

Conclusion

This chapter has offered a (necessarily) brief critique of three key points in the 'Castle Story'. It will be remembered that this story saw castle development in teleological terms: an evolutionary struggle between attacker and defender up to *c.*1300 and a military decline thereafter. As has been demonstrated here, there are now good grounds for seriously questioning this interpretative framework. Scholars have rejected the idea that the quintessential structure of the Anglo-Norman castle, the *donjon*, was always designed primarily for defence; have highlighted the chivalric and cultural factors that influenced the design of Edwardian castles in North Wales; and questioned the idea that the later medieval period witnessed the decline of the castle. It should not be thought, however, that scholars working in the field have now arrived at the 'truth'. As Matthew Johnson has recently pointed out, it could be said that we know less about castles than we have ever done before.[51]

One of the advantages of the 'military' interpretation of castles is that it did seem to provide a mechanism for explaining why the form of castles changed. Although the idea that the changing nature of siege warfare affected development in design has been rejected, we have not yet reached the stage where a detailed and nuanced alternative can be put in its place. A common buzzword is 'status' but this term is as problematic a term as 'warfare'; it can only superficially explain why individual builders chose to build in the way they did and is lacking in subtlety as an explanation for the changing form of castles over time.

To take a single example: in the late eleventh century some Anglo-Norman lords thought it acceptable and appropriate to display their lordship through the building of *burh-geat* type towers from which they could publicly display their lordship; but by the second quarter of the twelfth century the greatest lords were constructing larger buildings and engineering a complicated and intimidating approach to the lordly presence. This change can be explained

FIGURE 32.
Lulworth Castle, Dorset.

with reference to structural changes in the composition of the Anglo-Norman aristocracy in this period: it was a time of considerable dislocation and a desire on the part of 'true' nobles to assert their rank in the face of a generation of *arrivistes*.[52] Similar social factors can also be invoked to explain changes in castle design throughout the medieval period and it should not be surprising that aristocratic buildings were provided with the trappings of fortification. These were so important as signifiers of lordly authority that it was possible for a castle to be 'slighted' simply by the striking-through of emblems such as arrowslits.[53] Such actions open up a whole series of questions concerning the social dimensions of crenellation in this period and this refers us back to the question posed towards the beginning of this chapter: 'what is a castle?' The answer to this necessarily depends on definitions, and historians are now seeking looser classifications which are perhaps closer to the medieval reality. John Goodall has recently suggested that a 'a castle is the residence of a lord made imposing through the architectural trappings of fortification, be they functional or decorative'.[54] The real advantage of defining the castle in these terms is that it forgoes the need to somehow 'measure' the level of fortification at any given site. This is crucial because, as has been stated earlier, it is impossible to disaggregate 'war' and 'status' in castle architecture as building in a fortified style inevitably referenced a military vocabulary. And it is to this military vocabulary and the subject of warfare to which we will now turn.

FIGURE 33.
The gatehouse at Carisbrooke Castle, Isle of Wight. Were the arrowslits and gunports intended for effective defence, or were they part of a military architectural style?

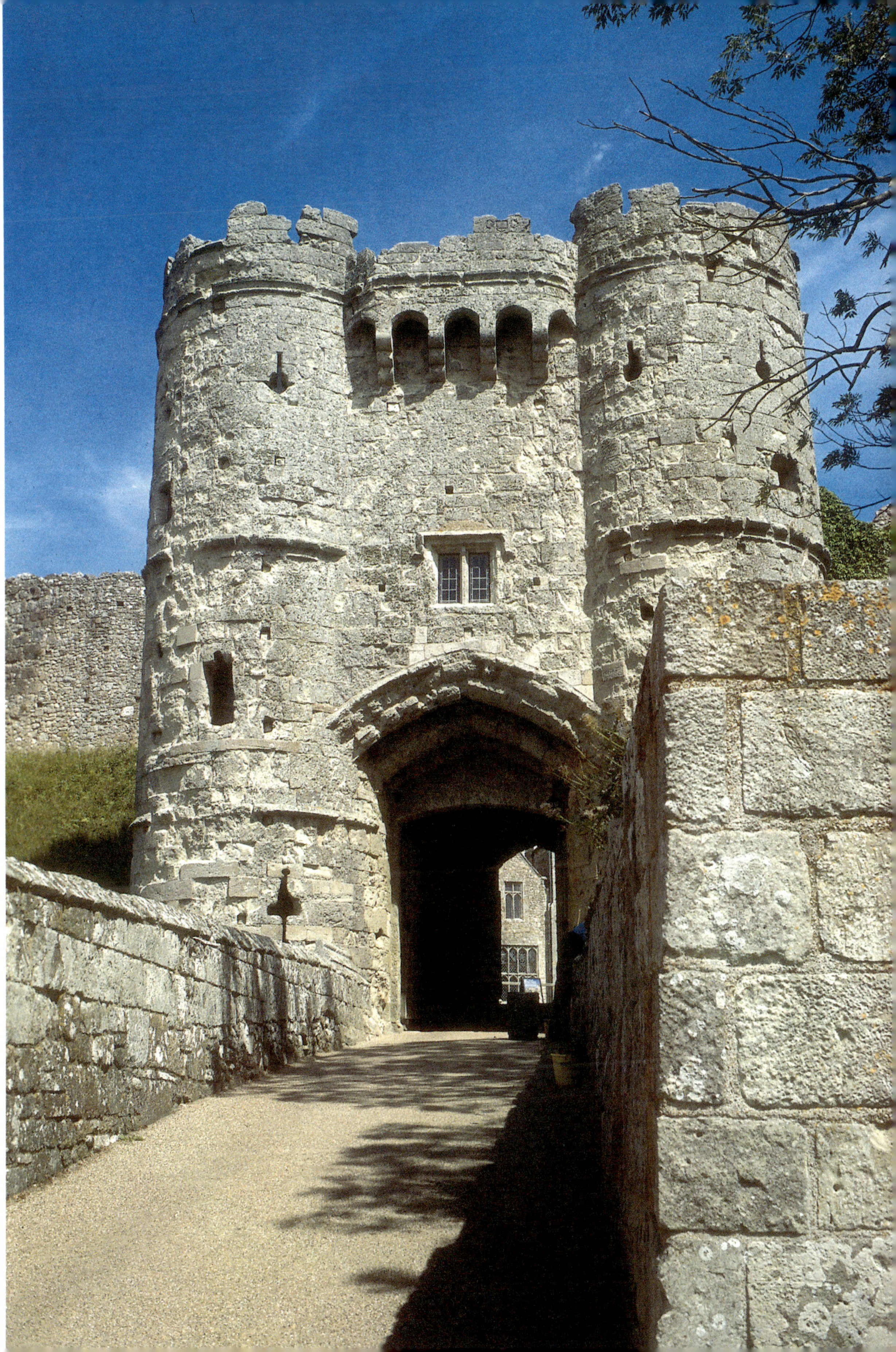

CHAPTER FOUR

The Castle at War

Perceptions of medieval war

Medieval warfare is popularly perceived as a chaotic and brutal activity. It is an image reinforced by countless films, books and heritage displays. While there may be much about the reality of medieval conflict that may appear distasteful or abhorrent, this should not lead us into thinking that hostilities in this period were necessarily disorganised or unsophisticated. In comparison with some of the civil conflicts that have taken place in Europe in the last decade some aspects of medieval warfare may seem more enlightened than we might care to imagine. Although the practice of warfare in the Middle Ages (even by its own standards) may have sometimes been characterised by acts of savagery and violence deemed to be beyond acceptable social norms, there were attempts to limit the brutality of conflict and to ameliorate its destructive effects. This was certainly true of siege warfare; far from being a story of battering rams and boiling oil (Figure 33), the reality of a medieval siege was frequently very different from the popular image presented by, for example, Hollywood.[1]

Medieval warfare has often occupied a somewhat ambivalent position within historiography. On the one hand, scholars in the early and mid twentieth century in particular were quick to highlight its supposedly barbarity and castigated the practice for its chronic lack of organisation.[2] At the same time, they were swift to praise the great military achievements of the Middle Ages (such as the successful First Crusade) as well as the skill and valour of 'national' heroes such as Richard I and Henry V. Modern historians have continued to celebrate the personal abilities of heroic warrior kings but have dispelled the idea that war leaders lacked the administrative and strategic capabilities of their modern counterparts. Rather, they have emphasised the professionalism of medieval commanders and fighting men; the military discipline that was frequently displayed on the medieval battlefield; and the often-complex logistical arrangements that were undertaken before and during campaigns.[3] Wider social studies of warfare in this period have also started to move away from interpretations of battles and sieges based on 'inherent military probability' – a concept derived from twentieth-century tactical principles – and instead have sought to place medieval conflict within the chivalric values that permeated elite culture at this time. Thus it has been possible to completely re-write the

The Castle at War history of individual engagements, as historians have come to appreciate both the complexity of medieval warfare and the social mechanisms that governed its conduct.[4]

While modern commentators have sought to rescue medieval warfare from some of the more patronising judgements of earlier generations, the status of the castle as an element sometimes crucial to organised campaigning in the Middle Ages has remained intact.[5] Despite the radical questioning of its military role, the castle is still central to our picture of the nature of conflict in this period. This is unsurprising, as castles are often represented as being of prime significance in medieval chronicles, one of our principal sources for siege warfare. Reading accounts such as the *Gesta Stephani* – a major

FIGURE 34. Map indicating attacks on castles in England and Wales, 1066–1652. The first figure for each county represents the number of castles raised over the course of the Middle Ages, and the second the total number of attacks sustained over the same period. Based on D. J. C. King, *Castellarium Anglicanum*, 1983.

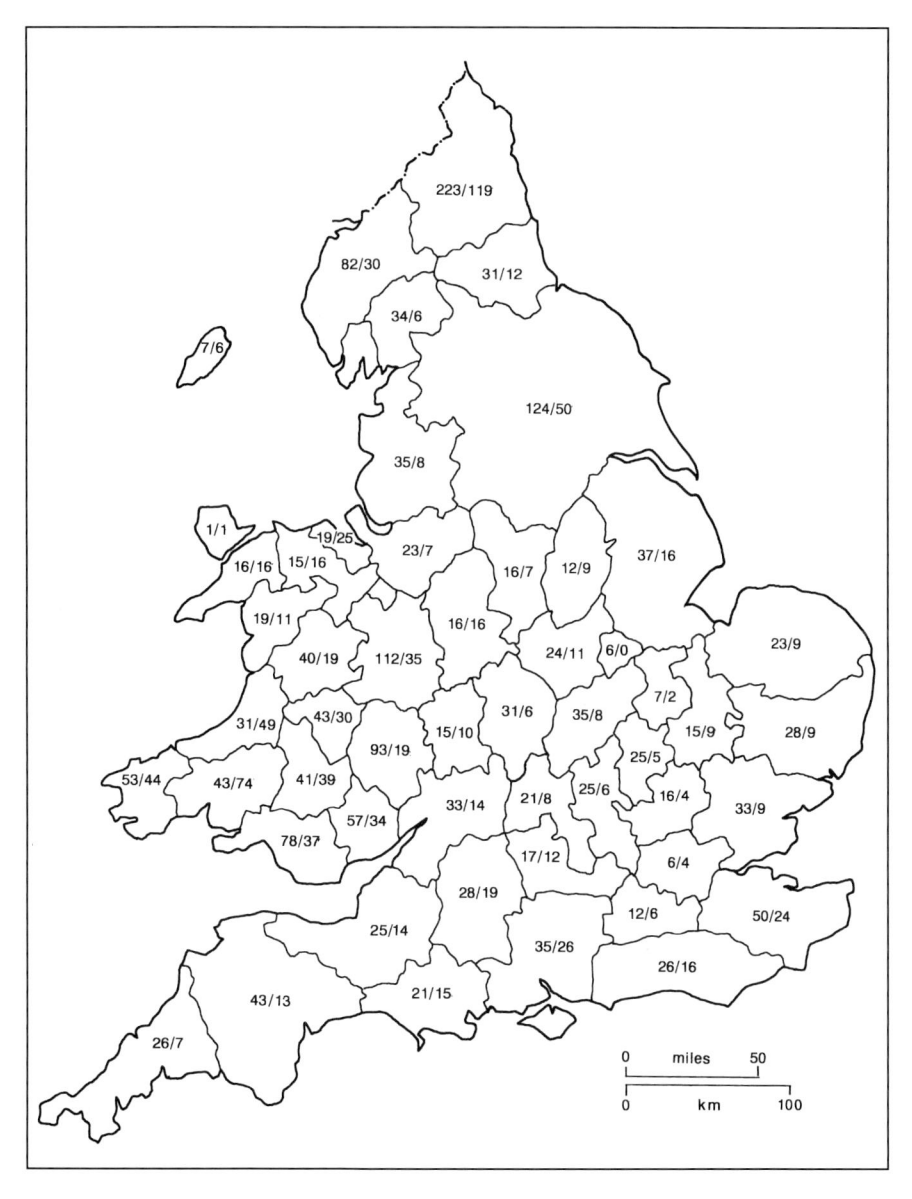

71

source for the civil war of Stephen's reign – one might be forgiven for thinking that sieges were commonplace, or that castles were permanently on a war footing.[6] This would be a mistake, however, as the majority of castles spent most of their time at peace. But quite why certain castles rather than others assumed military importance at specific times is sometimes difficult to establish and the subsequent course of events may defy modern 'military' logic or probability mainly because medieval siege warfare had an element of ritual: that is, it conformed to a set procedure and protocol. Sometimes this meant that physical fighting and, consequently, casualties were minimised. What appears to have proved a more important factor than the state and manning of the castle's defences in deciding the outcome of events, and whether fighting occurred at all, was the wider political context in which the siege took place.[7]

The frequency of siege warfare in England and Wales

Before we examine the role of castles in medieval warfare, it is worth raising the general issue of the extent to which castles *actually* saw violence during the Middle Ages. Although historians have pointed out that it was rare for a castle to experience a siege during its lifetime, there is still a widespread assumption that there was a likelihood of 'ever present' threat of attack which led aristocrats to fortify their homes. If it was possible to gain some idea of the level of siege warfare then this might tentatively allow us to assess the extent to which castle builders *expected* their residences to be attacked. It would also be possible

Castles in Context: Power, Symbolism and Landscape, 1066–1500

FIGURE 35.
Frequency of sieges in England and Wales. The peaks indicate relatively rare periods of organised campaigning (for example, during the 'Anarchy' of Stephen's reign and the civil war of John's reign) when castles could change hands rapidly. Based on D. J. C. King, *Castellarium Anglicanum*, 1983.

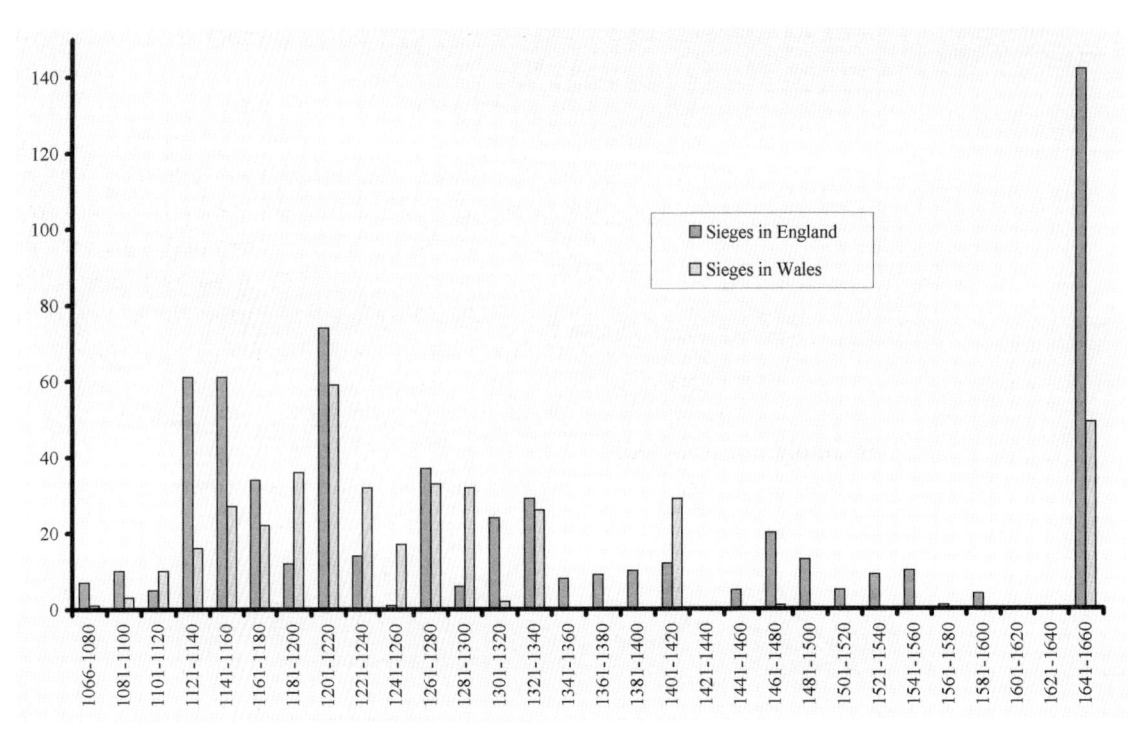

The Castle at War to detect whether some castles were more likely to be attacked than others, or whether those castles in border or coastal areas saw more armed force than those inland. We can potentially learn much from the frequency with which castles found themselves under siege.

Figure 34 represents an attempt to gain some idea of how often castles were involved in military encounters in England and Wales from the eleventh to the seventeenth centuries. Two sets of information are presented. The first figure indicates the total number of castles in each individual county and the second shows the total number of attacks that took place on those castles from the eleventh to the mid seventeenth century. This data is also presented in Figure 35, where the number of attacks for England and Wales is shown by decade. The limitations of this data should be noted, however: the information presented here has been compiled from D. J. C. King's *Castellarium Anglicanum*, a massive work which attempts to identify and list every castle in England and Wales.[8] *Castellarium Anglicanum* is an enormous feat of scholarship but the figures here derived from it obviously reflect the way in which King complied his work. Most importantly, he attempted rigidly to exclude those sites that were not 'real' castles. Inevitably this meant making arbitrary judgments about what was, and was not, a 'castle': he included artillery forts of Henry VIII and tower houses in his figures, but not fortified houses such as Acton Burnell in Shropshire. The total numbers of castles for each county presented here are therefore based on King's criteria and represent the sum of building over several centuries, rather than the level of fortification at any one point in time.

There are also problems in assessing numbers and frequency of attacks. At better-documented sites, King noted the number of times a castle was besieged, forced to surrender or dismantled. Needless to say, it cannot be known for certain how many assaults on castles went unrecorded. While it is unlikely that major sieges did not find their way into the historical record, lesser confrontations may well have escaped the attention or interest of chroniclers or government records. Sometimes it is known for certain that this is the case: the attack on Hen Domen by the Welsh in 1095 is not mentioned in any Welsh Annals; we only know it happened at all because it was recorded in the *Anglo-Saxon Chronicle*.[9] Additionally, chroniclers will sometimes simply state that all the castles of a given territory were attacked during the course of a campaign. Thus we know that the castles of Ceredigion and Dyfed were attacked in 1158 and 1159, but exactly which sites were targeted and how often is simply not recorded.[10]

It is also not necessarily the case that the military encounters recorded here always represent what we might define as 'sieges'. Due to the nature of much of the evidence, it is often extremely difficult to assess whether a particular confrontation should be classed as a 'siege', an 'attack' or simply a surrender involving no fighting. Some do represent full-scale siege operations, such as that at Dover in 1216 and Kenilworth in 1266, but these make up only a small proportion of the total. At the other extreme, many incidents hardly warrant the term 'siege' at all. That at Deddington in Oxfordshire in 1281 consisted merely of an alleged attack on the castle gates and doors.[11] Similarly, the taking of Warwick Castle in 1153 – although included by King – involved no fighting; rather, the Earl of Warwick's wife surrendered the castle when she mistakenly believed rumours that her husband was dead.[12] Far more common are occurrences where a castle garrison was persuaded – or intimidated – into surrender, or where the defenders backed down after a limited period of fighting. This happened at Tonbridge in 1147 when King Stephen and an army in full battle array appeared unexpectedly at the town. The rebel commander, Gilbert Fitz Richard, was forced to disguise himself in order to flee and Stephen 'by his sudden arrival and constraint and intimidation of the garrison, soon obtained surrender of the castle'.[13] The figures presented here are inclusive of minor assaults and other occasions where negotiations seem to have been backed by some kind of military presence and so (as far as our sources allow) are unlikely to drastically underestimate incidents, but they can only act as a *guide* to the number of times castles found themselves involved in extra-manorial events.

Immediately apparent, however, are the bursts of activity during periods of organised campaigning or national disturbance. The peaks in Figure 35 reflect

Castles in Context: Power, Symbolism and Landscape, 1066–1500

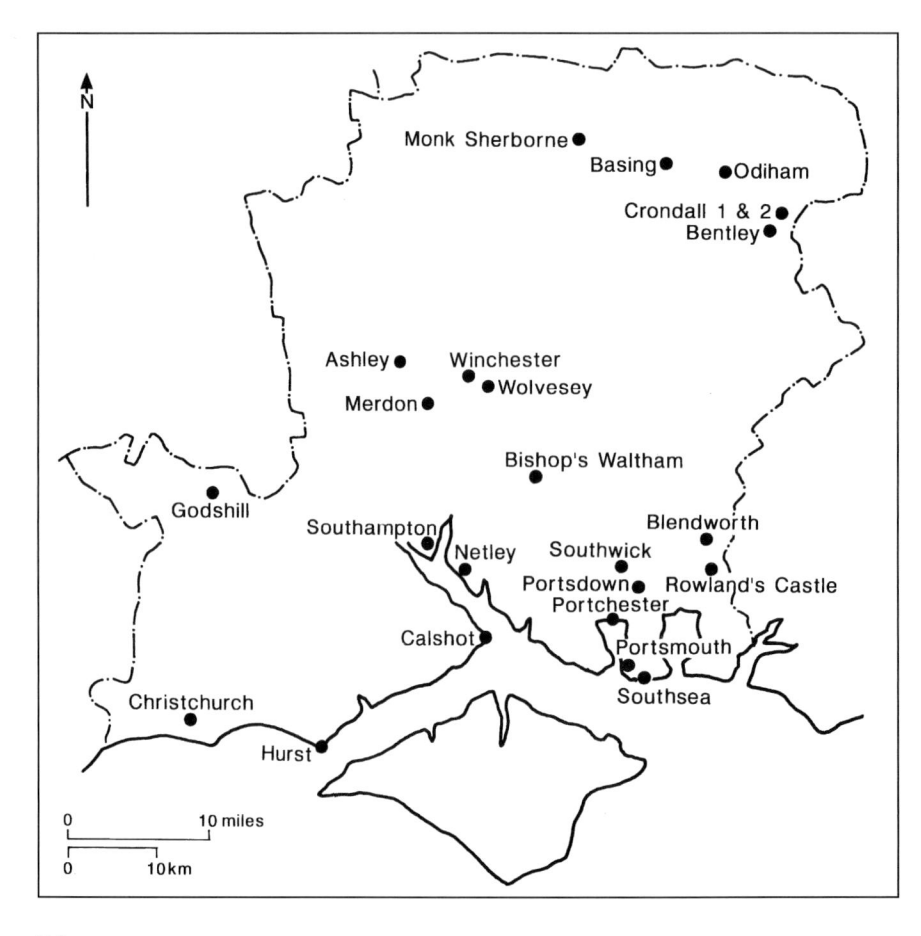

FIGURE 36. Distribution map of Hampshire castles. Based on D. J. C. King, *Castellarium Anglicanum*, 1983.

The Castle at War   major periods of conflict such as the Anarchy of Stephen's reign, the civil war during the reign of King John and the Barons' wars of the mid thirteenth century. These periods witnessed occasional episodes of organised campaigning where castles were often surrendered cheaply and could change hands rapidly. In the later medieval period, in contrast, the number of actions decreases sharply. However, the baronial rebellion against Edward II, Owain Glyn Dŵr's rebellion in 1400 and the Wars of the Roses serve to push up numbers in specific decades. Again, the seemingly high level of military activity at these times masks a more complex reality. Detailed studies of the 1320s and the Wars of the Roses have shown that castles played only a minor role in military events and Figure 35 represents the political and symbolic value in the precautionary manning of castles at a time of insecurity.[14] Peaks at these times contrast with longer periods where castles saw only occasional use or were at peace. The lack of activity in certain decades is also of significance: the howls of protest by chroniclers regarding the evils of castle-building and castle men in the 1140s may owe much to a slow fall in the number of castles and a failure to maintain existing fabric in the previous two decades.

A case study: Hampshire
High siege totals for some counties in Figure 34 do not necessarily equate with high levels of military activity. This is neatly exemplified by Hampshire, a county with 30 castles listed by King and with a total of 26 military encounters from the twelfth to the seventeenth century (Figure 36).[15] With due caution as to what these figures actually mean, these incidents took place at 12 castles, meaning that the remaining 18, as far as we know, never saw action of any kind. A breakdown of the recorded attacks reveals that there were three main periods of activity and these correspond with periods of national instability: eight attacks are associated with the Anarchy of Stephen's reign, ten with the civil war during the reign of King John and seven with the Civil War in the seventeenth century, with the one remaining attack being that on Odiham in 1321 by opponents of Edward II.

    The military record of these castles is not altogether impressive. In 22 of 26 cases the besiegers were successful; only in four cases did the castle in question manage to hold out, and the impression given is one of limited action and surrenders. Christchurch and Crondall changed hands twice in quick succession during the 1140s, control of the former passing firstly by stealth and subsequently by agreement.[16] Control of Porchester, Southampton, Winchester, Wolvesey and Odiham passed repeatedly between the forces of Louis of France and those loyal to King John during the course of 1216 and 1217. In this campaign there appears only to have been determined resistance at the barely-manned Odiham, but here the garrison was forced to surrender after three days. At the others, fighting appears to have been minimal and the majority were simply surrendered. During the Civil War of Charles I's reign, the siege of Basing House resulted in a bloodbath, but at Christchurch, Southampton and Winchester there were only minor incidents.

Even a brief analysis of a single county is instructive. At face value, a discussion of the military encounters at Hampshire's castles seems to contradict the 'revisionist' argument that castles were primarily residences; after all, here we see them involved in action. While the numbers of sieges may appear superficially impressive, it is important to remember that this is the *sum* total of military activity and does not amount to anything like a constant state of war. The impression is one of castles caught up in wider events and ill-prepared to meet the challenge.

Regional variation
The figures also highlight important regional variations in the frequency of attacks. Probably the most striking aspect is the rarity of attacks on castles in lowland England. Counties such as Essex, Buckinghamshire, Derbyshire, Oxfordshire, Bedfordshire and Suffolk all fail to reach totals in double figures. Even in some border or frontier counties where it is often assumed that castles needed to be on a war footing, attacks are surprisingly rare: Cheshire accounts for seven, Lancashire eight and Westmorland can only boast six attacks. Even allowing for under-recording, some of the totals seem low. Shropshire, for example, is often characterised as a dangerous border county, yet its one hundred and twelve castles only suffered attack on twenty-two occasions in five hundred years of castle-building.[17]

Those counties where there does appear to have been more sustained military activity are to be found in south Wales and northern England, in the counties of Brecknockshire, Cardiganshire, Carmarthenshire, Radnorshire and Northumberland. A higher level of military activity in the north of England is not surprising as, despite prolonged periods of peace, continuing Anglo-Scottish warfare throughout the medieval period ensured that castles were more likely to witness armed force than their southern counterparts. The high numbers of attacks in south Wales are more difficult to explain, but may be accounted for by the nature of the sources. We are fortunate in having a number of chronicle sources, such as the *Brut y Tywysogyon*, that relate in some detail not only the conflict between the Anglo-Normans and the native Welsh, but also those disputes between the native Welsh princes. Castles are frequently described as coming under attack and this inevitably produces higher figures than elsewhere. Whether this should be taken as evidence for high levels of under-recording nationally, however, is difficult to judge. The twelfth and early thirteenth centuries was the period of Norman settlement in south Wales, a long-drawn-out process that was resisted by force, which played a part in increasing the numbers of sieges. Certainly the reasons behind the high levels of attacks in this region and the role castles played in conflict would warrant further investigation.

Much of this analysis has necessarily involved calculations made with the benefit of hindsight. Concentrating on numbers of attacks and sieges inevitably creates an impression of military buildings constantly on a war footing. While castles clearly did figure significantly in some campaigns, what

FIGURE 37.
'Heynoe's Loop' at Carisbrooke Castle, Isle of Wight, from where the archer Peter Heynoe shot and killed the French commander during the siege of 1377.

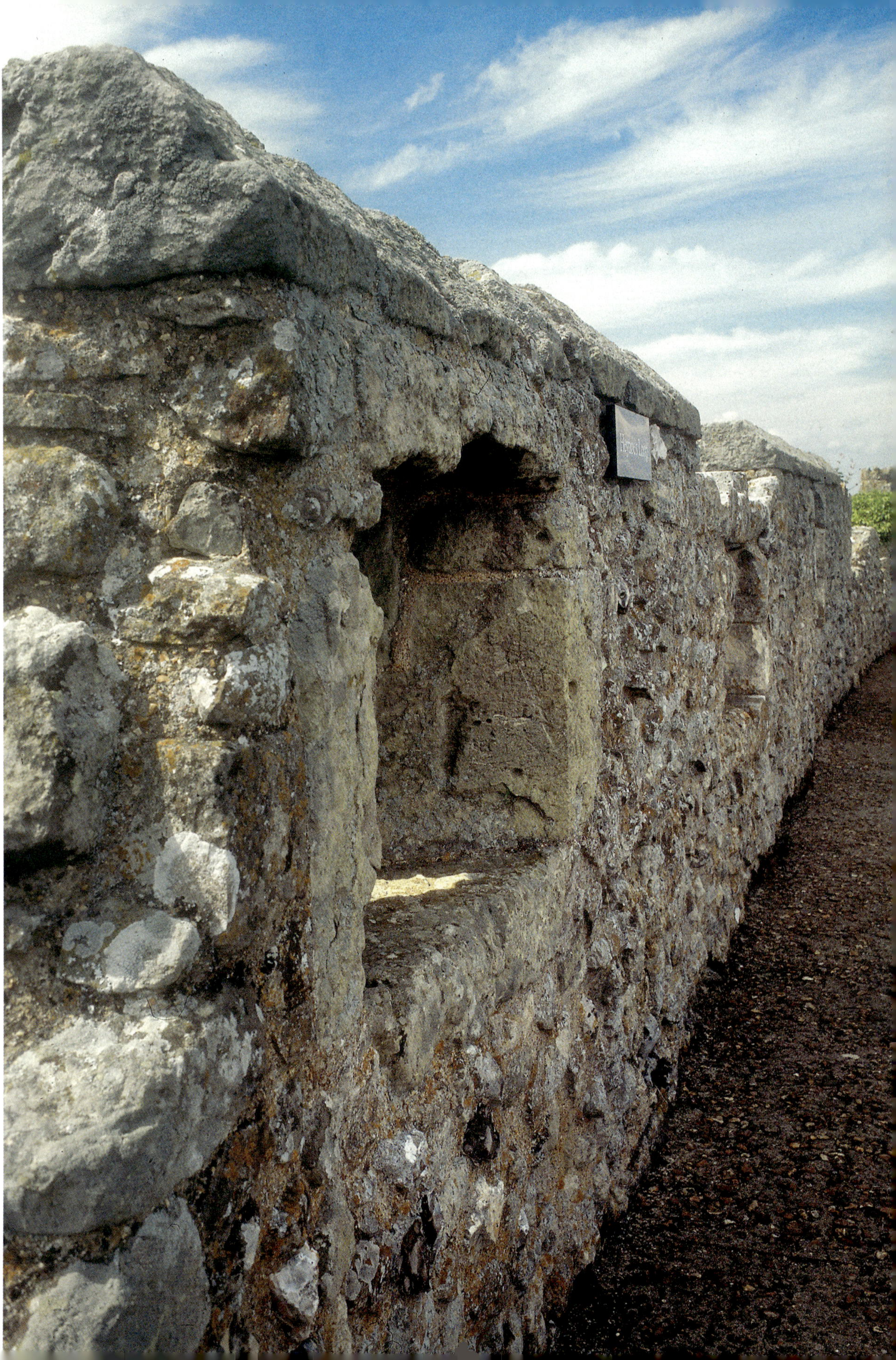

emerges most strongly is the number of castles which do *not* seem to have been attacked, the number which *failed* to feature significantly in wartime and how many times castles were given up *without* any fighting. While this may seem surprising, it becomes more explicable when sieges are placed within the context of medieval warfare. But before we can turn our attention to how exactly castles functioned (or failed to function) in war, we need to explore the nature of medieval conflict itself.

Aristocratic war

One of the greatest dangers in trying to interpret medieval war is the tendency to impose our own views of armed conflict onto a historical period when warfare was in many respects fundamentally different. Today, the majority of the population has never experienced military hostilities at first hand and our perceptions of war are inevitably coloured by the experience of the twentieth century: the age of 'Total War'. The First and Second World Wars have left us images of the Somme, mass citizen armies, panzers rolling across the Russian Steppes, *blitzkrieg* and so on. It is no accident that a military interpretation of castles gained momentum and then acquired the status of orthodoxy (particularly after 1912) during the century that witnessed Europe's two most destructive conflicts. Also not without significance is the fact that possibly the most powerful advocates of the military interpretation of castles in the decades after 1945 – John Beeler, R. Allen Brown and D. J. Cathcart King – were all military men, the latter two having served with distinction in the Second World War.

Medieval warfare was, by contrast to its modern counterpart, *aristocratic* war. Due to the expense of equipping an armoured soldier and providing him with a warhorse, from the early medieval period warfare had become the preserve of the social elite and consequently acknowledged as an aristocratic activity. Indeed, it was infringements of individual lordly rights that initiated most conflict in this period.[18] By the eleventh century warfare was considered the *raison d'être* of the aristocratic caste and permeated the whole culture of secular noble life.[19] Aristocratic conduct was chiefly focused around the concept of 'chivalry', an all-embracing term for a series of ideas on behaviour that to a greater or lesser extent impacted on the activities of participants during campaigning.[20] This is not to deny the importance of infantry, engineers and non-combatants to armies; rather, it is to say that an overall structuring principle of medieval war was that it was an activity that rightly belonged to the elite of society, and was governed by a noble ethos. It is this that helps explain some of the less recognisably 'modern' facets of medieval war, such as trial by battle, that were often highly important to the outcome of events.

This aristocratic mentality manifested itself in a number of ways. Although the recruitment of soldiers who served for pay was characteristic of campaigns as far back as the twelfth century, the idea of fighting for one's social superior exercised a powerful hold over fighting men. In the fourteenth century, for

Castles in Context: Power, Symbolism and Landscape, 1066–1500

example, English royal expeditions to France always recruited more heavily than those led by other nobles.[21] The loyalty of men to their captain or lord could often be the decisive factor in deciding the course of a battle or siege, and the death or capture of a commander frequently dictated the outcome of events. During the siege of Carisbrooke Castle in 1377, an English archer, Peter Heynoe, having observed the French commander's habit of reconnoitering the castle each morning and night, shot and killed him, at which point the demoralised French troops retreated.[22] (Figure 37) It was only in the sixteenth century that large armies chiefly composed of footsoldiers ousted the mounted warrior from pre-eminence and the numerical contribution of aristocrats to armies subsequently diminished. Warfare still retained its noble ethos, but the growing bureaucracy that was necessary to support increasingly organised and prolonged campaigning meant that it was fast becoming recognisably 'modern'.[23]

The distinctive attitudes that underpinned medieval warfare directly influenced the conduct of campaigns. Pitched battles, particularly in the eleventh and twelfth centuries, were rare. Following the advice of the Roman military manual *Epitome Rei Militaris*, medieval commanders only ventured directly into battle if they were confident of victory or had no other option but to risk a last roll of the dice.[24] It was the huge risk that battle entailed that led medieval commanders to err on the side of caution. Firstly, there was the possibility of death: in 1066 the battles of Stamford Bridge and Hastings resulted in the deaths of King Harold of Norway, King Harold of England and the latter's three brothers Tostig, Leofwine and Gyrth. Secondly, there was the risk of becoming a prisoner. When King Stephen (against the advice of his council) went into battle at Lincoln in 1141, his subsequent capture represented a political disaster. Finally, while a defeat could spell catastrophe, the benefits of victory might not always have been worth the risk. Even a successful engagement might not radically alter the wider strategic balance in the longer term. In short, battles were rare because they did not necessarily bring complete victory, but might spell ultimate defeat.

While armies may not have spent their time deploying against each other in the field, campaigns were often characterised by the practice of ravaging opponents' land. Due to the difficulties of supplying armies, commanders tended to let their forces live off the countryside: medieval soldiers often marched on what they had plundered. Advancing across Normandy in 1346, the English boasted that their army was despoiling the land for five or six miles around their line of march.[25] This tactic was not simply an example of raw brutality; rather, it was a considered strategy. By allowing their forces to forage over wide areas, commanders were not only keeping their troops fed but were also demonstrating in the most graphic way possible that their opposing lord was failing in his most primary duty: the obligation to protect his tenants and followers.

If despoiling the countryside had certain advantages it also presented an attacker with particular difficulties. The dispersal of troops across the landscape left them highly vulnerable to quick counter-attacks and thus attacking commanders constantly had to strike a balance between dispersing their troops in order to permit successful ravaging, while keeping them sufficiently close together to prevent small groups being ambushed and overwhelmed. Equally, a defender had to concentrate enough of his troops to hit a dispersed enemy hard but in turn had the logistical problem of keeping his own forces properly supplied. Thus medieval warfare was characterised by skirmishes and raiding as armies attempted to engage small numbers of opponents detached from their larger formations while the numerical odds were in their favour. It was within conflict characterised by such fluid tactics that the castle found itself placed in time of war.

Castles in Context: Power, Symbolism and Landscape, 1066–1500

Castles and war: The military record

There is a general agreement among military historians that castles could fulfil both offensive and defensive roles.[26] Offensively, castles provided logistical bases for operations and secure strong points for the seizure of territory. In 1165, it was from the castles of Shrewsbury and Oswestry (Croesoswald) that Henry II launched campaigns into Wales.[27] The royal army moving against the rebel Richard Marshal in south Wales in 1233 used the castles at Gloucester and Hereford as staging posts during their advance and it was on the night of 11 November while encamped at Grosmont Castle that they were surprised by Richard's troops and routed (Figure 38).[28] Defensively, castles could hold

FIGURE 38. Grosmont castle, Monmouthshire. It was while encamped here in 1233 that a royal army was surprised at night and routed by forces loyal to the rebel Richard Marshal.

FIGURE 39.
Clun castle, Shropshire. Clun was one of the few castles where the obligation of castle-guard retained its importance into the thirteenth century.

territory as, at least in theory, the troops within could exercise some degree of control over the surrounding countryside. For this to happen effectively, the troops in question had to be highly trained. Their role would be to skirmish with and harass enemy forces in the vicinity, a situation that called for individual initiative and skill in arms. It was for this reason that in 1145 Robert of Gloucester raised a castle at Faringdon in Oxfordshire 'strongly fortified by a rampart and stockade, and putting in it a garrison that was the flower of his whole army he valorously restrained the wonted attacks from the king's soldiers, who had been coming out of Oxford and other castles round about to harass his own side'.[29] Faringdon neatly illustrates that in wartime a castle could perform both an offensive and a defensive role at the same time: resisting attacks on the one hand, while providing a localised strong point for co-ordinating operations on the other. It should be noted, however, that Faringdon is unusual in as much as it is an example of a castle built specifically for a military purpose and therefore quite different from the majority of castles raised in the Middle Ages. It is important here to understand that contemporaries used the word 'castle' to describe structures such as that at Faringdon in the same way as they did other castles that served a more residential purpose. In the Middle Ages there was no equivalent of the Victorian word 'fieldwork', which referred to a purely military structure raised during the course of a campaign.[30] Faringdon provides the rare opportunity to

81

see a 'military' castle in action during organised campaigning and while it was potentially possible for any castle to exercise a similar role, most did not perform anywhere near so effectively. In fact, many failed so comprehensively that it is doubtful that they were ever intended to perform a military function.

Even in the far north of England or the Welsh marches castles do not always appear to have been successful in fulfilling a defensive role. The fluid tactics adopted by attackers ensured that they could simply bypass static fortifications and then ravage the countryside with impunity. The density of castles in the Welsh borders failed to stop incursions, as during major raids the insurgents simply entered England via high ground. Troops from castles sometimes caught the booty-laden raiders on their way back – but this can hardly be described as an effective strategy.[31] Although the earth and timber castles on the Welsh borders were intended to provide places of refuge for local communities, many could not resist determined aggression. In 1249, for example, Welsh raiders burned the mottes at Lydham and Brompton in Shropshire.[32] Larger castles provided more security but by themselves could do little in the face of a strong war party. In 1231, Montgomery Castle held out against a Welsh assault, but the resident staff could do nothing to protect the neighbouring town from the insurgents.[33] Equally, strings of fortresses did nothing to prevent Scottish incursions into England that sometimes penetrated as far south as Yorkshire; even major castles such as Knaresborough were no deterrent to ravaging Scots.[34] Thus even in supposedly 'militarized' areas castles could seldom do anything to prevent medieval armies from invading territory.

This frequent inability of castles to prevent raiding also stemmed from other factors. In periods of prolonged peace the provisioning and the condition of the buildings would frequently lapse. To judge from the endless stream of payments for building works on royal castles, many seem to have been in a state of disrepair.[35] Moreover, castles were frequently understaffed or unprepared for war. At Harlech, an inventory of 1403 records how the garrison had only three shields, eight helmets, six lances (with four missing their heads), ten pairs of gloves and four guns along with iron and lead for the defence of the castle.[36] Finally, although numbers fluctuated considerably, it was generally the case that the castle staff was small and so did not have the strength to sally out to defend the surrounding countryside. Permanent staffs were normally only three or four men strong, and consisted of a constable and a few watchmen. Even in an emergency, major castles sometimes had only a small staff. That at Conway in 1404–5 consisted of a constable, a man at arms and twelve archers.[37]

This level of unpreparedness was partly due to the fact that providing an adequate garrison and provisioning a castle for war was a hugely expensive operation. The cost of keeping a garrison at Nottingham for 18 months in 1267–68 came to £445, a sum made all the more telling by the fact that during this time their commander received less than £100 in income from his office.[38] At Criccieth, provisioning of 6 men at arms and 50 archers at the castle in

1402–3 amounted to a staggering £416 14s. 2d.[39] Similarly, the keeping of 159 men at Cockermouth Castle in 1316 to guard against Scottish raiding amounted to £100 for only three weeks.[40] The financial costs involved with garrisoning ensured that for most of the time castles had only limited manpower, so it is little wonder that so many played a negligible part in active campaigning. A small blockading force could thus be left around a castle by attackers, enabling the remainder of the army to continue on its way.

There were various mechanisms for assembling a larger garrison in wartime. In the eleventh and twelfth centuries, the basis of a garrison at a major castle might be provided by the feudal obligation of castle-guard, whereby tenants owed military service at the castle of their lord by virtue of their land tenure. There was considerable variation in the way in which this operated but it is clear that this was not a scheme for national defence – it seems more akin to suit of court – and in most cases could only provide a minimal number of men.[41] From an early date some services were commuted to a money payment that could then be used to hire a substitute. Castle-guard did retain its wartime importance in the Welsh Marches at castles such as Oswestry and Clun but over most of England it had become a military 'irrelevance' by the thirteenth century (Figure 39).[42] Much more important, particularly from the late twelfth century onwards, was the hiring of professional soldiers to perform garrison duty. This practice might raise numbers to between a dozen and two-dozen men for relatively important castles, but in actual wartime – that is, when armies were in the field and there was a likelihood of a serious attack – numbers might increase further still. The most reliable guide to the wartime sizes of garrisons comes from the few occasions where, after a castle had surrendered, the numbers of occupants were listed: the French garrison that surrendered at Colchester in 1216 and was given safe conduct numbered 116 (4 knights, 33 riding serjeants, 40 esquires and boys, 17 crossbowmen, 22 foot serjeants); that at Framlingham in the same year amounted to 54 (26 knights, 20 sergeants, 7 crossbowmen and a priest); while 41 individuals surrendered to King John at Nottingham in 1194, although this is a minimum figure. In the most recent survey it was concluded that, in the eleventh and twelfth centuries, the average garrison in peacetime was 12–15 men, rising to 140 in wartime.[43] It needs to be remembered, however, that the term 'garrison' is itself highly misleading in a medieval context, suggesting as it does a permanent standing force. The reality was that without an adequate source of manpower castles were rendered militarily useless. This ensured that castles were frequently *unable* to defend their surrounding countryside.

If all this was the case then why did castles find themselves caught up in war at all? The real value of the castle was that while it held out, no lord could make permanent claim to a conquered territory. If land was to be taken, all fortifications therein had to be reduced. When Louis of France invaded England in 1216, he was forced to leave part of his forces besieging Windsor and Dover Castles.[44] In the event, he was defeated in Lincoln and his invasion came to nothing, but if he had hoped to make his conquest complete both castles would have to have surrendered. Similarly, in his campaign of conquest against Normandy in the early fifteenth century, Henry V had to take, if necessary besieging, every strong point in order to make his gains permanent. While no castle was ever intended to withstand siege for an indefinite period, a determined and well-supplied garrison could hold out for many months, buying vital time in which a field force could be assembled to counter the incursion. This is the conclusion that emerges strongly from several studies: castles were most effective when they were used in conjunction with field armies.[45] In the north of England, for example, when not bypassed and ignored, some castles could hold out against the Scots and buy valuable time in which a field army could be assembled and led north to attempt an engagement. This is not to suggest that all castles had this function, or that they performed this task satisfactorily, but certain border fortresses such as Wark, Norham, Newcastle and Berwick did play an important role in border defence.[46] But for most castles, most of the time, there was little likelihood of an attack. On the rare occasions when castles did find themselves confronted with military forces outside their gates the form that sieges took was often complex.

Ritualised aggression: The conventions of siege warfare

The storming of fortifications was an invidious and dangerous enterprise that was potentially costly in terms of men and material. In much the same way that pitched battles were unpredictable affairs, unless the odds of victory during a siege were overwhelming, the outcome was far from certain. Strong-minded and well-supplied garrisons could potentially resist for weeks or months and the physical dangers that siege operations presented to attacking troops ensured that a particular status applied to towns or castles taken by storm. As late as the Napoleonic Wars, fortifications that had refused to surrender but which were subsequently taken could be sacked, the defenders deemed to have forfeited their right to quarter. In the Middle Ages contemporaries were well aware that prolonged sieges could result in death and injury for both attackers and defenders and often presented lurid details of the sometimes harsh realities of investing a castle.

In a situation where there was the potential for considerable bloodshed, a code of conventions quickly grew up which attempted to reconcile the interests of both besiegers and besieged. This chiefly took the form of what has been termed 'conditional respite': the besieging commander agreed to suspend operations for a set period of time while a beleaguered garrison petitioned its lord for aid.[47] If a relieving force failed to arrive then the garrison could surrender with honourable terms and expect reasonable treatment. Troops that ignored all calls to lay down their arms were taking a considerable gamble, especially if they were in revolt against the king; if their castle was taken by storm they risked harsh penalties from the victors. Conditional respite was a social response to the dangers of siege warfare. A castle might be won with no fighting and the

The Castle at War

FIGURE 40.
Corfe castle, Dorset. Even the mightiest fortress was vulnerable to treachery: Corfe was taken in 1646 after a Royalist traitor opened the gates to Parliamentary forces. Following its surrender, the walls were viciously slighted.

garrison's lives would also be spared. As a social mechanism it also reinforced the ethos of medieval aristocratic society. A garrison which was not relieved could surrender with honour intact; they had discharged their military obligations to their lord and he in turn had failed to come to their assistance. By the same token, by granting conditional respite a besieging lord was demonstrating his benevolence and augmenting his reputation as a noble warrior.

There were also more pragmatic reasons for negotiating some kind of truce. A castle or town might have to pay for the privilege of suspended hostilities and hand over sums of money to the besieging force. Additionally, attacking commanders were only willing to entertain a respite if there was little hope of the castle being relieved. If a fortress would eventually be surrendered without the need for a serious fight this was obviously highly advantageous; thus, on a general level, many of the 'rituals' of medieval siege warfare were designed to obviate the need for a major siege. This was partly due to the cost involved: a full siege could be prohibitively expensive. The three-month siege of Exeter in 1136 was reported to have cost fifteen thousand marks and the two month siege of Rochester in 1216, sixty thousand.[48] Some measure of the cost of the siege of Kenilworth in 1266 is to be gauged by the fact that the revenues of ten English counties were so exhausted that the sheriffs were unable to return any cash to the royal exchequer the following year.[49] It is therefore hardly surprising that full-scale sieges were not entered into lightly and that commanders were anxious to take fortresses by other means.

Although each military confrontation at a castle was unique, a set of common characteristics can be discerned. Initially, there might be a massive display of force in order to intimidate the garrison and persuade them to surrender. At Dover in 1216, the French army paraded several times in front of the castle walls in an attempt to sap the morale of the defenders. At this stage a state of siege had not been declared and the only fighting consisted of crossbowmen taking a few pot shots at the defenders.[50] The Norman besiegers at Ely in 1070 chose a more unorthodox way to intimidate their opponents. They acquired the services of a witch who advanced at the head of their troops and 'harangued the Isle and its inhabitants for a long time … casting spells for their overthrow; and at the end of her chattering and incantations she bared her arse at them'.[51] In this particular case, it brought the Normans no advantage. If it seemed that a castle was poorly defended then there might be an immediate assault. At Llanstephen Castle (Pembrokeshire) in 1146 a mixed force of Frenchmen and Flemings immediately attacked the Welshmen within 'when [they] saw how very few were the defenders, they raised ladders against the walls' but they were beaten back when their ladders were thrown from the walls.[52] Treachery was another means of gaining entry to a castle and accounted for many successful captures right through to the period of the Civil War. Corfe Castle in Dorset, 'one of the most impregnable in England', was only taken in 1646 when the Parliamentarians gained access due to a duplicitous royalist commander (Figure 40).[53] Robert Fitz Hildebrand chose a more unusual method in 1143 to gain control of Porchester Castle. He successfully courted the castellan's wife and then imprisoned her husband.[54]

If negotiation, treachery or immediate attack failed to get the necessary results, then a state of siege would be declared.[55] The firing of a single arrow into the closed castle gate might signal this event, but by the fifteenth century a single cannon shot might announce the start of the siege. At this point further negotiation would often take place and here a period of conditional respite might be agreed. A cessation of hostilities would only occur, however, if a garrison believed that it was unlikely to be relieved; thus in 1210 the English garrison at Llandovery (Llanymddyfri) was granted free passage and safety after surrendering because 'they had despaired of any kind of support'.[56] Within the period of conditional respite the garrison was not normally permitted to take any action that might give them an advantage, such as re-supply or fortify. However, this was not always respected; at Newbury in 1152 John Fitz Gilbert negotiated a respite from King Stephen and handed over his son William as a guarantee of his word. When he instead used the opportunity to replenish men and stores he put the young William in mortal danger. The child was placed in a siege engine and the royal troops threatened to catapult him over the castle walls. Fitz Gilbert replied from the battlements that he retained the equipment to make another son and entreated the besiegers to do what they wished. In the end William (later to have a remarkable military and political career) was spared only because Stephen baulked at hurling the boy to his death.[57]

The Castle at War

In other cases, if it became clear that they were faced with overwhelming odds a besieged force would back down at the very last minute in order to surrender. By the later Middle Ages this was usually the moment of the first cannonade, at which point it was obvious that the attacker meant business. This happened at Bamburgh in 1464, the castle yielding when 'all the king's guns [that] were charged to shoot upon the said castle'.[58]

A similar event took place in 1405 at the Earl of Northumberland's castle at Warkworth. Henry IV related the episode in a triumphant letter written to the Privy Council in London during his campaign, which is worth quoting at some length:

> We arrived at the castle of Warkworth and we sent to the captain ... [the letter is damaged at this point but the castle's surrender was obviously demanded] ... The said captain being well supplied with men as well as with victuals and other materials refused outright to do it, saying that he wanted to keep the castle for the use of the said Earl. And [he] sent us this as his last reply, we straight away set our cannons to that castle, which did us such service that before seven throws the said captain and all the men in his company, begging for mercy, submitted entirely to our grace and surrendered the aforementioned castle to us on the first day of this month of July, inside which we have installed our men. And all the castles of the said Earl have surrendered to us, except Alnwick, concerning which we trust that by the grace of God, after such great and glorious exploits with all the others, we will have our will and in a short time, if it please God.[59]

Situations such as these were common and make up a large proportion of the military incidents at medieval castles listed earlier. Both sides were often prepared to go through the motions of military conflict, but bloodshed could be, and frequently was, avoided.

If combat operations started in earnest there were three possible outcomes: the defenders could hold out; the garrison could be relieved; or, most commonly, the castle could be surrendered. When garrisons did choose to fight they did so because they believed they would be relieved or simply out of a sense of honour and loyalty to their lord. The attackers would then either have to mount an assault or begin a blockade. To this end, temporary siege castles were often built, examples of which still survive at Corfe in Dorset and probably at Bridgnorth in Shropshire (Figure 41). From these troops could plunder the surrounding countryside. At Tetbury (Staffordshire) in 1144, for example, royal forces besieging the castle despoiled the land around the castle.[60] At Mayette in Normandy, troops besieging the castle smashed walls and cut down trees and vines, although this was partly in response to an attempt on the life of William Rufus.[61] What eventually became of the garrison depended on the final outcome of events. A successful castellan had much to gain: for his defence of Dover, Hubert de Burgh gained renown across Europe. However, in the event of the castle falling there were, potentially, huge consequences. If the garrison was deemed to have fought well then they might leave with honour. The defenders of Hertford and Berkhamstead in 1217 were allowed to vacate with their arms and armour due to their stoic defence.[62] More usually, there would be a formal acknowledgment that defending troops had been defeated. The victor's banner was flown from the ramparts and trumpets were sounded as the defeated men left the castle. At Rochester in 1088, despite the surrendering garrison's protests, this was done as a public message of their defeat.[63] In some cases harsher treatment might follow. If a garrison had defied the king in person then this carried with it connotations of treason, for which punishments were more severe. This was certainly the case at Shrewsbury when, after a one-month siege where the defenders had refused numerous calls to surrender, King Stephen hanged the 94-man garrison, including the commander.[64] When the future Henry II took Crowmarsh in 1153 he spared the knights of the garrison but chose to execute 60 archers; these were men of humble status but their weapons could kill noblemen, and so they were deemed deserving of a sterner punishment. In

FIGURE 41. 'The Rings', Corfe, Dorset. The earthworks represent the remains of a siege castle constructed during the 1140s.

other cases, kings were persuaded to be more lenient. After the siege of Rochester in 1216 John was dissuaded from hanging all his captives as it was thought that this would only invite reprisals on captured royal garrisons and weaken their will to defend their castles; in the end, John hanged one crossbowman who had been in his household as a young man. However, in England and Wales throughout the Middle Ages it was not general practice to slaughter captured garrisons wholesale.[65]

What emerges as a key factor here is the role that negotiation played in determining whether a 'siege' resulted in actual fighting or an agreed surrender. By the Wars of the Roses this was such a truism that it had found its way into a proverb: 'The castle that speaketh and the woman who will hear, they will be gotten both'.[66] The number of defenders, the state of the supplies, the potential strength of the walls and the attitude of the garrison all had parts to play, but the wider political context of the siege was often the decisive factor in the course of events. This is amply borne out by an examination of three military confrontations at castles. Although quite different, each example illustrates how the precise context of an encounter often proved more important than military architecture or superior weaponry.

Conway 1401
Conway (Conwy) Castle in Caernarvonshire has rightly been described as 'one of the outstanding achievements of medieval military architecture', but its military record is not impressive (Figure 42).[67] Although it was occupied for several hundred years, the castle saw military action only on three occasions. The first was in 1294 when Edward I conducted a winter campaign against the men of Gwynedd who had rebelled earlier that year. As the English army moved along the North Wales coast the king pressed ahead of his army and found himself cut off in hostile territory. Edward was forced to fall back within the castle walls until the rest of his forces arrived. The Welsh attempted a blockade but soon fell back themselves when confronted by the main body of English troops. This was barely a 'siege' but does serve to illustrate how a castle could provide a level of security during organised campaigning. Nearly four centuries later, in 1646, Conway town was taken during the Civil War but the castle itself does not seem to have been subjected to attack. Once the Parliamentarians had secured the port (the Irish prisoners were tied back to back, thrown into the sea, and in the words of a Parliamentarian pamphleteer, 'sent by water to their own country') the castle was instructed to surrender and was yielded a few months later.[68]

These two events appear somewhat lacklustre, however, when compared to the most spectacular episode in the military history of Conway.[69] On 1 April 1401 (Good Friday) two brothers, Rhys and Gwilym ap Tudor, seized the castle and held it for nearly three months. In an elaborate *ruse de guerre* a group of about forty armed men entered the town while the English garrison were praying in the town's parish church. A Welsh carpenter then entered the castle on the pretext of undertaking routine maintenance work and killed the two

English watchmen on duty at the gate, whereupon the rebels then rushed into the castle and closed the gates. This proved a severe embarrassment to the English administration in Wales; not only had they lost the castle by a ruse, but the events had also taken place on one of the most significant days of the Christian calendar. The English then had to blockade the castle themselves while they negotiated with the brothers Tudor for its surrender. It was only returned to English control after Rhys and Gwilym had secured a pardon for their actions and agreed (somewhat harshly) to hand over some of their co-conspirators to be executed.

These events represent a stirring story from the Middle Ages, perhaps similar to the images of siege warfare we are familiar with from the popular media. But the significance of the siege should not be over-emphasised. The incident was 'the sort of daredevil act from which folk memories are quickly woven' but which, militarily speaking, 'had no immediate significance'.[70] However, the political context of the siege helps to explain a great deal. Rhys and Gwilym were driven to action by the fact that Henry IV had refused to pardon them for taking part in Owain Glyn Dŵr's rebellion the previous year;

FIGURE 42. Conway castle, Caernarvonshire. On Good Friday 1401 Conway was the scene of a major embarrassment for the English when a small group of Welsh rebels entered the castle while the English garrison prayed in the nearby church. The English were then forced to besiege the castle themselves and eventually forced its surrender.

MICK SHARP

The Castle at War the Good Friday incident was a desperate act by men who were increasingly becoming politically isolated in their own region. Moreover, once they were holed up behind the castle walls, their situation rapidly began to deteriorate. After the initial seizure the crown was forced to acquiesce to their demands but as time went on it began to take a harder line. With approximately 120 men at arms and 300 archers blockading the castle it was obvious that the rebels' negotiating position was tenuous and it was probably for this reason that Rhys and Gwilym allowed some of their men to be given over for execution. In return for their pardon, the crown could visibly punish at least some of the rebels for their actions.

The events at Conwy illustrate two important points. Firstly, even the largest and most magnificent castles were not constantly guarded strongholds. Secondly, possession of a castle was not always a military advantage; holding it could prove a liability and represented a constant drain on resources.

Bedford 1224
Bedford Castle was founded at some point in the late eleventh century. In the early thirteenth century it was acquired by the mercenary captain Fawkes de Bréauté, a major political and military figure in the war between John and his barons and during the minority of Henry III. Despite fighting on behalf of the Angevin cause, during the recovery of royal power in the aftermath of civil war Fawkes' power and wealth made him a target for Henry's supporters. He had made powerful political enemies and caused much resentment by his alleged usurping of royal authority in the lands over which he had control. While this might have been acceptable in the unusual circumstances of civil war, by the mid-1220s accusations of this nature could have serious consequences. When Henry de Braybrooke (the royal justice charged with dealing with complaints against Fawkes) was captured and taken prisoner in Bedford Castle, Fawkes' enemies moved against him.[71] Fawkes had certainly spent a good deal of effort in making Bedford Castle a fitting residence for a man of his station – in this case something of an upstart. He had demolished two churches to expand the castle site and added a new *donjon*, a large bailey revetted with stone and an outer barbican. Negotiations between Fawkes and Henry had been ongoing over previous weeks but were brought to a close when the garrison sent out a message to the king that they wished to receive no more royal heralds demanding their surrender. Fawkes himself went north in an attempt to rally support and charged his brother William with defending Bedford against the king.

The royal forces surrounded the castle and set to work building engines. Specialist engineers were sent to assist, one of whom, a Master Thomas, was reported to be 'skilled in such science'. Four mangonels (a stone-throwing engine) were stationed around the castle and two siege engines built and placed up against the walls; these were so effective that they forced the garrison to move around the castle in their armour. There followed four main assaults on the castle. First, the outer barbican was captured and, subsequently, the outer bailey, where the royal forces found large amounts of provisions (a valuable detail). Taking the inner bailey and *donjon* proved more difficult and miners under the protection of a large hoarding or 'cat' eventually managed to bring down the inner bailey wall. Finally the *donjon* was also mined and as the garrison sat down to their evening meal smoke filled the rooms and a large crack appeared in the walls. Knowing the game was up, the garrison sent out Fawkes's wife, her female household and the captive Henry of Braybrooke. As a sign of surrender they hoisted the royal standard on the tower and spent one more night in the ruined donjon before emerging the next day. They first received absolution from the archbishop of Canterbury, after which they begged for mercy at the feet of the king. One near-contemporary account suggests that Henry had vowed before the siege to hang the garrison; another relates how he asked his archbishop for counsel who in turn pointed his finger at the royal justiciar. Whatever the discussion, the whole garrison, probably in the region of eighty men, was hanged.

The siege had lasted for eight weeks and the garrison had resisted, in the words of the chronicler Ralph of Coggeshall, 'with foolish bravery and stubborn probity'. Fawkes had taken a huge gamble and had been pursuing a risky military and political strategy, although the decision to resist the king by force had partly been to buy time in which he could appeal to the Pope for justice.

FIGURE 43. Framlingham castle, Suffolk. Framlingham was the residence of the Bigod family and was substantially re-built *c.*1190. In 1216 the castle failed to offer any resistance to an army led by King John, despite a strong garrison. The 'siege' lasted only a matter of hours.

The Castle at War

FIGURE 44.
Rochester castle, Kent. In 1215 Rochester was the scene of a closely-pressed siege as King John spent nearly a month investing the castle; the garrison only surrendered after part of the *donjon* had been brought down by mining. Afterwards, a chronicler wrote, 'few cared to put their trust in castles'.

Eventually the Pope wrote to England, demanding an end to Fawkes' maltreatment, but the letters were dated three days after the surrender. Following his defeat Fawkes' castle was slighted and became the site of a manor house. Even though the castle had been physically broken, the fact that the walls were then torn down and the motte reduced in size speaks volumes about the symbolic power of crenellation in this period.[72]

Framlingham 1216

Framlingham Castle in Suffolk was the power base of the Bigod family, great East Anglian magnates, Earls of Norfolk and a family with a reputation as political troublemakers.[73] Hugh Bigod had seized Norwich Castle in 1136 and King Stephen was forced to move against him in the 1150s, as was Henry II in 1173. The original castle, founded around the year 1100, probably took the form of a motte and bailey, and was surrendered and destroyed following Hugh Bigod's involvement in the great rebellion against Henry II in 1173. Hugh's son Roger re-built the site in the 1190s and it is his work that stands today (Figure 43). Roger certainly chose to build in a military style, especially when compared to the newly-completed royal castle at Orford ten miles to the south east. There was no central *donjon*; rather, the castle took the form of a large stone ringwork studded with thirteen mural towers. Considerable provision was made for archery, with elaborate embrasures allowing for interlocking and flanking fire. At least in theory, any intruder could have been disabled before they reached the castle walls.

In the autumn of 1215 King John's war with his rebellious barons was at its height. While John set about trying to reverse the terms of Magna Carta by diplomatic means, he also gathered his troops in an effort to deal with the rebels militarily. Late in the year he left loyal lieutenants to blockade London while he himself set out at the head of an army that he took north to ravage the land of his opponents. In the midst of this campaign, he had spent Christmas at Nottingham, 'not in the usual fashion, but as one on the warpath'.[74] In the spring of 1216 John returned south and moved against East Anglia, specifically targeting Roger Bigod, one of the region's principal rebels; a chronicler who was probably in the royal host relates that John's troops paid particular attention to the lands of Roger – by which he means that they plundered them thoroughly. On or around March 11th, the leading royal scouts reached Framlingham. The Bigod honour was clearly on a war footing, as we know that Roger had a strong garrison at Framlingham consisting of 26 knights, 20 sergeants, 7 crossbowmen and a priest. All was set for what was potentially a major siege.

John himself appeared at Framlingham on 12th March and must have left the following day, because on the 13th March he is known to have been in Ipswich. Although we do not know exactly what happened on 12th we can surmise the course of events. On the 13th, letters of safe conduct were granted to two of Roger's knights so they could return to him and negotiate peace terms. Roger had clearly decided to surrender at once and there is no evidence of a 'siege' as such; rather, the castle had been given up without a fight, despite the undoubtedly strong defences and adequate garrison.

Again, we need to investigate the wider political context of early 1216 in order to explain the course of events. The previous year John had spent nearly two months taking Rochester Castle in Kent; in a very rare example of a siege prosecuted with vigour by both sides the defenders only surrendered when half the *donjon* was brought down by undermining and their provisions ran desperately low (Figure 44).[75] What had taken place at Rochester was clearly very unusual but the price of defying the king had been seen by the whole kingdom – he had shown his determination, if needs be, to press home a siege to the limit. The Barnwell Chronicler famously wrote of the siege that 'our age has not known a siege so hard pressed nor so strongly resisted, afterwards ... few cared to put their trust in castles'. This statement has been seen in the past as evidence of the beginning of the military 'decline' of castles but perhaps it should be interpreted to mean that defending castles as part of a *political* strategy was no longer wise. With the French prince Louis yet to arrive in England with an army and form a party capable of taking on John, resistance made little political sense. For John, the symbolic value of taking castles (and all that it implied about royal power) was more important than the holding of them as fortresses for himself.

The events at Framlingham are far more typical of the medieval siege than those at Bedford. The kind of incident at Framlingham accounts for the majority of 'actions' listed in the peaks in Figure 35. Similar events took place

Castles in Context: Power, Symbolism and Landscape, 1066–1500

when John moved into Essex shortly afterwards: Colchester surrendered without a fight and Castle Hedingham after three days. When viewed in this light, the high numbers of actions listed in Figure 35 appear less dramatic.

Conclusion

There is no escaping the fact that castles did find themselves under siege in the Middle Ages and that these confrontations could result in violence and bloodshed. This does not, however, mean that the primary purpose of castles was military or that there was an ever-present danger of attack. From what we have seen here, for most castles, for most of the time, attack was a vague and remote possibility. This was particularly the case in lowland England. Here, castles only became involved in actual war on two main occasions: during the Anarchy of Stephen's reign and during the civil war of the early thirteenth century. These conflicts were characterised by organised campaigning where armies were in the field and castles could have some effect on the outcome of events. But even here it is certainly not the case that all castles had the same significance; many took no active part in hostilities simply because their lords did not, and the castles themselves were simply surrendered. It is salutary to note that many of the examples of castle warfare in England and Wales cited above come from the reigns of Stephen, John and Henry III: if we seek to see how castles operated in periods of organised warfare we are necessarily forced to look at very atypical events.

Also notable is the surprisingly large number of sieges that took place at medieval castles during the Civil War. The military role of some castles in the seventeenth century is out of all proportion to their medieval histories. The defences of Pontefract Castle in Yorkshire, for example, were never put to the test from the castle's foundation in the eleventh century until it was attacked three times in the Civil War. Similarly, at Beeston in Cheshire the castle of the 1220s failed to see any major military action until the seventeenth century, when it was attacked twice. At Beeston today, it is these events that form the basis for the public display on the site. While the Civil War actions may be highly appropriate for the final episode in the castle's history they are certainly not representative of most of its occupation. Activity during the Civil War makes up a substantial proportion of military encounters in counties such as Yorkshire and Shropshire, which stands in contrast to the almost total lack of attacks in these areas since the end of the Wars of the Roses. The role of the medieval castle in the Civil War is a study in its own right, but the legacy that the seventeenth century bequeathed to the military perception of castles is certainly greater than has hitherto been suspected.

Nonetheless, it is important to place medieval sieges back into the context of warfare as a whole. It needs to be re-emphasised just how rare an occurrence a full-scale siege actually was in medieval England; much in the same way as pitched battles were avoided, medieval commanders deliberately eschewed major sieges. With this in mind, it is instructive that some of our best accounts of siege warfare in England and Wales come from only a handful of examples: Rochester in 1215, Dover in 1216, Bedford in 1224, Kenilworth in 1266. Because these were rare events at the time, chroniclers wrote about them at some length and in turn historians have let them dominate our perceptions of siege warfare as a whole.

However, although confrontations at castles may have been more numerous than were pitched battles over the course of the Middle Ages, we should not come to the conclusion that a military role was necessarily paramount or even important for the majority of castles. In his examination of the role of castles in the fourteenth century, Michael Prestwich has commented that 'it was not very often that the castles of medieval England were put to the test'.[76] This chapter has aimed to show not only how rare such a test was, but also how badly prepared many castles were to meet it.

Castles in Context: Power, Symbolism and Landscape, 1066–1500

CHAPTER FIVE

Lordly Landscapes

Introduction

In Chapter Two the ways in which the building of a crenellated residence projected a particular image of lordly authority were discussed. In this chapter, we will look beyond the limits of the bailey and examine the structures that surrounded the medieval castle and the activities that took place in its immediate environs. The impact of castles on the countryside could be considerable, not only in the exploitation of materials by lords for castle construction but also in the construction of adjacent settlements, parks, religious houses and other landscape features. A castle rarely stopped at its moat and certain aspects of castle-building can only be fully appreciated if we take a broader, landscape-based perspective.[1]

In the last two decades archaeologists and landscape historians have spent a considerable amount of time investigating the ways in which the building of a castle impacted on its immediate environment. Much of this innovative work has centred on the recognition and recording of what have been termed 'designed' or 'ornamental' landscapes at castle sites, and has led to the appreciation that some of the structures that surrounded castles were not constructed simply for utilitarian purposes, but had been contrived partly to improve the setting of the residential buildings. Thus features such as fishponds, mills, settlements and dovecotes may have been carefully placed in specific locations around the castle in order to enhance its aesthetic appeal. For this to be the case these structures must have been imbued with particular social or symbolic meanings that would have been highly apparent to people at the time, but which are not necessarily so obvious to us today. In addition, it needs to be emphasised that we are not talking here about a few isolated or individual structures placed adjacent to the castle gate; rather, the field archaeology suggests that at some of the largest castles the entire surrounding landscape had been manipulated to improve the setting of the buildings. Significantly, such designed landscapes have also been identified around medieval monastic houses and royal and ecclesiastical palaces, places which are clearly not designed primarily for defence. This means that castle landscapes might more profitably be compared to eighteenth-century pleasure grounds and parks, rather than the killing grounds of a warrior noble.[2]

The identification of designed landscapes of medieval date is now relatively

FIGURE 45.
Leeds castle, Kent. The castle stands at the centre of a 'designed landscape' of late thirteenth-century date. The detached building was known as the 'Gloriette', a term that referred to a private suite of apartments set within a park or garden. From here the beauty of the landscape could be fully appreciated.

97

straightforward, as enough examples have been investigated to allow some common elements to be discerned. The most elaborate landscapes comprised an 'inner core' of structures that could include a small enclosed garden (known as the *herber*), orchards and small ponds.[3] Beyond this lay an outer area which might include a park-like garden, further water features, religious buildings, rabbit warrens, mills and settlements. This is, of course, to over-generalise; the presence of all these elements and their precise spatial arrangement obviously varied immensely from site to site. Here, the significance lies not so much in the idea that these features have only recently been recognised (many have been known about since the birth of castle studies) but, rather, in the fact that our understanding of the mechanisms by which they were planned, arranged and understood has improved beyond all recognition. In terms of landscape *design*, the use of water to create artificial lakes, the provisioning of a park to provide a sylvan backdrop to the main residence, or the attempt to correct the effect of perspective when constructing a 'view' are all attested at medieval castle sites. Certainly enough information has been gathered to completely overturn the traditional – and often repeated – idea that landscape 'design' originated during the Renaissance.

Designed landscapes: some examples

Leeds Castle, in Kent, is a fine example of the way in which the use of water and parkland could be combined to stunning visual effect (Figure 45). In 1279 the manor of Leeds passed to Edward I and at this date the castle probably comprised a motte and bailey with an adjacent deer park. During the 1280s the castle was substantially rebuilt and surrounded by a large ornamental lake. The main focus of building was the tower, named the 'Gloriette', which was raised on what was probably the site of the Norman motte. By the late thirteenth century the term 'Gloriette' meant a suite of lordly accommodation within a park or garden and thus seems a highly appropriate description for a building set within an artificial mere. Additional ponds were constructed to the south, northwest and east, the last of which was clearly intended to be viewed from the Gloriette. Leeds castle in fact sits within a huge water garden of medieval date.[4] Edward I and his queen, Eleanor of Castile, made frequent visits to the castle and there is some suggestion that the design may have been influenced by the Islamic gardens Eleanor would have known in Spain. The whole *ensemble* was overlooked to the west by higher ground and it is possible a viewing platform was located in this area, from which the royal party and guests could appreciate the beauty of the castle in its watery setting.

A similar situation is found at Ravensworth in Yorkshire, a castle held by the Fitzhugh family throughout the Middle Ages (Figure 46).[5] Henry Fitzhugh II transformed the castle and landscape at the end of the fourteenth century, with water and parkland again being the dominant elements. A considerable effort went into damming a watercourse in order to create a lake around the castle. This arrangement, in turn, was enveloped by a park through which the

Castles in Context: Power, Symbolism and Landscape, 1066–1500

FIGURE 46.
Ravensworth castle, Yorkshire. Plan of the castle showing the approach into the castle and its immediate landscape context.

PAUL EVERSON/NATIONAL MONUMENTS RECORD

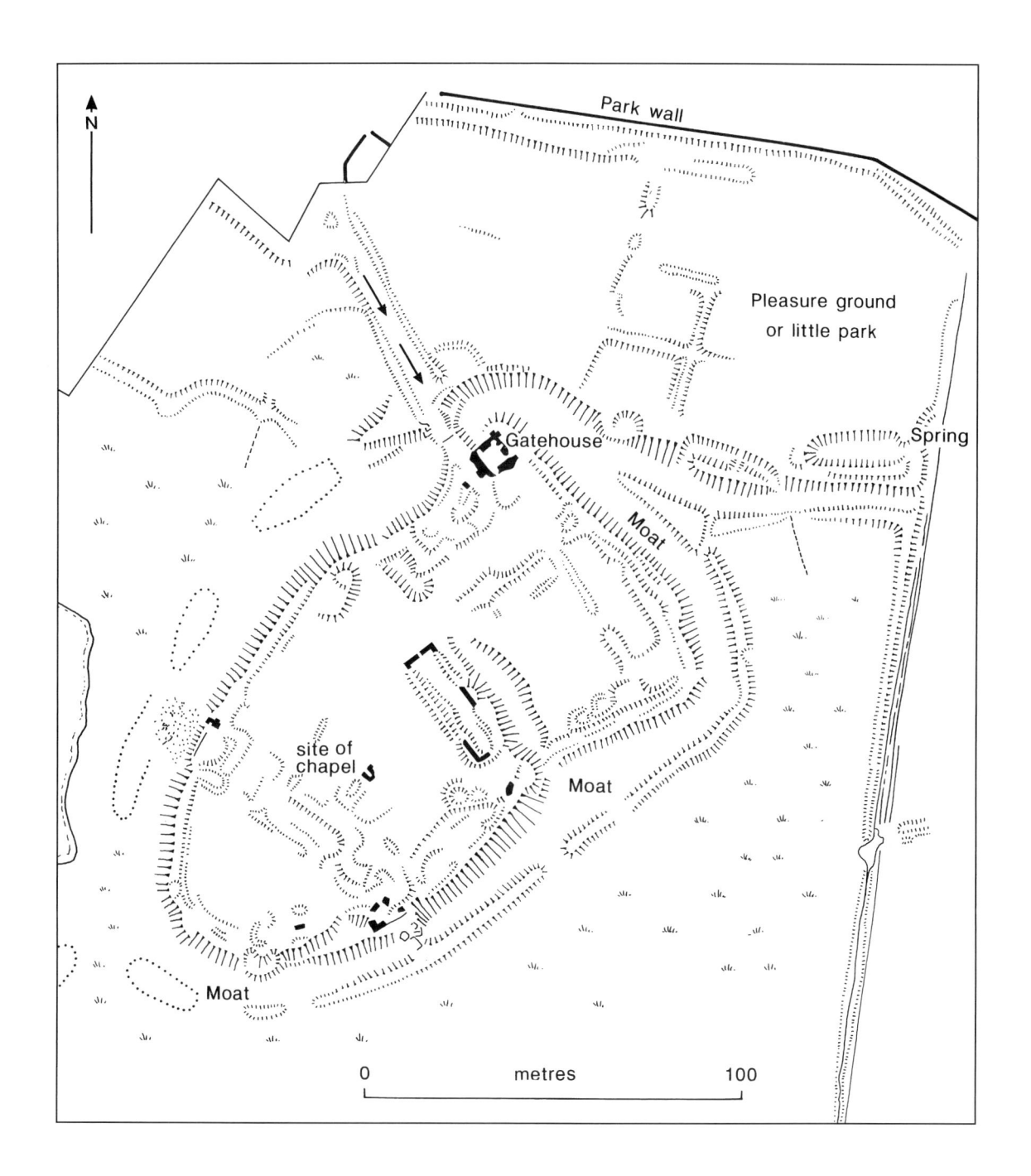

visitor had to pass before they could gain entry to the castle. The aesthetic and symbolic character of the site was made apparent by the chivalric emblems on the building as well as by the highly structured approach to the castle, the existence of a walled pleasure park and, probably, a walk around the castle itself. This is certainly not what we would expect to find in a part of England that is often characterised as an anarchic and war-torn border area.

Designed landscapes also characterised earlier periods, however; one of Norman date is to be found at Devizes in Wiltshire. Here, Bishop Roger of Salisbury (1107–39) constructed a new castle with an attendant borough and a deer park (Figure 47). This foundation seems to have been entirely new and the effect of such an imposition on the existing tenurial geography can be seen in the place-name Devizes, which derives from the Norman French *le devises*, meaning 'the divisions'. The borough took the form of a semi-circle with a market place and church that were overlooked by the castle. This 'public' space was mirrored by the more 'private' area of the deer park, which has the oval shape and bank and ditch typical of early parkland. Here, water features were not part of the scheme and, unusually for a castle of this size, an accompanying religious house was not founded, but the visual qualities of the whole site were nevertheless remarked on long ago by Beresford, who proposed that a fine view of the landscape would have been afforded from the castle tower.[6]

Such examples are typical of the kind of medieval designed landscape that have been recorded in recent years. However, while their identification is now relatively straightforward, aspects of their origins, workings and dating remains unresolved; landscape archaeologists are only beginning to appreciate their scale and complexity. While it may be possible to ascribe particular features to the medieval period, achieving closer dates and proper phasing of the various landscape features is extremely difficult. A castle and landscape occupied over many generations would naturally be adapted and altered as need or desire required, and additionally, while it seems apparent that the primary purpose of such landscapes was ornamental (i.e. they enhanced the setting of residential buildings) and, as such, they were intended to give pleasure to those who experienced them, it is clear that 'designed landscapes' were highly complicated enterprises that fulfilled a number of different roles, had complex histories and were experienced differently by different social groups. The discussion that follows will examine some of these issues and attempt to bring out the complex reality of landscape design in the Middle Ages.

Landscapes of production

The designed landscapes that surrounded castles fulfilled an economic role. During the Middle Ages it was expected that a lord's lifestyle should be commensurate with his status and this entailed, amongst other things, maintaining a retinue, taking part in elite activities (such as hunting), wearing certain clothes and consuming particular foods. The resources needed to sustain such a lifestyle ultimately came from a lord's landed wealth and the arrangement of landscape features around castles can be seen, at least in part, as a response by lords to the economic demands of their social rank. In one sense, then, we can 'read' designed landscapes in economic terms, with each component element providing a specific resource or service.

There is some evidence that lords were fully conscious of the economic

Lordly Landscapes   dimensions of their designed landscapes while they were still contemplating building. Individuals appear to have been keenly aware that their operations might well impinge on the interests of other landowners in the locality and thereby risk conflict. Bishop Alexander of Lincoln, in the early 1130s, was careful to pre-empt any action that might be taken against him before he made extensions to his castle at Newark. He ensured that he received a charter that specifically guaranteed his right to divert the king's highway and extend his fishponds – potentially the most difficult part of his plans.[7] Occasionally it is possible to glimpse the economic rationale behind developing other parts of the castle landscape. At Orford (Suffolk), in 1171, marshland near the castle was enclosed specifically 'to increase the farm' that is, the annual sum to be gained if it were let. The financial dimension of landscape design is also clearly attested by the attempts by lords to found settlements with attendant fairs and markets adjacent to their residences. This was particularly a feature of the eleventh and twelfth centuries and it has been estimated that nearly 80 per cent of all town foundations in the period 1066–1100 were associated with castles.[8] In some cases, such as Windsor and Arundel, the castle became the focus for new settlements as people moved close to the castle from existing farms in order to take advantage of the economic opportunities generated by the needs of the resident staff. In other cases, the settlement was part of the original design and castle-builders sometimes went to great lengths to ensure that towns or settlements were placed next to rivers or major roads so that potential trade could be exploited. Perhaps the most famous exponent of this practice was Robert de Bellême, who transferred the settlement of Quatford in Shropshire to a more favourable site alongside his castle at Bridgnorth.[9]

Numerous studies show that examples such as Bridgnorth were somewhat extreme instances of a more general lordly concern to exploit any commercial opportunities that castle-building offered. At Ongar, in Essex, the castle bailey was superimposed onto the main street of an existing settlement in order to exercise control over trade.[10] In a blatant act of economic appropriation, Robert Count of Mortain had the market of the monks of St Stephen's-by-Launceston in Cornwall transferred to his castle, clearly wishing to take a share of its revenue.[11] Sometimes these enterprises proved worthwhile: at Eye in Suffolk, the market of Robert Malet had by 1086 proved so successful that it was having a detrimental effect on that of the Bishop of Thetford at nearby Hoxne.[12] A similar situation pertained at Trematon Castle in Cornwall, where Robert of Mortain's market had ruined that of nearby St Germans.[13] In other cases castle settlements were failures. At New Buckenham in Norfolk, William D'Albini II acquired land from the Bishop of Norwich so that he could place his new castle and planned town (with some 40 burgesses) adjacent to the main Norwich to Thetford road in an effort to stimulate trade.[14] The venture was far from a success, however, and the fact that New Buckenham can now boast one of the best surviving examples of a Norman town plan is a legacy of economic stagnation and the settlement's failure to expand much beyond its initial bounds. But whether successful or not, it is the sheer number of castle settlements that demonstrate that lords saw their *capita* as a direct means of generating wealth.

If lords hoped that their towns and settlements would produce revenue, then other features that made up designed landscapes provided different kinds of resources. One of the most important was game, which centred on the rearing of deer – a prestige animal, the keeping of which was synonymous with aristocratic rank – but castle landscapes were also arenas for producing rabbits, fish, waterfowl and other game birds.

The primary area for specialised animal husbandry was the deer park. The association between park and castle went back at least to the time of Domesday and the deer park was a backdrop common to secular and ecclesiastical residences throughout the Middle Ages.[15] At the largest castles there was frequently more than one, with the 'Little park' close to the castle, and a larger or 'Great' park usually removed from the main residence, as seen at Fotheringay in Northamptonshire. A similar arrangement often pertained to fishponds; stews frequently appear in the sources differentiated into 'Great'

FIGURE 47. Devizes castle, Wiltshire. Devizes was raised in the twelfth century by Roger, Bishop of Salisbury. The juxtaposition of castle, planned town and deer park is a classic Norman arrangement.

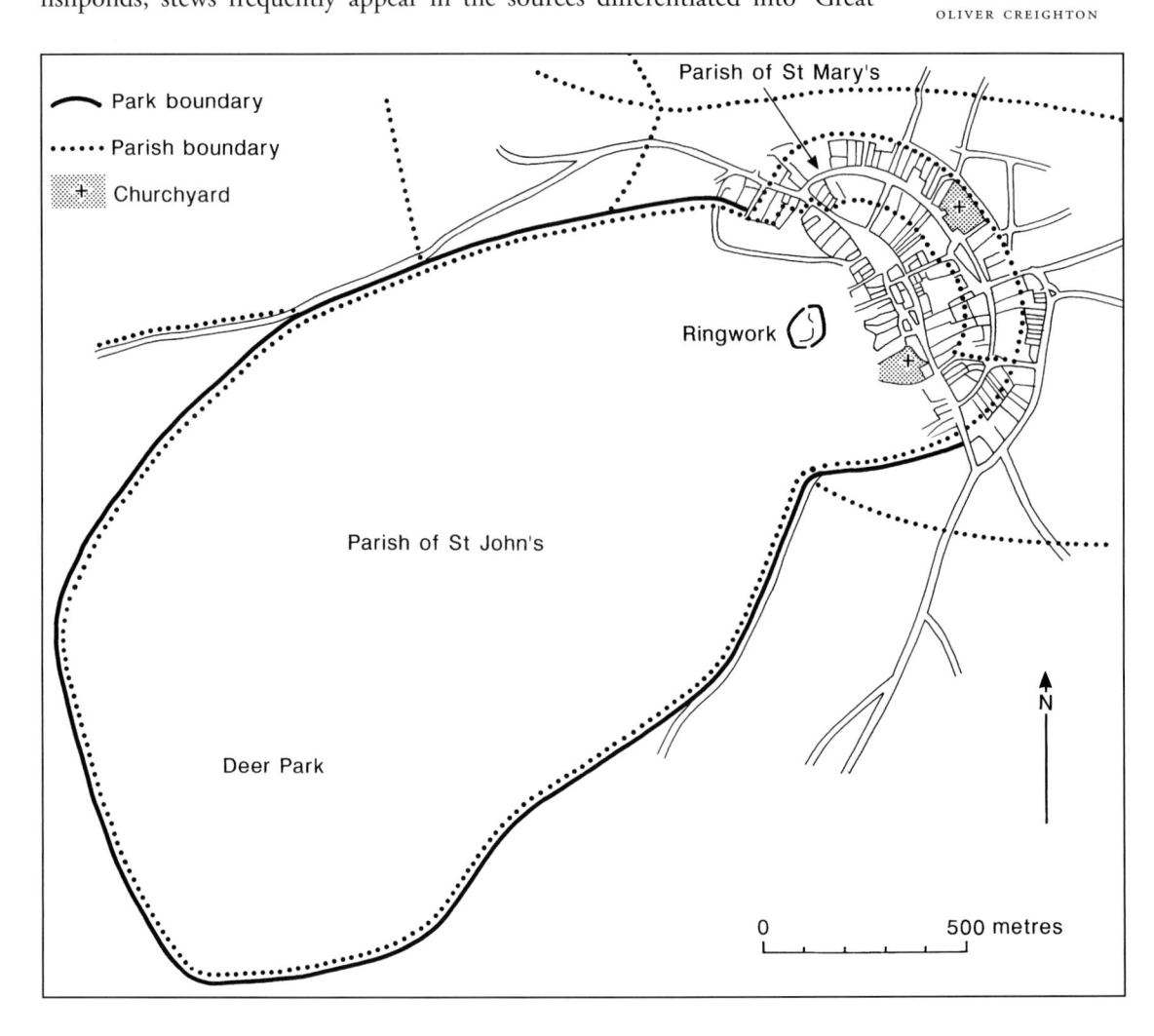

OLIVER CREIGHTON

Lordly Landscapes

FIGURE 48. Launceston castle, Cornwall. The history of the castle can be traced through the excavated bone assemblage. During the castle's heyday in the thirteenth century a vast array of game was being consumed on site. As the castle's importance diminished in the later Middle Ages, so too the variety of foodstuffs eaten became more restricted.

and 'Little' ponds. The larger ponds – *vivarium* – were probably reserved for large-scale breeding practices, and are often found in parks, but the Little Pond – *servatorium* – was usually closer to the castle. Alongside parks and ponds, rabbit warrens and dovecotes also had a place in game management. Dovecotes frequently appear adjacent to castles and at Stafford the warren was situated within the Great Park, while that at Castle Rising in Norfolk bordered the park and extended some five kilometres to the south-west of the castle.[16] Designed landscapes, then, served an important role in specialised food production.

At some castles game production amounted to something of an industry. For much of its history Barnard Castle (Durham) was at the centre of a huge trade in venison, where deer reared on neighbouring uplands were butchered and then transported across the kingdom.[17] Although perhaps not on the same scale, evidence for deer management can be found at other castles. Where there was more than one park this allowed stocks of deer to be separated or herded for rearing, fattening and for the selecting of beasts for hunting. At Clare (Suffolk), in the fourteenth century, the deer were rotated in the three castle parks according to their age.[18] Evidence from a variety of other sources indicates that the designed landscapes at other castles also functioned as game reserves and to judge from accounts of park-breaking, a wide array of species was being reared at castles. One such account of a break on Queen Philippa's parks at Knaresborough Castle stated that the intruders carried off deer, hare, rabbit, pheasant and partridges.[19] The frequency with which species such as peacock, woodcock and duck appear in other such accounts strongly suggests that at least some of these were being produced on site. It is possible to trace the changing fortunes of Launceston castle through its bone assemblage: during the castle's heyday in the thirteenth century a wide array of game species are represented, but the range of taxa dramatically falls away as the castle became less important in the fourteenth and fifteenth centuries (Figure 48).[20]

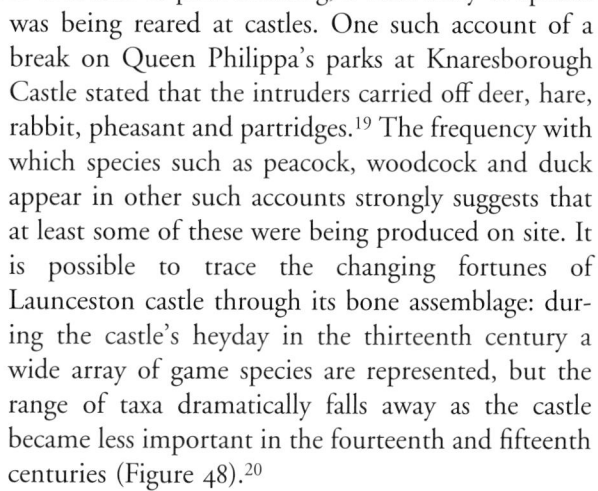

Features such as parks and warrens were valuable assets but they also required a tremendous amount of investment and management. Most parks were surrounded by a pale: a large earthwork bank with ditches on either side, topped by a fence or hedge. Pales were intended to prevent the deer from escaping and also offered a degree of security from poachers or other unwanted guests. For a park to function effectively, the pale had to be kept in constant repair; consequently, lords spent vast sums on their upkeep. At Stafford castle, in the fourteenth century, there were payments nearly every year for repairs: in one year replacing 200 pales required expenditure of £9 1s 9½d – a price comparable to the construction of a new mill.[21] Similar investment went into keeping the banks and walls of warrens secure. Despite all this, however, in many cases parks and warrens were loss-making enterprises; they were valuable because of the social *cachet* they conveyed. As such, they are a reminder of the complex motivations underpinning landscape design in this period.

Alongside the management of game, designed landscapes supported a diverse range of other activities. Most medieval parks contained a mixture of standard mature trees, coppiced underwood and sections of open grazing, thus providing an ideal environment for a variety of other interests. The keeping of non-game animals within parks was a common occurrence: at Skipton, in 1307, it was reported by a royal official that the king's deer had suffered due to the former keeper, Richard Oysel, over-grazing the castle park with seventy horses.[22] In 1357, at Peckforton Park in Cheshire (attached to Beeston Castle), the Black Prince was obliged to let some of the deer free as there was not enough pasture to support their great number.[23] Studs are known from Knaresborough and, again, Skipton parks. Another important activity was the production of timber. Extents and surveys show that parks were often great forestry enterprises and sometimes there were also associated industrial activities; Knaresborough was the scene of ironworking and in 1385 charcoal burning took place in Framlingham castle park in Suffolk.[24]

Castle landscapes were, therefore, 'productive' areas, which provided lords with a range of services and material goods. This was not simply a straightforward matter of economic potential; as intimated above, more complex strategies were clearly involved. Some elements, such as parks, appear not to have justified – at least in strictly economic terms – the resources spent on them, whereas other features, such as towns, seem to have been more pragmatic enterprises. Quite whether lords expected to 'offset' the expense of one part of their elite landscape by the profits of another is, at present, impossible to tell, but detailed work on individual lords in the future might help to reveal particular strategies. But on any reading of the evidence, economic factors were clearly at work in castle landscapes and while designed landscapes may have been intended to provide a scenic backdrop to residential buildings we must also remember that they had a very direct economic role, from which standpoint many of their other meanings were derived.

Landscapes of recreation

Designed landscapes were the pleasure grounds of the medieval aristocracy. Documentary sources make it abundantly clear that medieval men and women enjoyed walking in and around their formal gardens and took delight from the animals, plants and ponds that were contained within.[25] The wider setting of the castle's associated landscape was the scene for more energetic pursuits. Jousting, archery, boating and fishing all took place at castles, but the chief

Lordly Landscapes

pastime, for which many of the larger designed landscapes were engineered, was hunting.

Given their role in producing game, it is no surprise that the largest designed landscapes contained some kind of hunting ground. It is difficult to underestimate the importance of this activity to medieval aristocrats, both as a source of pleasure and as a social ritual. William the Conqueror was famously reputed to 'love the deer as if they were his own' and his son Henry I was said 'to study the footprints of deer with a high degree of science'. Alexander Neckham, writing in about 1200, commented that 'the pleasant bark of the hounds is more delightful to the ears of our nobles than the sweet harmony of musical instruments'.[26] The ecclesiastic John of Salisbury, writing at about the same time, was more scornful of the time that nobles put into the hunt: 'In our days, the scholarship of the aristocracy consists in hunting jargon'.[27]

The practice of hunting was important for a number of reasons.[28] To begin with, aristocrats simply enjoyed the activity: the chase was physically exhilarating. It was also a method of preparing knights for war; indeed, it was so dangerous that hunting accidents led to many deaths, of which that of William Rufus in the New Forest in 1100 is only the most well known. It kept the participants active, a fact seized upon by moralists as it was believed that idleness led to sinful behaviour. There was also a strong religious element to the pleasures of the chase. It was believed that Man had once had the same level of senses as the animals but that this had been lost at the Fall; thus the appreciation of the quarry's skill and dexterity during the chase represented a way of getting closer to the perfect nature of Mankind that had existed in Eden. There was also a strong sexual dimension to hunting. Hunts were often elaborately planned and staged activities, involving hundreds of men and women, and the themes of pursuing and capturing the quarry readily lent themselves to the ideas of courtly love and sexual largesse. The keeping of deer was emblematic of noble rank and consequently the process of hunting ennobled the participants; it demonstrated their skill in horsemanship and in handling weapons and, no doubt, was intended to imply that they were the masters of worldly beasts. Hunting was also closely connected with hospitality. It provided an excellent opportunity for entertainment on the part of the king or baron and there were no doubt many social aspirants who advanced their position or political standing by forging relationships during expeditions or the feasting which ended the day. It is impossible to understand some aspects of medieval designed landscapes without reference to this crucial facet of noble existence during the Middle Ages.

Given the significance of hunting, it is not difficult to see the important place of parkland in landscape design. Unsurprising also is the fact that there was a close correlation between the royal itinerary and royal forests. Several important castles, such as (Old) Wardour in Wiltshire and Odiham in Hampshire, were effectively grand hunting lodges. At places such as these the castle parks were often huge and certainly large enough to permit a substantial hunt. Where the castle bordered the royal forest, hunting parties could leave for days on end, staying at large purpose-built lodges, such as that at Haverah in Knaresborough, during the expedition. In other cases, the arena of the Little Park could provide a venue for a more stage-managed hunting scene, a point returned to below.

Somewhat less violent was the activity of boating. The artificial meres that were adjacent to castles such as Kenilworth, in Warwickshire, or Framlingham, in Suffolk, may have been able to support large quantities of fish and fowl but they also provided excellent boating lakes. At Kenilworth part of Henry V's extension to the mere involved creating a double moated enclosure that was only accessible by boat. Whether fishing and fowling were as popular as hunting is difficult to tell but these activities certainly also took place; for example, in 1255 it was recorded that men fished in the moat at Gloucester castle.[29]

Alongside their economic and recreational purposes, designed landscapes sustained a variety of symbolic meanings. Worthy of emphasis is the sheer scale of designed landscapes at the largest castle sites. This is of some significance, as many are simply *too* big to be *purely* functional and must have had additional meanings beyond the mere utilitarian. Obviously, the use of such symbolism varied from site to site and must have been more apparent at some castles than others, but there is strong evidence that the social messages displayed through landscape manipulation were deliberately articulated and not lost on contemporaries.

The seigneurial landscape

One of the most important symbolic messages conveyed by castle landscapes was that of manorial lordship. This powerful visual vocabulary of seigneurial power was particularly potent since in a society where large sections of the population were vulnerable to the catastrophic effects of harvest failure, control and display of resources were crucial ways in which to demonstrate differences in status. Much in the same way as it is possible to 'read' designed landscapes in economic terms, so too each element can be shown to have had some kind of connotation with authority. As well as expressing lordly power some of the meanings inherent in landscape design were more practical. Mills, for example, were a sign of one of the most crucial monopolies in the medieval economy and the placing of buildings such as barns in close proximity to the castle (a fine example remains at Manorbier in Pembrokeshire), evidenced productive manors.

As we have seen, the keeping of game (and particularly deer) was the *sine que non* of aristocratic rank. Thus the area in which they were kept – the park – was itself emblematic of lordship. Needless to say, the larger the park, the more 'noble' the owner, especially as emparking took land out of direct agricultural production and gave it over to an activity that was, economically speaking, far from profitable. This association between landscape and

Lordly Landscapes

seigneuriality also extended to other features. The keeping of doves had, since the eleventh century, been the preserve of manorial lords. As a consequence the dovecote became emblematic of lordly status and was often displayed in a prominent location, usually near entrances or next to roads, or more occasionally adjacent to rivers (Figure 49). At Caister Castle in Norfolk (built *c.*1440), the dovecote was placed directly to the north of the castle immediately adjacent to the main Norwich to Yarmouth road.[30] At Manorbier the dovecote was again outside the walls, in this instance alongside the roadway leading up past the castle from the nearby bay.

Similar lordly status pertained to fishponds. In the Middle Ages freshwater fish was an expensive and therefore a high-status food and the area in which they were kept inevitably carried connotations of lordship. Ponds were often directly linked with the lord himself, this close interest being reflected in the name 'Earls Pond' or 'Earls Pool' at castle sites and similarly 'Abbots Pond' at monastic houses. At Castle Acre Castle, in Norfolk, the 'Earls Pond' lay below the castle, while at Clare, in Suffolk, the fishpond immediately beyond the outer bailey was also referred to by this term in the 1260s (Figure 50).[31] The direct association between private fishponds and personal lordship is best illustrated by the actions of Abbot Sampson of Bury St Edmunds in Suffolk, related by the Abbey's chronicler Jocelin of Brakelond. Sampson had taken the decision in 1182 to create a new fishpond, with subsequent adverse effects on neighbours and fellow monks:

> He has so raised the level of the fishpond at Babwell, for the new mill, that there is not one man, rich or poor, who has land next to the river between the town gate and the east gate, who has not lost his garden and orchards as a result of the flooding. The cellarer's pasture, on the other bank, has been ruined, and the neighbours' arable land is spoiled. The cellarer's meadow has been destroyed, the infirmarer's orchard is submerged, and all the neighbours complain about it. But when the cellarer tackled him in chapter about the damage, the abbot replied, with a flash of anger, that he was not going to sacrifice *his* fishpond for the sake of *our* meadow [my italics].[32]

The personal identification of landscape features with individuals also extended to settlements. If towns were expected to generate revenue for the lord, then they also became a prime target during major political disturbance. Sacking an opponent's town demonstrated in the most dramatic way possible the inability of a lord to protect his tenants – the primary duty of lordship. During the Anarchy of Stephen's reign, Robert, Earl of Gloucester, burned Worcester, the town of Waleran, Count of Meulan, in a deliberate attempt to undermine his rival's political standing and reputation. The count himself rode through the ruins a week later fully aware that this was a slight on his personal authority. The eyewitness John of Worcester commented that 'as he [Waleran] looked at the gutted part of the city, he was much moved, he realised it was done to harm him'.[33] The castle itself had held out – indeed it

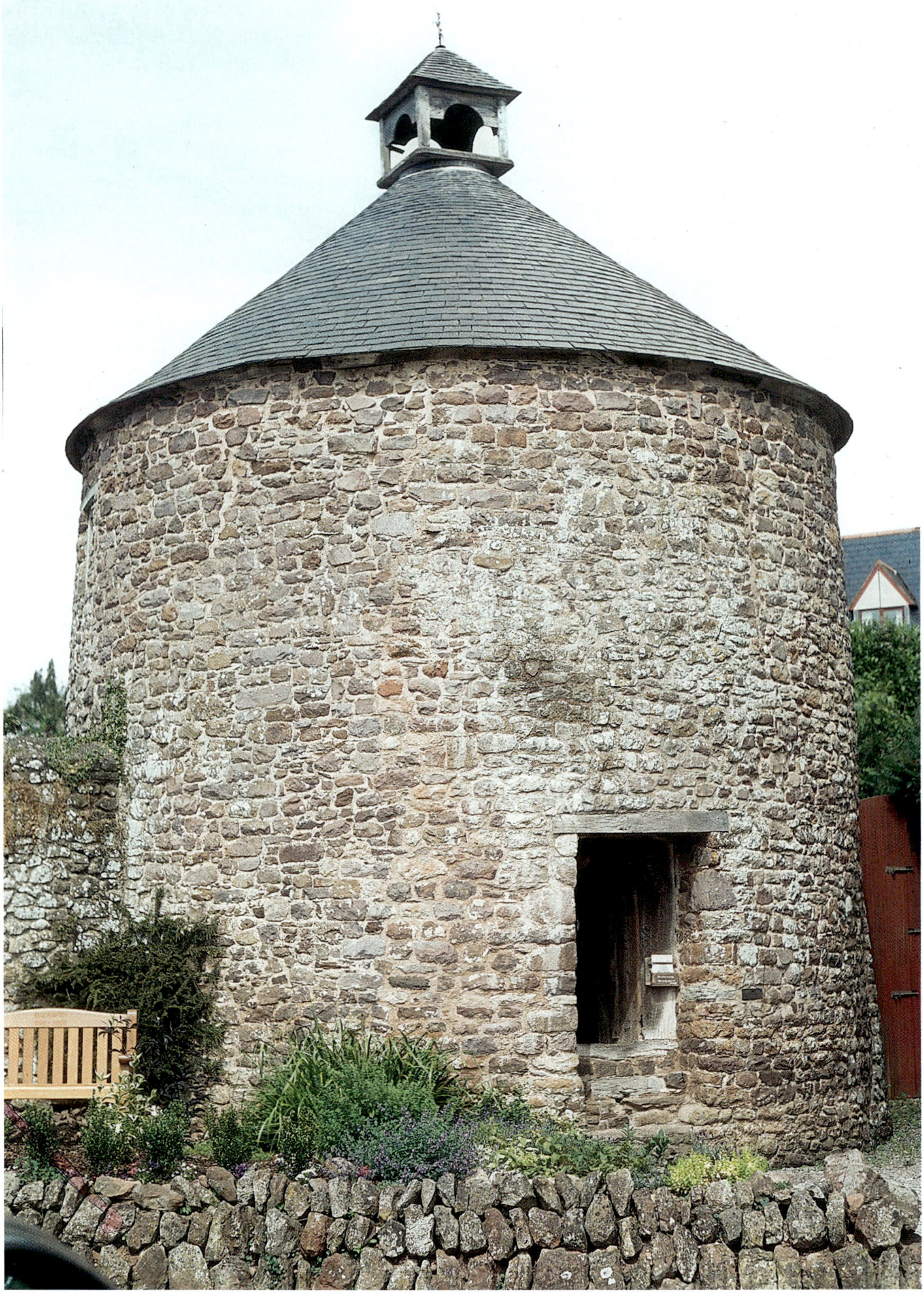

Lordly Landscapes

FIGURE 50.
Clare castle, Suffolk. The unusual arrangement of ponds to the east of the castle bailey probably represents the remains of a fourteenth-century water garden.
SUFFOLK COUNTY COUNCIL

FIGURE 49 (*left*). The medieval dovecote at Dunster, Somerset. Dovecotes were important symbols of manorial status at ecclesiastical and secular residences in the medieval period. This example probably dates to the fourteenth century.

seems not to have been targeted – the Angevins seemingly content that their actions against the town were sufficient to make their point.

Medieval designed landscapes therefore carried their own symbolic meanings and embodied specific messages that pertained to aspects of lordly authority. There is little doubt that in a visual society where allegory and symbolism pervaded everyday rituals at all levels, this seigneurial vocabulary was entirely comprehensible to contemporaries of all ranks.

The religious landscape

Religious buildings were an integral part of the largest medieval designed landscapes, as the foundation and patronage of a church or the foundation of a religious house all demonstrated the piety and charity of the builder. The twinning of castles and religious houses was a phenomenon characteristic of the medieval period and there was also a close association between castles and churches at parochial level.[34] Both monastic institutions and churches were important elements in landscapes of any pretension. The most elaborate castle landscapes, however, as well as containing buildings that served a direct spiritual purpose, were permeated throughout by religious symbolism. Although hard to believe now, from the twelfth century rabbits were considered to carry connotations of religious salvation; thus the placing of a warren adjacent to the seigneurial seat symbolised the owner's religious devotion.[35] This religious imagery appears (unsurprisingly) to have been particularly redolent in ecclesiastical landscapes. At Stow Palace in Lincolnshire, described in the twelfth century as 'delightfully surrounded with woods and ponds', the approach of St Hugh of Lincoln was greeted by a flight of swans, a bird with Christian connotations of the Virgin and Creation.[36]

The religious symbolism associated with water also helps to explain why moats, ponds and artificial lakes form such an important part of castle landscapes. Christ himself was a Fisher of Men and the fact that water sustained all life ensured that ponds could readily lend themselves to Biblical imagery. In the medieval theory of the 'four humours', water was also associated with the feminine, which was inevitably linked to the image of the Virgin. The feminine dimension to landscape design is found particularly in castle gardens. As Roberta Gilchrist has shown, gardens were identified as feminine space and some of the gardens that formed part of designed landscapes owed their existence to female patronage.[37] Perhaps the most well-known female patron was Queen Eleanor of Castile, who took a close interest in the gardens of Edward I in North Wales and, as we have seen, Leeds in Kent. One of the most famous in Wales was at Rhuddlan, in Denbighshire, where there was a courtyard garden with 6000 turves, fenced with staves (Figure 25). The garden was also used as a metaphor for the female body, with enclosed gardens representing chastity. This meaning was ambiguous, however: in literature, gardens were the venue for sexual encounters and flirtation. In a thirteenth-century description it was noted that 'it is delight rather than fruit that is looked for in the pleasure garden'.[38] Gardens with water features and fountains may have been symbols of paradise or the Garden of Eden, but they also carried with them connotations of sexual temptation and the treachery of Eve. Thus certain elements found at designed landscapes in the Middle Ages were imbued with overt and complex religious symbolism.

Medieval landscape design was clearly imbued with multi-layered meanings; however, quite what it was that made such landscapes seem pleasurable and precisely why elites poured their resources into setting their residences off to best visual advantage are intriguing questions. Indeed, the contention that residential surroundings had a clear *aesthetic* appeal was initially one of the most controversial aspects of the 'discovery' of medieval designed landscapes. Nonetheless, while aesthetic elements may be difficult to discern with any precision, there is some evidence that sheds light on this area of landscape design.

The aesthetic landscape

In 1123 Ranulf, the king's chancellor, was travelling with the king to Ranulf's castle at Berkhamsted in Hertfordshire (Figure 51). This probably generated some nervousness on Ranulf's part as Henry I seems to have been genuinely feared by his contemporaries and the chancellor was no doubt anxious to entertain the king according to the correct protocol. The chronicler Henry of Huntingdon relates what happened as the party neared the end of their journey:

> Now as he [Ranulf] was conducting the king on the way to giving him hospitality, and had reached the very top of the hill from which his castle could be seen, in his exaltation of mind he fell from his horse, and a monk rode over him. He was so badly injured by this that after a few days his life ended.[39]

This incident, while unfortunate for Ranulf, throws light on a number of aspects of the aesthetic landscape of the twelfth century. The fact that the accident occurred within site of Ranulf's castle is somewhat ironic, since when the party of travellers came to the point in their journey from which their host's castle was first visible the overwhelming emotion should have been one of some satisfaction. Additionally, the link with hospitality suggests that the entertainment of the king was something that began not merely at the castle gate, but in the wider countryside. From what we have seen about the role of designed landscapes as hunting grounds this is not surprising – it may not be without importance that adjacent to Berkhamsted Castle was a large park. But the precise wording used by Henry of Huntingdon also suggests that there is more of significance here; namely that the castle could also be a thing of beauty and that the ensemble of castle in its setting could be appreciated – exulted in – for its own sake.

The idea that castle landscapes were intended to be aesthetically pleasing is also suggested in other sources. One of the most famous is that of Gerald of Wales who, in 1188, described Manorbier Castle in Pembrokeshire as 'delightfully set about with orchards and ponds'. The description may be a stylised portrait of the castle where he was born – it echoes that of Stow Palace, discussed above – but it was one that was clearly intended to convey the impression that it looked visually appealing.[40] Well known, too, is the fact that the construction of a balcony at the royal palace of Woodstock in 1354 stemmed from Princess Isabella's wish to view the park.[41] However, there is now increasing evidence from castles such as Kenilworth (Warwickshire), Old Wardour (Wiltshire), Harewood and Middleham (Yorkshire) that the arrangement of some buildings and architectural features such as windows only make sense when placed within the context of residential surroundings, as opposed to seeing them in a military context. At Old Wardour, for example, the first-floor private chambers overlooked an adjacent lake, the backdrop to which was provided by a deer park.[42] Equally, the fourteenth-century fenestration in the great hall at Kenilworth provided spectacular views of the adjacent mere and the chase that surrounded the castle.

Although we can appreciate the spectacular views often afforded from castle walls even today, proving that such effects were actively sought after by castle-builders, rather than being mere by-products of the raising of tall buildings, is difficult. The evidence of elaborate windows at the highest levels of upstanding structures, however, strongly suggests that visual pleasure was the intention. In a rare reference, William of Malmesbury relates a story (in all probability untrue) of how, as a young man, the future Henry I invited the captured rebel Conan up to the top of Rouen castle to admire the view from the battlements. As they looked out over the countryside Henry told his companion that the lands they could see would one day belong to him. This conversation was, to use the chronicler's words, 'a bitter jest', as Henry then promptly pushed the unsuspecting Conan off the wall to his death.[43] While Malmesbury was clearly making a political and moral point about the character of the young Henry, his words are valuable evidence not only that the landscape was viewed from castles, but that viewing the landscape in this way could be directly linked with notions of power and territoriality.

There is more direct evidence for the aesthetic appreciation of medieval

FIGURE 51. Berkhamsted castle, Hertfordshire. It was while on the way to the castle in 1123 that Ranulf, the King's chancellor, was killed when he fell from his horse. The castle park lies beyond the motte, on the high ground sloping up away from the site.

Lordly Landscapes

FIGURE 52.
Raglan castle, Monmouthshire. View of the deer park. At Raglan it is possible that the sylvan, 'ordered' view of the park was to be contrasted with the 'wild' landscape of the mountains in the distance.

landscapes embedded within the countryside itself. Although research in this area is still in its infancy, there is growing field evidence which suggests that major castles were provided with set ornamental views, or 'vistas', that were constructed with considerable attention to detail, much as happened in eighteenth-century country house landscapes (Figure 52). As we have seen, parkland frequently formed a backdrop to major castles, with the 'Little Park' often being situated immediately adjacent to the castle itself. These parks are of some significance since they are now being interpreted as pleasure parks, in contrast to the rather more utilitarian 'Great' parks, which were usually at some distance removed from the castle itself.[44] An indication of their status as far back as the twelfth century is suggested by their arrangement with Anglo-Norman keeps. At castles such as Castle Rising, Castle Hedingham and Mileham (Norfolk), the 'private' chamber faces the park, whereas the hall faces the 'public' area of the castle village. Moreover, little parks frequently appear in contemporary descriptions in particular ways, often described in Latin as *parva parcum subtus castrum* – 'the little park under the castle'. This cannot literally be 'lower' than the castle as in many cases the park itself is situated on higher ground above the residential site. Rather, it is indicative of a particularly close relationship between the two.

At New Buckenham, in Norfolk (*c.* 1146), the notion that the little park formed part of a 'view' from the castle is suggested by its spatial arrangement. The park was situated to the north of the castle, laid out on the sloping ground above the site. The boundary pale bows out away from the castle producing an 'amphitheatre' effect whereby the park looks physically larger when viewed from the keep. Additionally, the pale runs over the skyline and then abruptly stops when it is no longer visible from the castle – giving the illusion that the park runs on for a considerably greater distance without incurring the additional expense of actually making the park larger. The shape of the park is deliberately intended to enhance the view from the keep. This is probably a very early arrangement, as a surviving charter shows that the park was in place during the lifetime of the builder. Other examples are to be found at Castle Rising in Norfolk (where evidence from aerial photographs suggests that the park boundary had been deliberately shifted back to create this effect), Framlingham Castle in Suffolk and Ludgershall Castle in Wiltshire.[45] Similar attention to detail can also be seen in the manipulation of fishponds. At Clare Castle in Suffolk the pond complex that lay immediately beyond one of the baileys was laid out on a geometric pattern, an arrangement that could be most appreciated when viewed from the castle motte (Figure 50).[46] The date of these ponds is open to question but comparison with sites elsewhere suggests that they might conceivably date to the fourteenth century and therefore would be

FIGURE 53. Framlingham castle, Suffolk. Here, the castle overlooks a former garden and fishponds (foreground) with a mere forming a watery backdrop. In the fourteenth century the mere was more extensive and was provided with an island on which stood a dovecote.

associated with the occupation of the great widow Elizabeth de Burgh. Optical techniques aimed at moulding landscapes to achieve aesthetic effects have long been recognised in the study of post-medieval gardens, but evidence from sites such as Buckenham and Clare suggests that they have a longer pedigree.

The spatial arrangement of certain landscape features also suggests that close attention was paid to the creation of ornamental 'views' at the largest castles. At Framlingham, the Great Hall overlooked a formal garden (probably of enclosed type) with the mere providing a watery backdrop beyond (Figure 53). The mere was also furnished with an island on which stood a stone dovecote. All this was certainly in place by the fourteenth century, with the possibility that it may date to the late twelfth century, at which time the castle was substantially rebuilt.[47] Something similar is also suggested at Yielden in Bedfordshire, where the artificial lake surrounding the site was provided with an island on which a probable medieval dovecote was excavated.[48] Possible contexts for such vistas are also provided by evidence from the castle buildings. At Saltwood in Kent a view of the water garden would have greeted anybody waiting in the lobby before being allowed to enter the hall.[49] The view from the upper hall at Knaresborough – looking out towards Haverah Park – was perhaps intended for the private enjoyment of Piers Gaveston, for whom the *donjon* was constructed in the fourteenth century.[50]

All of this demonstrates that medieval castles were frequently surrounded by landscapes with a strong ornamental dimension. More difficult to determine with any confidence, however, is quite what it was that made these landscapes appealing to the medieval mind. As has been hinted above, the answer is inextricably bound up with (amongst other things) medieval attitudes to nature, authority and the countryside, all of which were complex and very different to our own. A recent analysis of the landscape around Ludgershall Castle points the way forward, in which it is suggested that the 'ordered' environment of the park was perceived differently from the 'untamed' wilderness of Salisbury Plain that formed a distant backdrop to the castle.[51] This contrast was probably reinforced by the activities that took place within such landscapes, which might also help explain why they were intended to evoke pleasure. Of these activities, hunting was foremost and it is within this context that the spatial arrangement of some landscape features, particularly Little Parks, is best interpreted. We should not perhaps envisage large hunts; to judge from medieval romance we should probably imagine displays of hawking or small set-piece hunting rituals where an individual or small group demonstrated their horsemanship to an audience in the castle by taking an individual deer. Such hunting scenes were familiar to medieval audiences and the inherent symbolism within them was well understood: Alexander Neckham (writing *c.*1200) relates a story of how, while enjoying the chase, a king and his entourage witnessed a goshawk kill an eagle and the king rebuked his attendant nobles for cheering on the smaller bird as according to the laws of nature – from which his own power was derived – the kingly bird should have emerged victorious.[52]

The conjunction of sport, pleasure and the viewing of the landscape –

particularly that of the Little Park – is made explicit in the fifteenth century in John Coke's *Debate between the Heralds*, where the English herald says to his French counterpart that 'we have also small parkes, made onely for the pleasure of ladyes and gentylwomen, to shote with the longe bowe, and kyll the sayd beastes'.[53] Here too we are reminded of the feminine elements in castle design, here not just confined to the formal garden, but extending outwards into the wider landscape.

Another factor that may have imbued medieval designed landscapes with a strong aesthetic appeal was their association with production. This suggestion is certainly borne out by the famous description of Owain Glyn Dŵr's castle at Sycharth (Llansilin) in Denbighshire (Figure 54). Here it is not so much the castle that draws most admiration but, rather, the surrounding landscape:

> Each part full, each house in the court
> Orchard, vineyard and whitefort.
> The famed hero's rabbit park ...
> And in another, even more

Castles in Context: Power, Symbolism and Landscape, 1066–1500

FIGURE 54. Sycharth, Denbighshire. An elaborate description of Sycharth castle and its landscape was included in a fourteenth-century Welsh poem. English forces destroyed the castle in 1403 during the latter stages of Owain Glyn Dŵr's revolt.

© CLWYD-POWYS ARCHAEOLOGICAL TRUST

FIGURE 55.
Castle Rising castle, Norfolk. The castle was raised c. 1140 following the marriage of William D'Albini II to the royal dowager queen, Alice of Louvain. It is possible that both castle and its attendant landscape were badges of royalism at a time when England was engulfed by the civil war of Stephen's reign.

Vivid park, the deer pasture …
A fine mill on strong water,
A stone dovecote on a tower.
A fishpond, walled and private,
Into which you cast your net
And (no question of it) bring
To land fine pike and whiting.
A lawn with birds for food on,
Peacocks and sprightly heron …
No hunger, disgrace or dearth,
Or ever thirst at Sycharth.[54]

There is much of interest here. The similarity between the features described in the poem and the field archaeology found at castle sites is striking: the landscape described is that of a well-ordered and managed estate that can produce a variety of foodstuffs in abundance; moreover, the reader (or listener) is invited to enter this landscape and partake of the lord's benevolence by fishing in his pond. The themes of lordship, chivalry and status along with the harsh realities of medieval food production were all represented and became conflated in castle landscapes.

Furthermore, by the end of the Middle Ages a large body of opinion maintained that the earth and the beasts had been created by God for Mankind's use. Man's duty was to tame and cultivate what God had provided, and by so doing he became civilised.[55] Thus parts of the countryside that were not cultivated had unpleasant associations: in literature, moorland was frequently connected with travellers having unwelcome experiences with evil spirits. By contrast, those landscapes that were fertile, well cultivated and which exhibited the features of a well-run estate, such as mills, dovecotes and barns, denoted Man's *dominion* over nature. This theme emerges most strongly in monastic writings, but such sentiments must also have been present in the minds of secular lords. In a twelfth-century description of the abbey of Clairvaux in France it is the gardens, orchards and vineyards that draw praise, and they do so partly because they offer such a contrast with the rocky wilderness beyond the monastic estate.[56] It is also worth noting that medieval notions of the Divine order were closely allied to the planning of residences. From the twelfth century onwards, advances in mathematics and geometry meant that planners could conceive of, and divide up, the physical landscape in a way that was impossible before. To plan and execute a complex geometric building or landscape was not only to create something physically beautiful, but also to construct a monument to the word of God. As Keith Lilley has shown, the idea of a 'sacred geometry' manifested itself in the planned form of some medieval towns, particularly those based on an elaborate grid plan.[57] This kind of metaphor is probably also applicable to castle landscapes, particularly those with attendant urban areas. It might not be too fanciful to suggest that the very highly structured landscapes which, even to the modern eye, look elegant in plan were partly designed with the ultimate viewer in Heaven in mind. That designed landscapes were associated with a particular kind of social or moral order is also suggested: Anglo-Norman writers drew a strong contrast between England and France, where towns and particular forms of agricultural exploitation (particularly arable cultivation) were associated with civilisation, and Celtic kingdoms whose social structure and relationship with the land rendered them barbarians.[58]

Much of the discussion here has centred on elite perceptions of landscape, and non-elite groups may well have seen things very differently. To a lord, his park might represent an area for pleasure, recreation and entertainment, but to his tenants, literally beyond the pale, as Matthew Johnson has put it, it could represent resources and a lifestyle denied to them by their social superiors. To judge from evidence of peasants' poaching, illegal fishing and park-breaking, designed landscapes were also contested landscapes and could be landscapes of exclusion. This is most vividly seen during the events of the Peasants' Revolt in 1381. Much in the same way that the rebels actively selected which lords to target and which manorial records to burn, so too we see the deliberate destruction of specific landscape features. Dovecotes, mills, warrens, fishponds and parks were singled out for attention, strong evidence that the seigneurial imagery discussed in this chapter resonated right across medieval society.

Designed landscapes may also have carried with them political statements of a different kind. In the seventeenth and eighteenth centuries it was well known to contemporaries that the particular style of the formal gardens of men such as Robert Walpole reflected their political affiliation.[59] Can something similar be seen in the designed landscapes of the medieval period? One hint comes from Castle Rising in Norfolk (Figure 55). The castle was built *c.* 1140 by William D'Albini II, following his marriage to the royal widow Alice of Louvain – whose money allowed the construction. Its landscape conforms to all that has been discussed here: a park, warren, planned settlement and religious house all lay immediately adjacent to the castle earthworks. The design of the *donjon* is interesting: it is a smaller version of that at Norwich, which was then the only royal castle in East Anglia. D'Albini was attempting to associate himself with the royal dignity, something also suggested by a chronicler's comment that, in William's view, 'apart from the king everything in the world was worthless in his eyes'.[60] The construction of Rising took place at a time of great political disturbance, as England became engulfed by the civil war of Stephen's reign. Recent work on the D'Albinis has shown that the family, over several generations, took their lead from the crown in terms of their religious patronage, marriages and alliances.[61] Is it possible, therefore, that we also see at Rising a royalist landscape, built as a statement of political intent at the start of a dynastic dispute?

Medieval landscape design?

It is now accepted by scholars that medieval aristocrats went to some lengths to manipulate the landscapes that surrounded their castles, and that this was partly a result of a desire to provide a pleasurable backdrop to their residences. Whether these landscapes can be described as 'designed' in the modern sense – that is, representing the deliberate intentions and grand design of a particular lord at a specific point in time – is more difficult to decide. Despite the evidence presented here, it could still be argued that at castle sites we are simply observing the piecemeal accretion of features over time, rather than any attempt by a single castle-builder with a 'master plan' to construct castle and landscape together, or even a set of social ideas and norms which led to the creation of particular landscapes in time.

Therefore, the problem of dating is a crucial one. If the suggestions that medieval aristocrats were capable of the planning of high-status landscapes, and did indeed execute these plans, are accepted, then it becomes necessary to show that the archaeological features we find at castle sites do indeed date from the same time as, or very soon after, the construction of the main residential buildings. Needless to say, this type of information is frequently unforthcoming. In many cases it is difficult enough to ascribe a specific date to a castle itself, let alone its landscape. There is also little doubt that many designed landscapes are indeed the result of piecemeal change over time. This should not be surprising, however, as it is difficult (though not impossible) to point to a castle that is itself of one single build or that has not been altered or adapted over subsequent centuries. Indeed, this situation was the norm.

Kenilworth, in Warwickshire, is a case in point. The castle was raised *c*.1125 by royal administrator Geoffrey de Clinton and, typically for the twelfth century, there was an attendant park, priory and mere.[62] Thanks to a detailed series of charters, we can see that soon afterwards a planned town was added and that the mere was enlarged several times during the twelfth century. John of Gaunt radically altered the castle in the fourteenth century and in the fifteenth, Henry V built the double moated pleasance at one end of the mere. During the sixteenth century the castle was the venue for Elizabethan pageants and the surrounding landscape was again subject to massive alteration.[63] The field archaeology around Kenilworth castle is therefore a true palimpsest dating from many different historical periods. Although the castle stands at the centre of a landscape that has been altered for aesthetic effect, it could be suggested that as the component features of this landscape all date to different times, it is inappropriate to couch it in terms of 'design'.

Yet despite the fact that much of its archaeology dates to different periods, Kenilworth provides some of the best evidence that the term 'designed landscape' is highly appropriate. There is a planned 'core' to this landscape that dates to the earliest phases of the castle. In the foundation charter of the priory of *c*.1125, Geoffrey de Clinton specifically stated the ground on which the priory was to be built 'except that which is reserved for my castle and my park'.[64] Although elements such as the town were to follow in his lifetime, this, it seems, is evidence for 'design' in the modern sense: Geoffrey clearly had an idea of how his whole residential complex would be spatially arranged and so therefore how it would be experienced on the ground.

To this we could add other examples where parts of a castle's attendant landscape can be dated to the very earliest phases of building. At Denbigh, in North Wales, within a year of the known date of the initial building work John de Lacy wrote back to England requesting deer for the stocking of his park. When the compact spatial arrangement of the castle, town and park at Denbigh is considered there is no reason to doubt that all these elements were part of the original design.[65] There are also instances where a castle was never completed and part of its relict landscape remains intact. At Kirby Muxloe, in Leicestershire, the castle was left unfinished following the execution of William Lord Hastings in 1480. Alongside the newly-raised castle walls was a dovecote – presumably intended as a sign (if any were needed) that a man of lordly status was raising the new castle.[66] Evidence from licences to crenellate also hint that such features were planned at the initial stages of construction. From the early thirteenth century the recording of parks, mills and ponds in licences also suggests that there was an 'ideal' range of structures which were considered appropriate for the residence.[67]

Although there is evidence to suggest that castles and landscapes were sometimes planned together, there remains a problem of definition. The term 'designed landscape' is not without its difficulties. Most notably it fails to distinguish between elite pleasure grounds and other kinds of landscape that can be, arguably, termed 'designed'; for example, the complex open-field systems of medieval England. The term 'ornamental landscape' has gained currency, but this suffers from the implication that the landscapes under discussion have a single function, something that is patently not the case. In referring to elite landscapes of the eleventh and twelfth centuries, the term 'landscape of lordship' has been used, but this too implies a single, simple, explanation for very complex structures.

Perhaps part of the problem comes from how the study of medieval designed landscapes has evolved: ideas about designed landscapes have been pushed further and further back chronologically by the results of fieldwork and a theoretical framework has not been properly developed as a result.[68] Given that castles have traditionally been studied as military buildings, some have doubted the existence of landscape design in the Middle Ages and this has brought into sharp focus the problems of definitions and dating. Yet we should perhaps be wary of pursuing the definition at the expense of the explanation. Post-medieval designed landscapes – even those of the nineteenth and twentieth centuries – are frequently difficult to date, are often of many different phases, and are subject to continual and sometimes wholesale change over time.[69] In many respects, the problems encountered in the study of medieval designed landscapes are inherent in the study of high-status landscapes of any period. Providing there is an awareness of these difficulties, a common definition may serve to highlight continuity and facilitate study across broad periods of time, rather than pose unanswerable problems.

A more serious difficulty arising from the development of the subject is the danger of importing seventeenth- and eighteenth-century ideas of landscape design back into a medieval world where conceptions of landscape were very different. The challenge now is to interpret the landscapes of the Middle Ages within the context of the society that created them and its attendant systems of belief and visual imagery. Not to do so risks the development of a teleological argument which sees the history of landscape design in straightforward 'linear' terms that would inhibit the study of the individuality of landscape design in this period. It may well be the case that a view of parkland from residential buildings was something that was seen as desirable from the eleventh to the nineteenth century, but why this was the case and what meanings were to be derived from such a view doubtless changed dramatically as parks themselves changed. Eighteenth-century aristocrats viewing their parkscapes may well have found them pleasing for reasons which would have been alien to their Tudor or Norman ancestors, who looked out over sylvan deer parks centuries earlier.

This chapter has attempted to show how castles often stood at the centre of landscapes that had been elaborately contrived for many purposes. One of those purposes was simply the visual pleasure which such landscapes provided the builder and his or her peers. In the next chapter we will see how they might have experienced the buildings and landscapes into which they poured so much time and effort.

CHAPTER SIX

Experiencing Castles: Iconography and Status

So far we have examined the castle in a number of contexts. We have seen how during the Norman conquest castle-building legitimised the succession of a new elite; how during the medieval period the building of a crenellated residence was not necessarily a response to military insecurity; how rare it was for a castle to be attacked; and how castles were often surrounded by complex designed landscapes. In this chapter we shall try to link some of the themes explored earlier and examine how contemporaries may have perceived and experienced castles. It hardly needs stating that this is an extremely difficult task; as has been seen, the word *castrum* could be used to describe a diverse range of buildings that were themselves open to many different interpretations. Moreover, an individual's perception of any castle would have been conditional on a range of factors including age, gender, social rank and political status. Nevertheless, the ways in which these perceptions diverged and overlapped can reveal much about why castles were built at all, what they were intended to represent and what they might have meant to medieval men and women (Figure 56). Although these are complex issues, some answers may be found in the depiction of the castle in medieval literature – a source curiously under-exploited by castleologists.

Castles and literature

Medieval romance literature can often seem bizarre to the modern reader.[1] The stories are frequently set in exotic locations and usually revolve around the themes of chivalry, courtly love and aristocratic honour. Descriptions of castles or palaces are often very lengthy and describe in some detail the appearance of particular buildings. These are seldom helpful for architectural historians, however, as they commonly consist of highly stylised accounts of the size and splendour of rooms within the castle rather than a dispassionate, 'accurate' description of architectural features. The point, rather, is that the castle had a specific role as a literary device within romance literature. The *dramatis personae* of this genre are fantastical creations to whom the normal constraints of worldly life do not pertain, and whose role is to embody the values and themes noted above. The castle performs a precise function within the genre; specifically, it allows the major characters to show off these virtues

Experiencing Castles: Iconography and Status

against a suitable backdrop. This is extremely useful as, although descriptions of buildings in medieval romance are essentially stereotypical and idealised (explaining why in different poems certain themes occur again and again), they do suggest an idea of the perfect castle. So, while the representation of castles in literature is an under-studied topic, it is one with real strengths: not only is the source material contemporary with many of the buildings themselves, but it also allows us to glimpse the ideals which castle-builders strived to achieve. Even a brief examination of these sources can shed much light on elite perceptions of castles and the themes that emerge are strikingly similar to those drawn from different kinds of evidence elsewhere in this book. In the following discussion literary evidence will be used in conjunction with the upstanding archaeology of castle buildings and landscapes in order to gain some impression of the perceived place of the castle within medieval society.

The castle site

It is as well to start with the castle site. As we have seen, it was extremely rare for castles to be sited exclusively for military advantage, and the small numbers that *were* positioned for tactical reasons were usually short-lived campaign fortifications or siege castles. The overwhelming majority of castles occupied lowland situations which provided ease of access to estates and efficient communications, and they were fully integrated into a wider patterns of medieval settlement. However, while such factors underpin the location of most castles it should not be thought that social or ideological concerns were always subordinated to these somewhat 'functional' requirements. The visual appearance of a castle within its landscape was not only of importance, but in some cases it also seems that builders actively utilised the local topography to their advantage. In the eighteenth century this was known as realising 'the genius of the place'; that is, exploiting the opportunities provided by the immediate environment in order to create a particular, and heightened, sense of place. Although it is difficult to pin down, there is some evidence to suggest that medieval builders showed a similar level of concern when it came to placing their castles within the landscape.

FIGURE 56 (*overleaf*). Tintagel Castle, Cornwall. From the twelfth century Tintagel was associated with Arthurian legend. In the thirteenth century Richard Earl of Cornwall acquired the site and his associated building programme can probably be interpreted as an attempt to associate himself with its mythical past.
JEAN WILLIAMSON

The idea that the castle should be a prominent landmark within its hinterland appears time and again in the sources. A castle that could be seen from a great distance certainly attracted praise; Manorbier in Pembrokeshire was 'visible from afar because of its towers and battlements', a characteristic noted approvingly by Gerald of Wales in 1188 (Figure 57).[2] This aspect of design is also singled out for commendation in numerous descriptions of castles in literary sources. In *Le Conte de Floire et Blancheflor* (c. 1150) the tower of Babylon was worthy of praise because 'when one sees it from twenty miles away, it would seem only a mile away'.[3] So too in *The Romance of Fergus*, where the castle owned by a lucky peasant (the idea of such a role reversal would have delighted medieval audiences) was visible for thirty miles. The poet was anxious to communicate the impression made by this sight, and

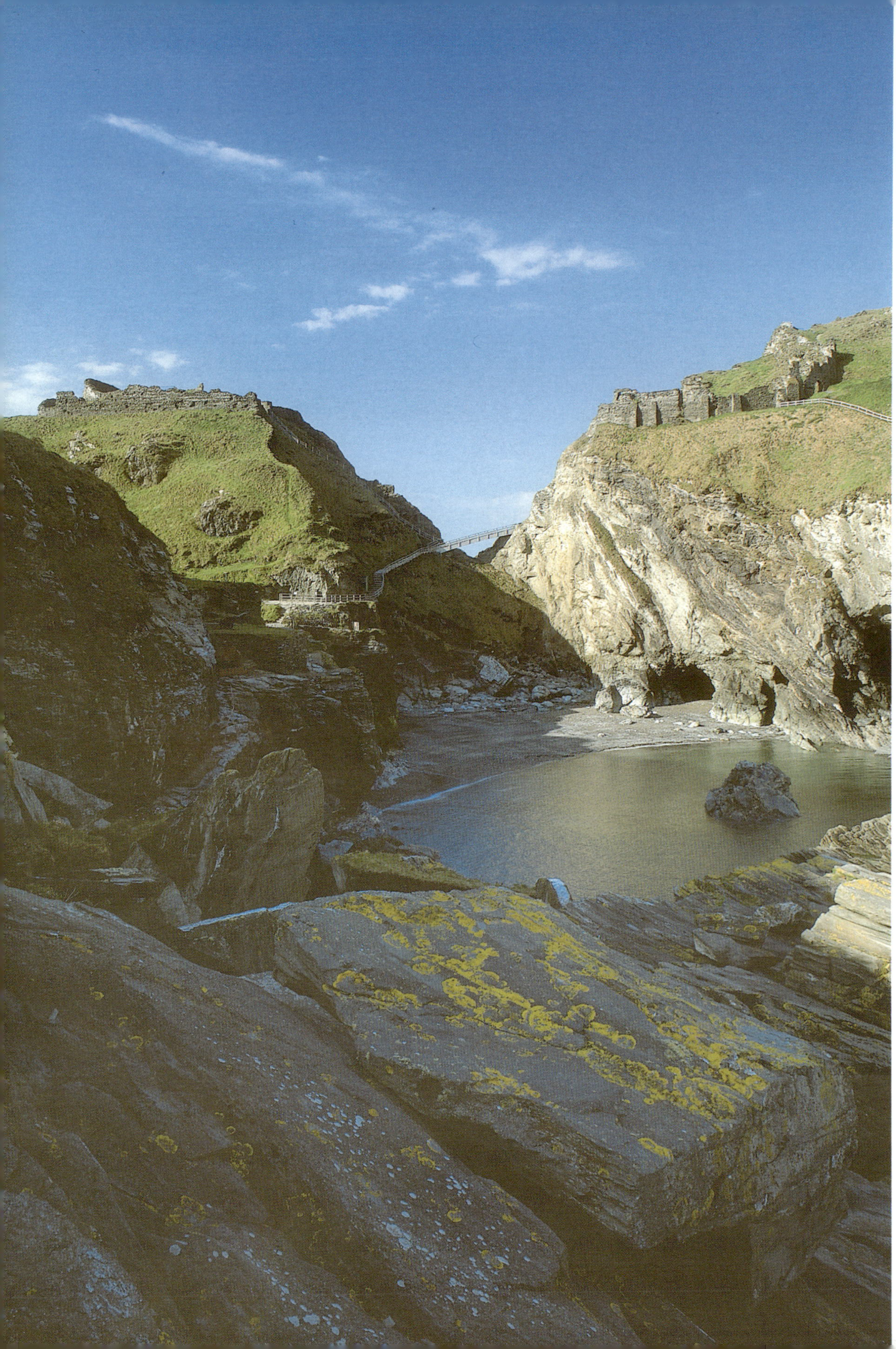

FIGURE 57 (*right*). Manorbier castle, Pembrokeshire. Manorbier was the birthplace of Gerald of Wales and in 1182 he described the castle as 'visible from afar because of its towers and battlements'. The castle was a prominent landmark for sea traffic.

FIGURE 58 (*below*). Dinas Brân, Denbighshire. In the same way as the spires of medieval cathedrals rose up to God, castle-builders could show that they too had an elevated position within society. Although it occupies a classic position in the landscape, Dinas Brân is in fact atypical in terms of its siting.

JEAN WILLIAMSON

described the reaction of a passing king: 'You should know that he looked a lot at//the fortress and the castle//which was so well and beautifully made'.[4]

The siting of a castle on high ground which commanded a wide area was the most obvious way in which such visibility could be achieved; to give just a single example, Dinas Brân in Denbighshire commands the Vale of Llangollen and would have been highly visible to those travelling in the Pass below (Figure 58). Thus the advantages of a hilltop site were not, as might be expected, simply military; rather, the placing of a castle on an elevated site was a metaphor for physical strength. The description of Ylion (the fortress at Troy) given in the *Roman de Trioe* is revealing:

> There was situated Ylion
> from which one could survey the whole country
> the rock was so high that to anyone looking at it
> from below, it would seem
> that it could reach the clouds ...
> With its appearance, it threatened everyone
> it could threaten, because it was not afraid of anything
> except of what could come out of the sky.[5]

In the same way as the spires of medieval cathedrals rose up to God, castle-builders showed that they too had an elevated position within society.

It was only rarely that lords were in a position to raise a castle in locations such as Dinas Brân; indeed, most never had this opportunity. But this did not mean that builders were unaware of the ways in which a castle could be sited in different landscapes for visual advantage. Where a potential site lay on the slope of a river valley it was possible to position the castle on what is termed the 'false crest' – that is, a location not on the highest available point of a river valley system, which would be out of sight when viewed from below, but one which forms the skyline when observed from the valley floor. One such example is Launceston Castle in Cornwall which, when viewed from the Tamar valley – where medieval settlement was situated – gives the impression of being raised on the highest point of its immediate landscape (Figure 48).[6] Higher ground in fact lies to the south and was occupied by the castle deer park, but this fact could only be appreciated from the castle itself. In the thirteenth century Richard, Earl of Cornwall, the builder of Tintagel (Figure 56) further enhanced the visual impact of this castle by raising a stone tower on the Norman motte. This ensured that the castle was immediately obvious to anybody crossing the county boundary from Devon, some miles to the east, and is a sight striking to this day, the tower appearing framed by the surrounding hills. The impressive visual effect cannot have been lost on Richard; as a statement of authority to anybody entering his Earldom, he could hardly have done better.

At other sites it is possible to observe different strategies. At Castle Camps, in Cambridgeshire (Figure 15), the castle lies at the head of (and overlooks) a small valley forming a tributary of the river Cam, and any travellers

Experiencing Castles: Iconography and Status

approaching from the county town of Cambridge would have seen the castle above them framed by the sylvan backdrop of the park, which extended onto higher ground to the east. At Leeds, in Kent, the placing of the castle in a hollow not only ensured that it could be surrounded by water, but also that the observer looked down on the castle from the park. It has been suggested that the visitor would have approached Leeds via a circuitous route and that this may have been linked with ideas of cosmology and microcosm – the castle at the centre of its circular landscape as Jerusalem was at the centre of the universe.[7] A number of other castles seem albeit superficially to relate to this theme. Castle Hedingham, in Essex, lies at the heart of a 'bowl' in the landscape, framed by adjacent interfluves, with the *donjon* rising at the centre. Carreg Cennen in Carmarthenshire (Figure 59) stands on a valley spur that is dominated on either side by mountainous terrain; the siting of the latter could be tentatively compared with that of monasteries in the Pyrenees or the Alps. The relationships of castles to topography is a fascinating topic and detailed work on more sites in the future will help reveal the strategies of individual lords.

The martial front

Positioning a castle so that it visually dominated a particular area was only one way of advertising the seigneurial presence. If castle-builders were conscious of the visual benefits to be gained from their choice of site, then it is abundantly clear that they also took a great deal of trouble to ensure that the buildings themselves presented a particular image to the outside world.

The 'show front' or 'show facade' is often thought to be an invention of the Renaissance period, but the provision of providing an elaborate facing to the parts of the building observed from the main approach was common in high-status buildings of the Middle Ages. One example, at Stokesay, was seen in Chapter Two but in other places there also seems to have been a real effort to tailor the visual appearance of a castle depending on whether the observer approached the building from the hinterland, or was viewing the castle from within the walls or from key points in the surrounding landscape. One of the best examples of this is Okehampton Castle in Devon (Figure 60).[8] As a result of a major programme of excavation in the 1980s we can see in some detail a major remodelling of the site by the Courtenay family that took place in the fourteenth century. The 'public' front of the castle (visible to anybody using the road to the north) comprised a strong military façade with *donjon*, substantial walls and narrow windows. The rebuilding of the southern side of the castle was more domestic in character. The buildings on the Norman motte were upgraded and a vast new range of accommodation was constructed, all of which enjoyed a view over adjacent parkland.[9] That some kind of vista was desired is shown by the provision of elaborate fenestration, window seats in upper chambers and a low curtain wall, all of which ensured a view of the park. The more 'private' face of the castle therefore presented a

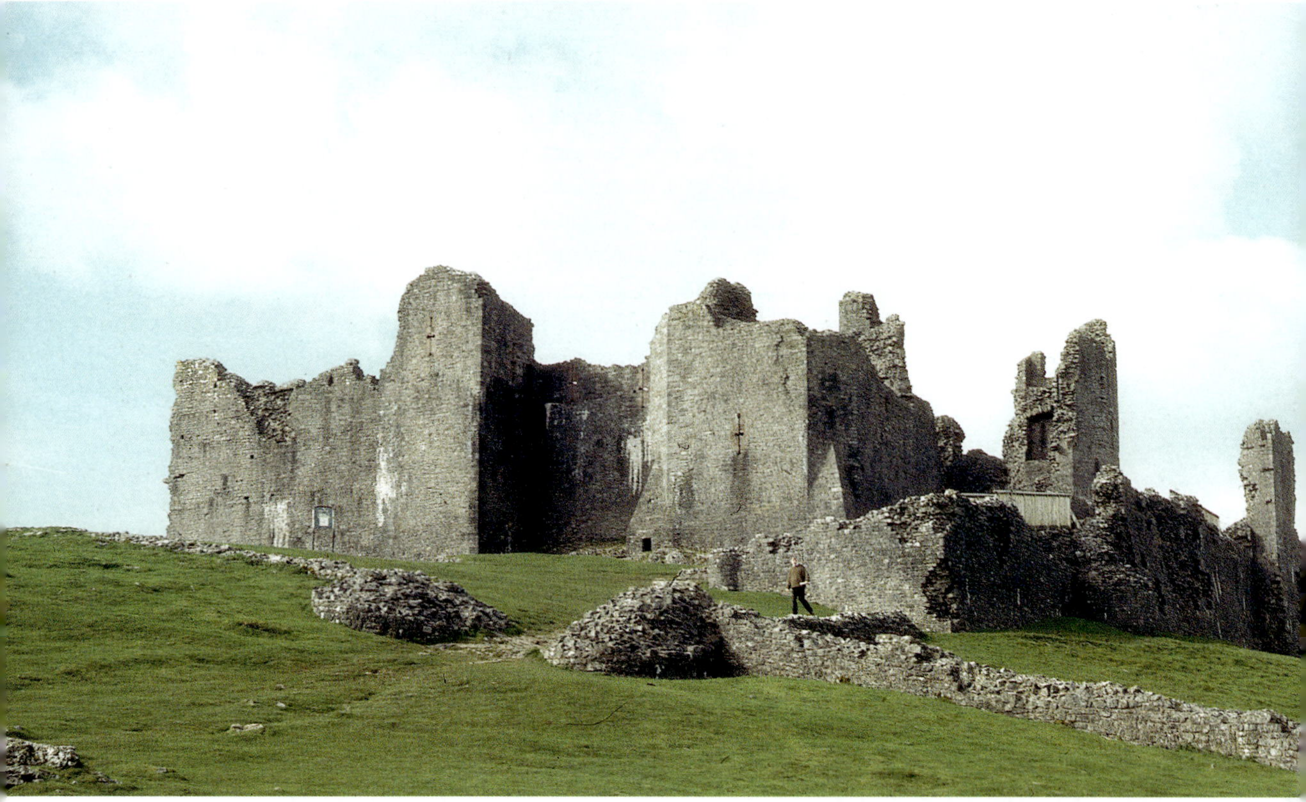

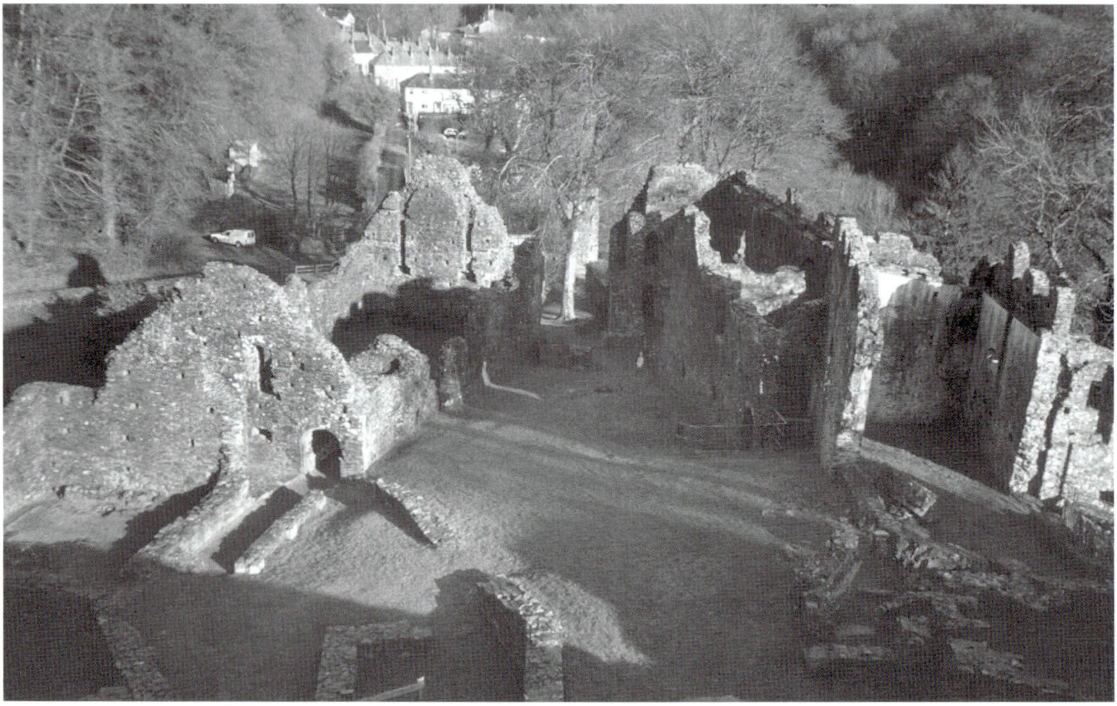

FIGURE 59 (*left*). Carreg Cennen Castle, Carmarthenshire. The placing of castles in dramatic locations may have reflected wider concerns than simply making the building difficult to approach.

FIGURE 60. Okehampton castle, Devon. In the fourteenth century the castle was substantially re-built. The external face offered a more martial prospect than the interior, which enjoyed views over the castle deer park.
© OLIVER CREIGHTON

FIGURE 61 (*below*). Warkworth castle, Northumberland. The Percy lion on the north face of the *donjon*.
© OLIVER CREIGHTON

different image to that which faced the outside world. This would have been the case not only for those with privileged access to the interior of the castle itself, but also those allowed to enter the castle park and look back onto the new Courtenay residence.

Such 'martial fronts' are seen elsewhere. At Ludlow, in Shropshire, the north side of the castle, which faces towards Wales, is studded with towers, presenting an altogether more militaristic face than that which faces the market place (Figure 2). The seat of the Percy family at Warkworth, in Northumberland, presents a less subtle image: on its north face, overlooking the main town street, is a huge depiction of the family heraldic badge, the rampant lion (Figure 61). Another interesting case is Haddon Hall in Derbyshire (Figure 62), the familial seat of the Vernons, which was substantially rebuilt in the fifteenth century.[10] Here, the main approach to the early medieval manor house (interestingly, a steep descent; here the site is compromised by higher ground) was completely altered and the lower court rebuilt. This ensured that the building was approached along the valley bottom from where the wooded backdrop could be fully appreciated. The new main facade was rebuilt in military style which contrasted sharply with the sumptuous accommodation within the castle. Emery perhaps captures the intention of the rebuilding in his comment: 'seen from the fields opposite the Hall, Haddon is as close as it is possible to see in England those houses depicted in fifteenth-century illuminated manuscripts'.[11]

It would be possible to describe many more of the kind of examples above at almost infinite length. While this would provide a whole series of case

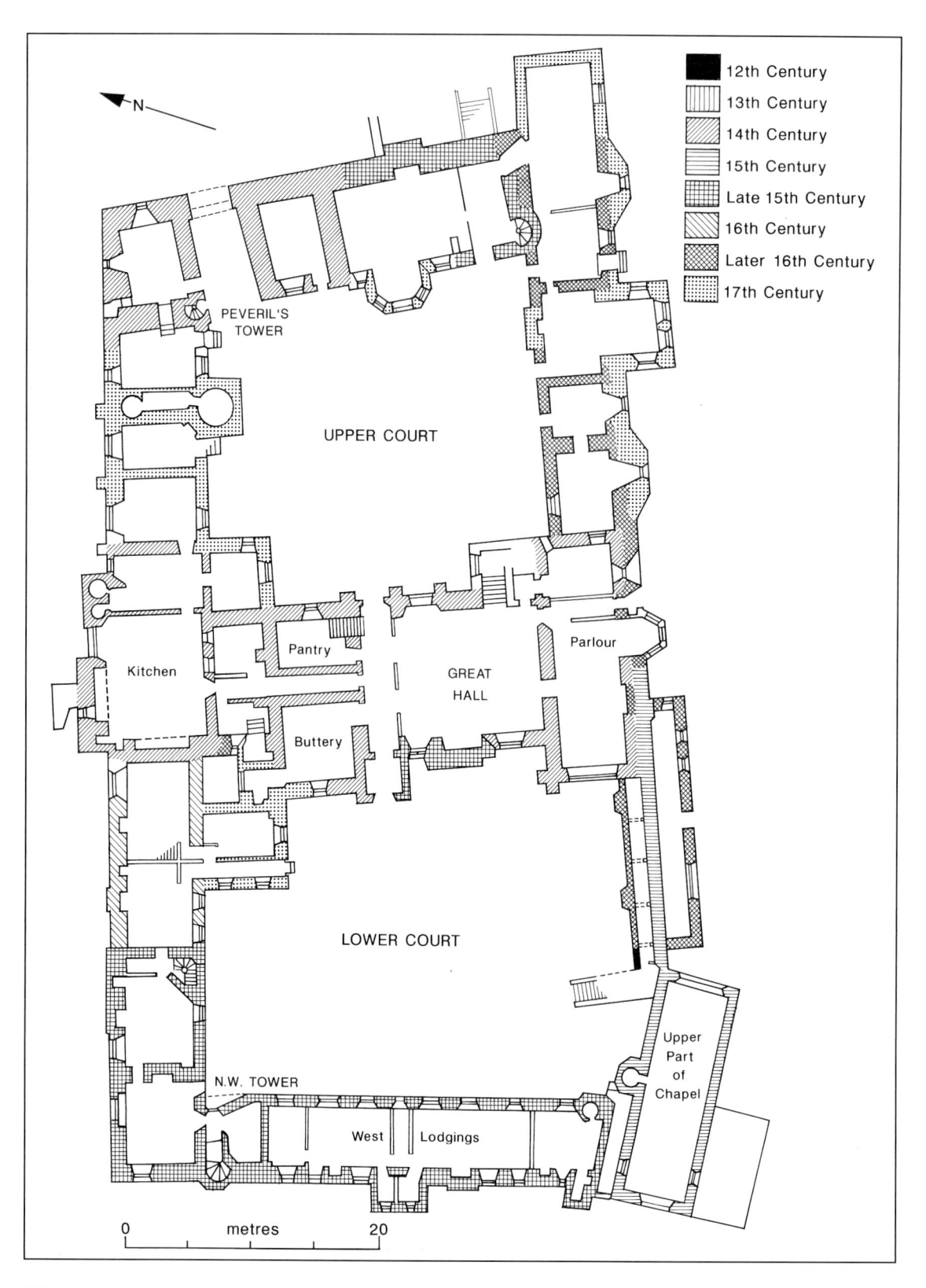

	12th Century
	13th Century
	14th Century
	15th Century
	Late 15th Century
	16th Century
	Later 16th Century
	17th Century

PEVERIL'S TOWER

UPPER COURT

Kitchen
Pantry
Buttery
GREAT HALL
Parlour

LOWER COURT

N.W. TOWER
West Lodgings
Upper Part of Chapel

0　metres　20

Experiencing Castles: Iconography and Status

studies demonstrating that castle-builders were not primarily concerned with keeping intruders at bay, it is unnecessary, since the real challenge is to gain some understanding of exactly *why* it was deemed so important to engineer castles in this way and what all this effort was meant to convey to contemporaries.

Reconstructing castles

Recent years have seen a determined effort on the part of castle scholars to reconstruct approach routes to medieval castles in order to gain some impression of how they may have appeared to the (usually high-status) visitor. Research in this area has opened up a whole series of important questions over the ways in which access to the castle lord was negotiated and how castles and landscapes were planned in unison in order to enhance the visual appearance of the building.

In order to judge the visual effect an approach would achieve it obviously needs to be known what form the residential buildings actually took, but this is frequently not straightforward as upstanding remains rarely belong to one period and thus we cannot be precise about the structures any visitor would have seen. While the location of windows, elaborately decorated stones or fireplaces may give valuable information on the hierarchy of space within a castle, it is more difficult to decide how a room may have appeared to visitors. Indeed, it should be said that much of our evidence for the function of rooms comes from the post-medieval period, many centuries after the buildings were first constructed. Additionally, the direction from which the castle would have been approached needs to be known, and this can also be far from clear. At Bodiam, perhaps the most famous case in castle studies to date, the approach route has been extensively reproduced by many writers (including this one), but the evidence on which this interpretation is based is far from problem-free. Moreover, as was seen in the previous chapter, the areas around castles are palimpsests with many phases of development superimposed onto the immediate hinterland. It is often impossible to know what landscape features were contemporary with the castle and which may have been prominently displayed to visitors in any given period. Despite this, by using a combination of evidence such as aerial photographs, maps, fieldwork, documents and the ruins themselves it is sometimes possible to reconstruct with some degree of confidence the approach to a medieval castle. We shall now embark on three such journeys.

FIGURE 62.
A plan of Haddon Hall, Derbyshire, indicating the phases of building. The building was transformed in the later medieval period with a 'martial front' facing the visitor.

Ruthin Castle, Denbighshire

Ruthin (Rhuthun) was raised during the initial phases of Edward I's conquest of North Wales, but is less well known than other Edwardian castles as there is little left of the original fabric and the site is now a privately-owned hotel.[12] Ruthin was the administrative centre of the *cantraf* of Dyffryn Clwyd and following Edward's conquest of 1282 it became the *caput* of the lordship of the same name. Ruthin's importance meant that it would have been furnished with a native Welsh residence or *llys* which, to judge from excavated examples elsewhere, would have consisted of a hall and ancillary buildings surrounded by an enclosure.[13] That there was such a manorial complex at Ruthin is suggested by the fact that the Welsh lord Llywelyn ap Iorwerth is found issuing documents there in the late thirteenth century.[14] The castle was probably raised over the existing seigneurial seat, placed on a sandstone ridge that rose above the valley of the river Clwyd and commanding a view down the valley and over the surrounding hills. The visual appearance of the castle and its surrounding landscape was clearly striking; its name *Y Castell Coch yng Ngwernfor*, 'the red castle in the great marsh', is easily explicable given the red sandstone used as building material and the extensive boggy ground to the east of the castle.

In 1277 Edward granted Drffryn Clwyd to his ally, the Welsh prince Dafydd ap Gruffydd, and work began on the castle in that year.[15] There is little written evidence for the progress of the building work in the Exchequer records, suggesting that Dafydd was responsible much of the work, although he probably had access to Edward's masons who were then employed at the building of Flint and Rhuddlan. Dafydd unsuccessfully rebelled in 1282 and later in the year Reginald de Grey, the Justicier of Chester, was granted the lordship by King Edward. This event seems to have marked an important point in the castle's history. Edward himself visited Ruthin and there are references to his master mason, Master James of St George, who probably directed the building work. From this point, Ruthin castle became a major residence of the de Greys and many of the features in the surrounding landscape can be attributed to their occupancy.

The castle itself was situated at the centre of a complex landscape much like those discussed in the previous chapter (Figure 63).[16] To the north of the castle a new borough for fifty burgesses was laid out around a market place and, following Owain Glyn Dŵr's revolt, town defences with gates were added. A parish church was also part of the original town plan and in 1310 John de Grey founded a college in memory of his father within the bounds of the borough. Between the castle and the town was the 'lord's garden' which was probably of *herber* type and which provided a view down to the east where the 'lord's orchard and pond' were located. The latter is of some interest as a small mound now lies in this location. The status of this feature is unknown but it is most likely to be the remains of a viewing mount or other ornamental feature. It does not resemble a post-medieval garden earthwork and a sixteenth-century or medieval date is most likely. The 'lord's pond' probably refers to a large fishpond now preserved in earthwork form to the south of the orchard. The town's mill lay to the west of the castle and was fed by a canalised stream 400 metres in length, cut from the Clwyd, that entered into a large mill pond which also probably served as an ornamental feature. To the south lay the castle park that encompassed the orchard, ponds and mill and provided a sylvan backdrop to the residential buildings. This was known

FIGURE 63.
Ruthin castle, Denbighshire. The castle is in the centre of the photograph with the attendant borough on the right and the deer park to the left. The mound at the middle right of the photograph is possibly a medieval garden feature and the remains of the castle fishponds can also be seen.

© CLWYD-POWYS ARCHAEOLOGICAL TRUST

as the 'little park', presumably to distinguish it from the four other castle parks that were situated several kilometres away at Bathafarn, Polpark, Clok and Brenk; these probably had a more direct association with hunting. In addition to this we also hear of gallows to the east of the town and further fishponds, which probably lay on the low ground either to the east or west of the castle.

Given this evidence, it is therefore possible to reconstruct the journey into Ruthin during the early fourteenth century. The principal approach route was probably from the east from Cheshire through the Pass of Penbarrass and, sited on its ridge, the castle would have been a major landmark. This is especially the case on the final approach to the castle, where the road bends from the east and runs up the Clwyd valley from the north. As travellers moved towards the town they would have passed the gallows, a highly potent reminder of the role of the de Greys' as dispensers of royal justice. From here they would have entered the town and passed into the market place. From the late thirteenth century all trading within the lordship had to take place here and this economic control was reinforced by the presence of a pillory in the market square.

Those visitors going on to the castle would then have travelled past the houses of the wealthiest burgesses (which lay closest to the castle) and then on towards the main gate. From this point the journey was far more structured. Before entering the castle, visitors were first taken into the deer park and would have passed the orchards and ponds before finally entering the castle through the gatehouse. Due to the present ruinous state of the building it is difficult to judge the exact spatial arrangement of the castle itself, but it probably consisted of a courtyard space with the main accommodation contained in the gatehouse and further chambers in the towers. From the gatehouse, there would have been views east and west over the water gardens and south over the deer park.

Ruthin exemplifies the potential of this type of analysis. As we have seen, although there is no such thing as a 'typical' medieval designed landscape, Ruthin – with its combination of parkland, water features and attendant town – does exhibit some characteristics common to other thirteenth-century examples. As more examples are found with this kind of structured approach the possibility that they were deliberately articulated in this way becomes more likely. Yet Ruthin also points up some of the difficulties inherent in this type of analysis. Although is it certain that the features that surrounded Ruthin castle were in place by the early fourteenth century, it cannot be known for certain if they were ever integral to the original design – although in this case the town and mill must have been as they appear in the original borough charter. A complicating factor here is that the castle was probably raised over an existing Welsh lordly residence and that a Welsh lord undertook the initial building work. We simply do not know if the de Grey landscape represented something entirely new or was an elaboration of existing features although, since it has been suggested that at Chirk existing systems of exploitation were inherited and extended by incoming English lords, the latter may have been the case.[17]

Castle Acre, Norfolk

Castle Acre in Norfolk occupies an important place in castle studies due to excavations in the 1970s which demonstrated that the unfortified double hall of the Warenne family dating to the 1070s was radically altered seventy years later (Figures 64 and 65). Alongside the castle, the Norman foundation consisted of a planned settlement, a Cluniac priory and, probably, a deer park; the whole *ensemble* has long been seen as a classic example of the impact of the Norman Conquest on the English landscape. The castle straddles two significant communication routes: the river Nar and the Roman road known as the Peddars Way. The former constituted a major east-west waterway that eventually drained into the Little Ouse, while the later was a major roadway running north-south along the western edge of East Anglia.[18]

Of some interest here is the relationship between the castle and the Roman road (Figure 64). To the south of the castle, the Peddars Way deviates

FIGURE 64. Castle Acre. The deviated course of the Peddars Way.

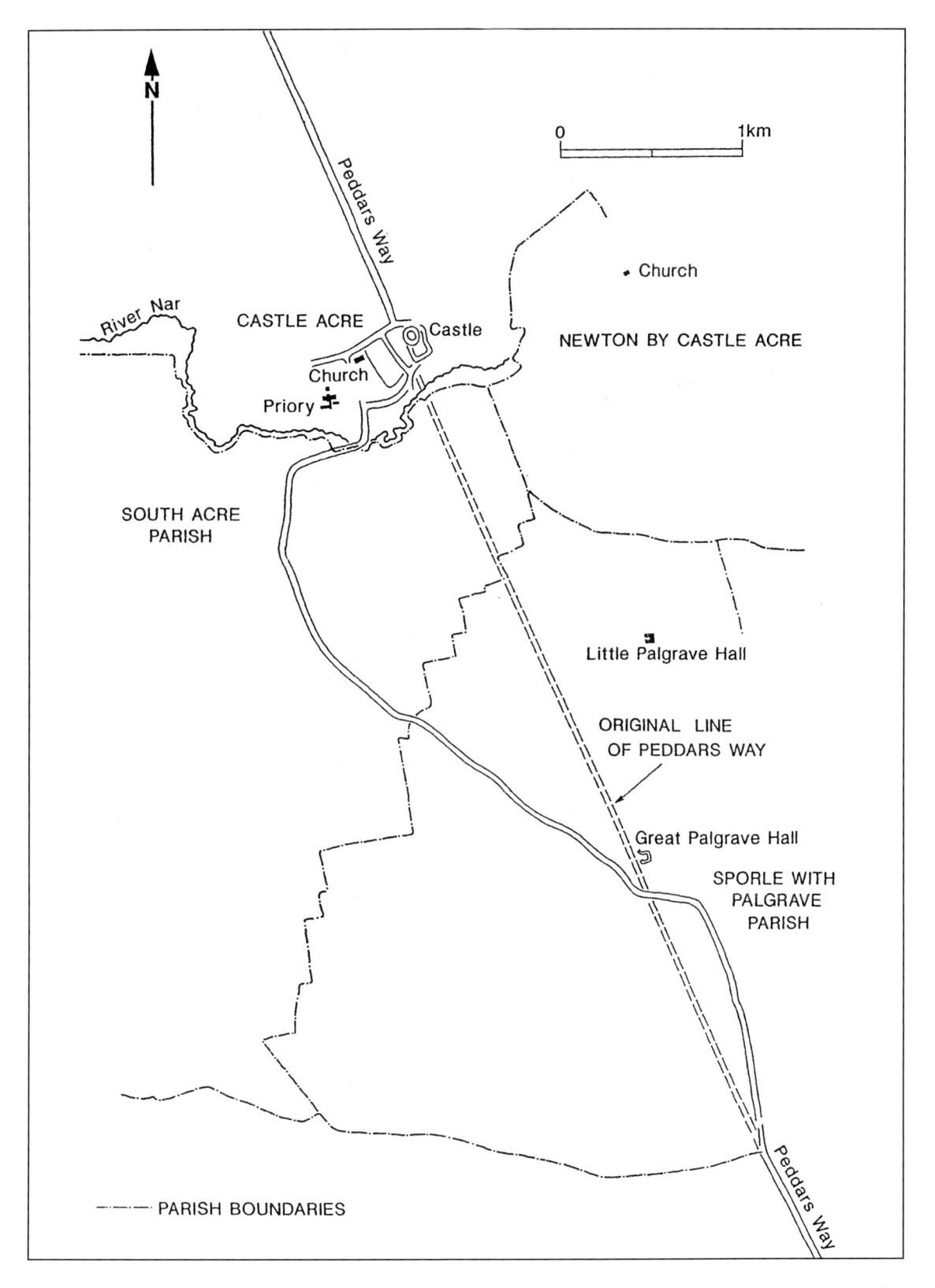

markedly from its original course. Originally the road ran along what is now the castle bailey ditch but the line of the road is truncated by the substantial flint wall which connected the castle to the settlement defences. Although it is impossible to date this wall with any precision, it is undoubtedly Norman in origin and is of similar construction and proportions to the masonry connected with the 1140s rebuilding located in the upper ward of the castle. This suggests that either this section of the Peddars Way had fallen out of use by this date, or that it had been subject to a diversion at an early date. There are a number of indications that the diverting of the road was part of an attempt to deliberately manipulate the way in which people experienced the castle.

An early date for the re-routing is suggested by the fact that the majority of the field boundaries to the south of the castle do not respect the original

FIGURE 65.
Castle Acre castle, Norfolk, regional *caput* of the Warenne family. The remains of the 'country house' of the 1070s can be seen in the centre of the picture, subsumed by later works.

Experiencing Castles: Iconography and Status

alignment of the road (we might expect, for example, the parish boundary to follow its course); indeed at nearby Sporle the parish boundary follows the line of the deviated course. Moreover, the manors over which the diversion runs were all Warenne land at the time of Domesday in 1086, again suggesting a connection with the castle. A reconstruction of the journey into Castle Acre via this route suggests a degree of conscious manipulation of the landscape in order to present a suitably impressive tableau to the visitor.

As travellers approach from the south, the first indication that they are entering an elite landscape is not the presence of the seigneurial seat but, significantly, a statement of piety, the Priory (Figure 66). The road then drops into a hollow, obscuring the Priory, and it is only as the visitor begins to cross the valley floor and climbs onto the opposite slope that the full visual effect becomes apparent. Here the viewer is presented with a vista consisting of the priory, town and castle; despite all the changes in the landscape over nine hundred years the effect today is still dramatic. The Priory occupies the foreground; the planned town sits in the centre, while the castle dominates the *ensemble* in the background. One imagines that this is the point at which the visitor might pause to view the scene before riding on and, if the view from this point showed the observer what was to come, then the rest of the approach made sure the impact was hammered home.

FIGURE 66.
Castle Acre priory, Norfolk. The Cluniac priory dominates the approach into Castle Acre. Any visitor was obliged to skirt round the precinct wall before entering the settlement.

137

Following this part of the journey, travellers were taken directly past the priory, crossing the river Nar immediately under the shadow of the precinct wall and then skirting along the southern side of the town wall. Here, they passed by the castle fishpond – known here as the 'Earl's Pond' – before entering the town via a gatehouse, travelling up the main street and turning right onto 'Toll Green' (where anybody on horseback probably had to dismount). They then passed under the bailey gate into the castle's lower ward. To enter the castle from here it was necessary to cross a ditch and pass through another gatehouse, and at this point the traveller would be standing immediately in front of the great tower. The building was accessed via a staircase. We do not know the exact arrangement of rooms in the tower in the 1140s, but if we take the contemporary *donjon* at Castle Hedingham in Essex as a possible model, then our visitors would have had to pass through an entrance hall before gaining entry to the upper hall and meeting the lord.

Although some care seems to have been taken over the principal approach, other approach routes were not neglected. The Peddars Way was also diverted on the northern side of the castle but to a much lesser extent: it makes two ninety-degree turns before entering the settlement. Any traveller approaching the castle from this direction would also have had to pass the park, the warren and probably the castle dovecote which, as we have seen, are all potent emblems of lordship. Equally, the riverine route up the Nar from Lynn must have had a similar visual impact as the principal approach from the south. Again, it is the Priory that assumes some significance, as the first landmark passed before entering the castle.

Castle Acre represents one of the earliest possible examples (as far as the author is aware) of a deliberately-planned approach route to a castle. While the evidence seems to point to a date in the Norman period it is unclear whether the road diversion belongs to the earliest phases of Norman occupation in the 1070s or the remodelling in the 1140s. Much depends on the date at which bank and ditch that connects the castle with the settlement was constructed. Excavations in the 1970s on the northern side of the castle did not provide an answer to this question but there is no reason to discount a date in the eleventh century. Other evidence, however, points to a later date. Initially, the Cluniac monks brought to England by William of Warenne were housed in the castle bailey and were moved out to their new site by the 1090s at the latest. The building of the priory clearly took some decades to complete as the abbey church was dedicated in the mid 1140s, around the same time as the castle was undergoing its transformation. As much of the approach route discussed above only really makes visual sense when the building of the priory was well underway and the new *donjon* towered above the landscape it may not be feasible to date this particular approach to an earlier period. Perhaps we should envisage the initial Warenne *caput*, then, as consisting of William's manor house, built on the site on its Anglo-Saxon predecessor, with the Roman road running alongside and an embryonic settlement to one side. This site was continually developed and the monastic house was subsequently

Experiencing Castles: Iconography and Status

moved onto a new site. In the 1140s the whole castle was transformed and the priory church neared completion; perhaps it was at this point that it was deemed necessary to divert the main approach road to the castle.

The changing social and political context of the 1140s may provide a clue as to why it was felt necessary to radically alter the way in which the castle was experienced. The usual reason given for the remodelling of Castle Acre at this time is the military insecurity during the 'Anarchy' of Stephen's reign. This makes little sense in a local context, as Norfolk saw no major campaigning throughout this period. At this time, however, several other baronial families were becoming increasingly powerful within the region, a situation that must have been greeted by the established Warennes with some alarm, particularly at a time of national political disturbance. The late 1130s and early 1140s saw the building of Castle Rising and New Buckenham castles by the D'Albinis and the construction of the *donjon* at Castle Hedingham in Essex by the newly created Earl of Oxford, Aubrey de Vere. Given that the banorial *caput* partially functioned as a visible sign of wealth, ambition and political standing it is easy to see why, in the context of the 1140s, a major magnate singled out Castle Acre for special attention.

Dover

Dover castle in Kent is the largest in England and probably holds the record for the longest occupied fortification in the country – it was in the 1950s that the British army finally departed. The castle has a complex history and the oldest fortifications on the site date back to the Iron Age. William the Conqueror added to pre-Conquest fortifications in the week after the battle of Hastings but more major work was carried out on the castle in the later twelfth century by the Angevin kings, notably Henry II.[19] His main works commenced *c.*1182 and consisted of a massive stone *donjon* and the inner bailey wall with mural towers. Parts of the outer curtain wall were also built in stone. The expenditure involved was massive (between £6000 and £7000), and the result was a potent statement of Henry II's political power in a part of the kingdom that controlled the shortest sea crossing to his continental lands. The significance of its location was later emphasised in 1216 by castellan Hubert de Burgh, who said that Dover was 'the key of England'.[20]

Recent work on the keep by English Heritage has yielded much new information about the building and John Goodall has reconstructed the approach.[21] Moreover, in this case it is known that Dover *was* a showpiece monument that was intended to be deliberately shown off to visitors and (hopefully) experienced in a particular manner. In 1247, when Gaucher de Châtillon came to England, Henry III ordered the constable of Dover that:

> when Gaucher de Châtillon shall come to Dover he shall take him into that castle and show the castle off to him in eloquent style, so that the magnificence of the castle shall be fully apparent to him, and that he shall see no defects in it. And Gaucher is to be allowed to enter the King's

park of Elham, and to hunt there two or three does as a gift from the King.²²

This interesting passage demonstrates not only that castles could act as cultural markers – in this case Dover is a metaphor for the realm – but, with the reference to the park, also points up the link between castles and hospitality. To judge from what he would have seen, Gaucher was probably impressed with his journey.

The castle would first have been seen while Gaucher was out at sea. Particularly noticeable would have been the proliferation of towers on the curtain walls together with the turrets on the *donjon* which were unusual for a castle of this date. After disembarking at the dock at Dover Gaucher would then have to ride up to the castle along the 'way between the hills' before turning to enter the castle from the north. This would also be the approach for any visitor coming from London and the route into the castle from this point was highly contrived.

Our visitor would have passed through one gate and then approached the barbican via a wooden ramp. At this point Gaucher would be looking at what would have seemed a triple-towered gateway and would then have passed through a twin-towered gatehouse, probably one of the first of its kind in

Castles in Context: Power, Symbolism and Landscape, 1066–1500

FIGURE 67. Dover Castle, Kent. The *donjon* was the centrepiece of an elaborate approach to the castle and its visual appearance was enhanced by the use of coloured bands of stone. From here the visitor would have been taken round the building and entered via an elaborate forebuilding.

England. At this point the visitor's field of view is entirely dominated by the squat *donjon*. Work on the fabric has shown that the design of the *donjon* was constructed partly to form a facade or display front. Originally, coloured building stones were coursed in layers so that on three sides the donjon appeared to have been constructed in striped bands. Although now lost due to infilling, originally the *donjon* would have sat on a mound of earth, raising it above its immediate surroundings. Other buildings were arranged around the internal face of the inner ward, giving the impression of a 'shell keep', although the idea may have been to give the impression to any visitor that they were entering a double *donjon*. From here, our visitor would have to travel around two sides of the tower before entering via an elaborate forebuilding, which, in turn, gave entry to an upper-floor hall. On his way up through the forebuilding, the visitor had to pass through two gates and as he did so he may have seen the king or some other dignitary above; over the entrance to the forebuilding are the remains of a probable balcony (Figure 67).

The forebuilding is also of interest for another reason. Unusually, it contained two chapels. The upper chapel probably served as a private chapel for the king, whereas the lower was clearly visible (and indeed was open) to anybody moving up the stairway. The architectural detail on both matches that in the shrine of St Thomas Becket in Canterbury Cathedral, which was completed immediately prior to the construction of the *donjon* at Dover. Later documentation suggests that at least one of the chapels at Dover was dedicated to St Thomas. This raised the intriguing possibility that Henry II (who did public penance for Becket's murder) deliberately appropriated the image of the Saint and incorporated it directly into his new castle, which stood on the pilgrimage route to Canterbury.

Experiencing castles

It could be argued that one of the inherent weaknesses in the kind of analysis undertaken in the three cases above is a lack of historical context. Currently we can really only speculate about the occasions on which the lord might be visited, how the use of space may have been managed, and how room function might have differed depending on whether the lord was, or was not, in residence. One avenue of research that would prove useful in this area of castle studies would be the identification of the exact occasions on which stage-managed events such as feasts took place. At present, however, it could be suggested that at royal castles the solemn ceremony of the royal crown-wearing was probably the most important ritual activity. During these occasions, the kingly authority was displayed to the assembled local nobility by a ceremony that took the form of a coronation without the royal anointing. William the Conqueror famously wore his crown three times a year at various towns across the kingdom; the ceremony at York in Christmas 1069 took place after the Harrying of the North and was intended to impose his authority following rebellion.[23] Given the classical imagery that castles such as Colchester,

Norwich, the Tower of London and Chepstow appropriated, it is easy to see why such buildings were deemed to be appropriate settings for these rituals.[24] At baronial level, activities such as the meeting of the honour court or the celebration of ennoblement provide likely contexts for lavish entertainment, but the exact role of the building on such occasions is difficult to pin down with any confidence. While it might be difficult at present to determine how some castles were approached and how social space was negotiated, it should not be thought that the type of analysis undertaken here is completely ahistorical. Again, contemporary literature makes it abundantly clear that castles were perceived in a highly structured way and that the idea of following a delineated approach route to a castle which reveals the building by stages is certainly not a figment of our imagination.

Structured approaches

The literary sources do make it clear that there was some notion of the 'correct' way in which a noble guest should enter and experience the castle. As has already been noted, the ideal castle should be visible as a landmark from a considerable distance but then, on approach, only reveal itself gradually to the viewer. Usually, visitors spend a good deal of time simply looking at the castle and its attendant structures before moving forward. In the *Roman de Waldef*, for example, the visitors stop and gaze at the castle and town that lie before them. One is immediately reminded here of the approach to Castle Acre discussed above, where the vista of castle, town and priory is situated at a convenient turn in the journey (the comparison may not be too fantastic a claim as the *Roman de Waldef* was written for an East Anglian audience). Some time is usually spent admiring the building and after a suitable period a messenger will often appear and lead the guests forward. The travellers are usually taken through the castle town but this represents merely an intermediate stage in the journey. Before gaining entry to the castle itself some kind of symbolic boundary was crossed. This might be a river or moat and, given that the medium of water was used to separate different orders of men in the medieval period, this moment was of some significance. On other occasions the castle gate marks the cultural boundary between the castle and outside world. For example, when the hero Fergus visits Lidel Castle he meets a nobleman with a hawk and a female companion at the castle gate and it is at this point that his horse is taken from him and he is led into the hall.[25] Sometimes these pleasantries are dispensed with altogether; the visitor might find the gates open so that he can pass effortlessly through the rows of towers and gates before meeting the host.

Once inside, the ubiquity of fireplaces, the quality of the fenestration and the splendour of the interior design are all emphasised. The domestic arrangements, such as piped water, well-lit rooms and general cleanliness might also draw praise. As is to be expected, a fine prospect was to be gained from the upper chambers; in the *Roman de Waldef* King Atle, at the castle that took his name, 'had the donjon made//from it one could survey//the whole country around'.[26] Also of interest were the features which could be surveyed from the upper levels of the buildings. In the tower that Atle raised it was said that 'from it one could survey//the whole country around//and in the distance the deep sea//where the boats used to come//and on the other were the woods//and the forests for all his choice'.[27] We are reminded here – by a totally different type of source – of the public and private division seen in the landscapes of the previous chapter. With the sea on one side and forests on the other, this could be Castle Rising, a further reminder of this romance's connection with East Anglia.

In the more fantastic tales from later medieval literature the castle will sometimes appear with the aid of supernatural forces. In *Sir Gawain and the Green Knight* the castle appears almost by magic just after Sir Gawain has been praying that he and his horse will find shelter and a place where he can hear Mass.[28] The castle is set in the midst of a meadow (shades here, perhaps, of Beaumaris in Anglesey: literally, the 'fair marsh') and is surrounded by a moat and enclosed by a park. From the edge of the moat Sir Gawain surveys the castle and notes tantalising visual hints of the 'handsome turrets in matching style' and the 'many chimneys pale as chalk gleaming whitely upon the tower roofs' that lie behind the wall. Gawain then hails the porter who tells the resident lord that he has a visitor. Within a moment the drawbridge comes down and, as Gawain enters through the open gates, the staff all kneel down before him. He lets them rise and as he proceeds into the castle a host of servants take his saddle and horse. They bring him into the hall where Sir Bertilak – needless to say, a man fitting of such a home – receives him. From here, Gawain is escorted into a private room. He also receives similar hospitality on his departure; on his exit the porter again kneels and prays for his safety as Gawain rides out.[29]

Partonopeu of Blois

What emerges most strongly from the depiction of castles in literature is their capacity to amaze. This is partly down to size – bigger nearly always seems to be better – but it is the sheer display of wealth and the consequent lifestyle thereby sustained which leaves visitors so staggered they think they are the victims of enchantment. The most impressive castles are constructed from materials that are not only intrinsically expensive or precious but also unchanging; they never fade or become tarnished. As the castle itself will never fade, so the builder too seems invincible. In the most fantastic castles the visitor simply wanders around of his own accord and experiences, without any guide, the riches on offer.

Thus the experiences of Partonopeu of Blois, when he visits the castle of Melior (the daughter of the Emperor of Constantinople), are worth quoting at some length. Melior's castle is on an island (again, the castle is approached over water) and Partonopeu arrives on a ship that is powered by magic. Like any castles with pretensions it has an attendant town, and the hero gazes up at this as his boat draws near: 'He sees the walls of the city//which shine against the sky//they are marvellously straight and tall//and do not lack in beauty'.[30] Inevitably, Partonopeu then has to go through the city before reaching the castle. What impresses him here is the cleanliness of the streets. He enters a street which is miraculously spotless and the poet explains 'It could not have any mud//for it was entirely paved//and the more it rained//the brighter the pavement would become'.[31] Having explored the town, Partonopeu then makes his way to the castle. What happens next is of some interest, particularly since it must have been read or heard by many nobles, as this Romance was one of the most popular of its day:

> He turned the head of his horse//retraced his steps in the great street//and went up towards the castle//There isn't such a beautiful one in the whole world/It has great ditches and tall walls//which do not fear catapults and assaults//He found the gates open//there were two towers tall and secure//From them one can defend the gates//neither king nor emperor could take them//He entered in the castle//there is plenty of wealth//there is a tower in the castle//made of brand new polished marble//the castle is made proportionally//and is neither too tall nor too low//the tower is enclosed in the middle//no one ever saw a nicer thing//the castle around the tower//was about a mile all around//inside there are mills and aviaries//and large gardens and lawns.[32]

It needs to be stressed again that examples such as this are from literature and part of the rhetorical function of the castle in medieval literature was to allow the real nobleman to show his true virtue and character.[33] Thus Partonopeu needs no guide or messenger to explain to him why the building is so magnificent or what it represents. The fact that Partonopeu is a true noble not only means that he understands all the nuances of his journey, but his whole experience of the castle demonstrates his intrinsic aristocratic virtues.

What we have been discussing here is an ideal, rather than, in all likelihood, the reality. While there must have been times when the visual appeal of buildings matched the aspirations of the owner these may not have lasted for very long. To judge from the descriptions of castles taken by the crown, many were in a sorry state. Time and time again we hear of crumbling walls, leaking roofs, ruined buildings and disrepair. At Restormel (Cornwall), in 1337, we get a vivid impression of what had become of the magnificent building raised two centuries earlier: 'One chapel where the glass of the large window is broken for the most part and needs speedy repair if it is not to become worse ... three chambers above the gateway in a decayed state covered with lead and the leaves of the gates at the entrance of the said castle are weak and insufficient ... also there are there three chambers with cellars below and a decayed bakehouse. And two old ruinous stables for twenty horses on either side of the gateway'.[34] To judge from similar accounts elsewhere, this was not an uncommon occurrence.

The cultural castle

The highly elaborate arrangements that some castle-builders engineered in order to create a specific sense of place highlights the fact that castles could stand for a variety of social metaphors. One of the most important cultural markers that castles represented was that of antiquity. Much in the same way as the urban elites of medieval England created elaborate lineages for their towns, so too could castles stand for the pedigree of a noble family.[35] The Welsh poet Iolo Goch described the castle of Criccieth in vivid terms: 'the fair wall you will see, and the bright fortress on the clifftop, and on the red stone on the edge of a field, that is Cricieth, a fine old building. And the old battle-scarred warrior is Sir Hywel with his wife, and her handmaidens sewing silk in the sunlight by a glass window. The splendid standard that you see is Sir Hywel's pennoncel with its three fleurs-de-lis on a black background'.[36] The noble residence could thus be a powerful embodiment of chivalry, reputation and ancestry. This sense of nostalgia and history helps explain why so many castles, despite being substantially rebuilt over the course of their occupation, retained some of their earlier fabric. Goodrich, in Herefordshire, is a particularly good example of a castle where part of the older fabric was deliberately left in place. Here the castle was almost totally rebuilt in the late thirteenth century by William de Valence.[37] However, the twelfth-century donjon was retained, and at the time (as today) must have stood out as being older that the rest of the fabric. By preserving this existing symbol of lordship Valence was advertising the fact that although much of his Marcher residence was new, the authority vested in the building was of a longer pedigree.

At other castles there appears to have been similar connections with the past. An intriguing example is Middleham, in Yorkshire, where the original motte was deserted in favour of a nearby low-lying site at some point in the mid twelfth century. Despite their abandonment, the earthworks of the old castle retained some meaning for future generations as they could be seen from a viewing balcony on the new *donjon*.[38] A more direct case of interpreting the past in the present is seen at Tintagel castle in Cornwall (Figure 56). The site was a trading centre in the early medieval period but became notorious after 1125 when Geoffrey of Monmouth's *History of the Kings of Britain* established Tintagel as the birthplace of King Arthur – a myth that persists to this day. Richard, Earl of Cornwall, acquired the site partly through exchange soon after he was raised to the Earldom and the castle he subsequently built on the site must be interpreted as an attempt to associate himself with the legend of Arthur.[39]

At other castles the element of 'courtliness' or the specific form of the buildings hints at the strategies of individual builders. As has been seen at Stokesay, in designing his gatehouse Lawrence de Ludlow was anxious to show an affinity with those buildings raised by the crown. At Cooling, in Kent, the placing of the licence to crenellate on the exterior facade of the gatehouse

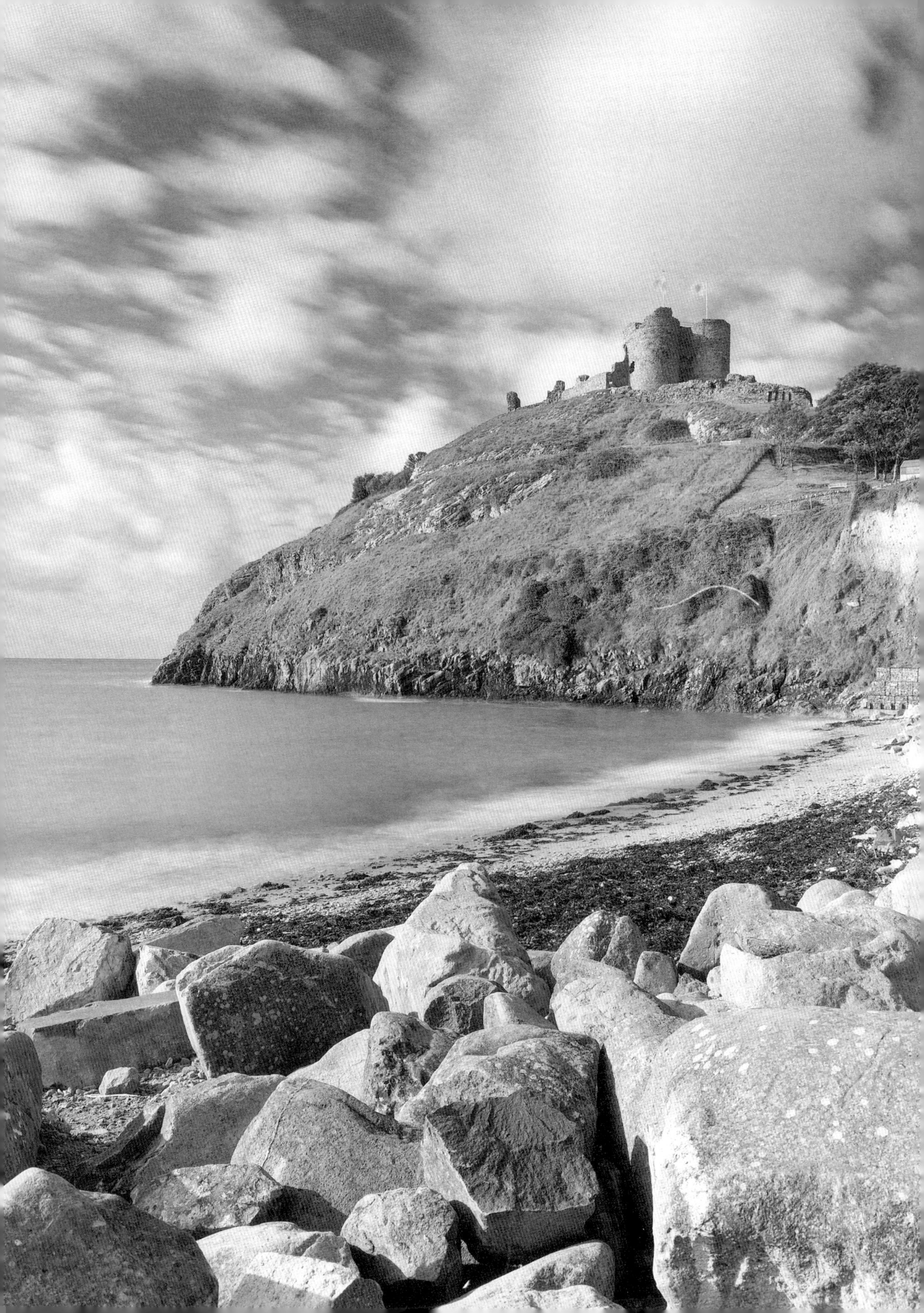

Experiencing Castles: Iconography and Status

identified the builder not only with the crown, but also with the national struggle against the French.[40] Roger Bigod III at Chepstow in the thirteenth century seemed almost too concerned with creating a martial image. Four giant crossbows were placed on the great tower (a special crane was constructed to winch them into position) but how this was ever intended to have practical application is not entirely clear.[41]

Despite the trend to downplay the castle's role in war, it should also be remembered that one of the most potent metaphors of castle architecture was that of warfare. Building a residence in a particularly overt martial style could be an excellent way in which to display potential physical power – indeed, the message of a grand crenellated building was by definition inherently militaristic. Where there was a close approximation between the actual effectiveness of military architecture and residential needs this was a powerful political statement on the part of the builder. For example, Beeston was a clear assertion of magnatial power by the Earls of Chester in the early years of the minority of Henry III. Something similar could be said about Criccieth (Figure 68). Here the castle would have been approached under the watch of the 'Engine Tower', so named on account of the siege engine that would have been placed upon the roof. The work at Criccieth can probably be attributed to Llywelyn ap Gruffudd (Llywelyn the Last) and seems to the fit the image of the charismatic and militaristic Welsh prince whose followers, an English chronicler said, stuck to him like glue.[42]

Castles and society

Quite what non-elite groups thought about the castles of their lords is difficult to establish. Undoubtedly there were some, such as artisans and masons, who profited from castle-building – others must have resisted the imposition of labour services and resented the resources of those who resided within the castle walls.

It goes without saying that the experience of the castle would have been different for those who lived within the shadow of its walls compared with others who lived some distance away. In some places the tenurial arrangement of the baronial honour and the existence of castle-guard created a sense of 'castle community'. At Clun, in Shropshire, the castle and its borough stood on the Welsh frontier for much of its existence; here the seigneurial presence potentially offered refuge and protection. The vills from which castle-guard was owed all lay to the east, towards England, and the castle formed the focus for the border community.[43] In other cases we might surmise that local inhabitants never saw much beyond the castle gate. At least in the Anglo-Norman period, lords seem to have appeared to their tenants at their gateways and it was here, it seems, that much business was conducted. In a twelfth-century reference at Castle Acre in Norfolk, a charter was witnessed 'outside the door of the bailey of the castle of Acre'.[44] It would be interesting to know how much access non-resident staff were granted to areas behind the castle gate,

FIGURE 68.
Criccieth castle, Caernarvonshire, perched on an imposing cliff top. Much of the surviving masonry can probably be attributed to Llywelyn ap Gruffudd (Llywelyn the Last).

MICK SHARP

and on what occasions. Those on business were obviously allowed access; we have already seen how, at Conwy in 1401, the Welsh broke in because two of their number pretended to be carpenters, and the ease with which they did so suggests that access for artisans must not have been an uncommon occurrence. Such incidents also highlight the role of the porter or watchman who was responsible for granting admission into the castle. It is significant that the role of the gatekeeper is one that is prominent in the depiction of castles in literary sources.[45] Given the numbers of castles which were surrendered or were taken by treachery this fact is not without consequence. Like most porters (as anyone working in a university will know only too well) the medieval doorman was frequently a surly and distrustful character who would only allow entry when satisfied of the identity and business of the entrant. The abundance of doors and portals for porters at castles throughout the medieval period suggests that, at least when the lord was in residence, access could be easily restricted or denied.

Those living close to a castle might never have got into the inner core of buildings, unless they had any specific business that would have necessitated entry. One incident which illustrates this is the case of a Welsh woman, Maud Vras, who died at Montgomery castle on New Year's day 1288.[46] Maud had gone to the castle to retrieve a kettle she had loaned to the under-constable and, as she waited in the passage under the gatehouse, a stone dropped on her head from a room above and she was killed. A jury later heard how the under-constable had been in an upper chamber trying on a new cloak when it touched the stone and apparently sent it down one of the murder holes onto the unfortunate widow beneath. While, even after seven hundred years, there is a lingering suspicion over whether this was an accident or not (a jury decided it was), it is significant that Maud was kept waiting at the gate. Clearly she had some connection with the resident staff and this may account for the fact that she was at the juncture between the inner and the outer ward of Montgomery castle. Whether such access arrangements were typical is a subject for future inquiry.

As noted above, for the peasantry castles often meant an unlooked-for drain on their time and energy: frequently tenants' labour services involved the upkeep of castle earthworks and walls. The exact obligations were often laid down quite precisely. At Pickering in Yorkshire the tenants of the honour were obliged to upkeep the area of the outer ward know as the herisson (literally, the hedgehog, so named because it bristled with stakes), each being responsible for one perch, or five and a half yards.[47] Where it is possible to tell, labour services on castles appear to have been highly unpopular. Despite the existence of well-defined labour services on fortifications in the pre-Conquest period, the protests in the *Anglo-Saxon Chronicle* over castle-works speak of widespread resentment. Similar complaints were made during Stephen's reign. In 1147 Hugh de Bolebec was found to be forcing wrongful labour services on his neighbours for the enlargement of his castle.[48] The thirteenth-century chronicler Matthew Paris also provides some insight into the attitude of those

Castles in Context: Power, Symbolism and Landscape, 1066–1500

FIGURE 69. Interior view of gunport at Raglan Castle, Monmouth.

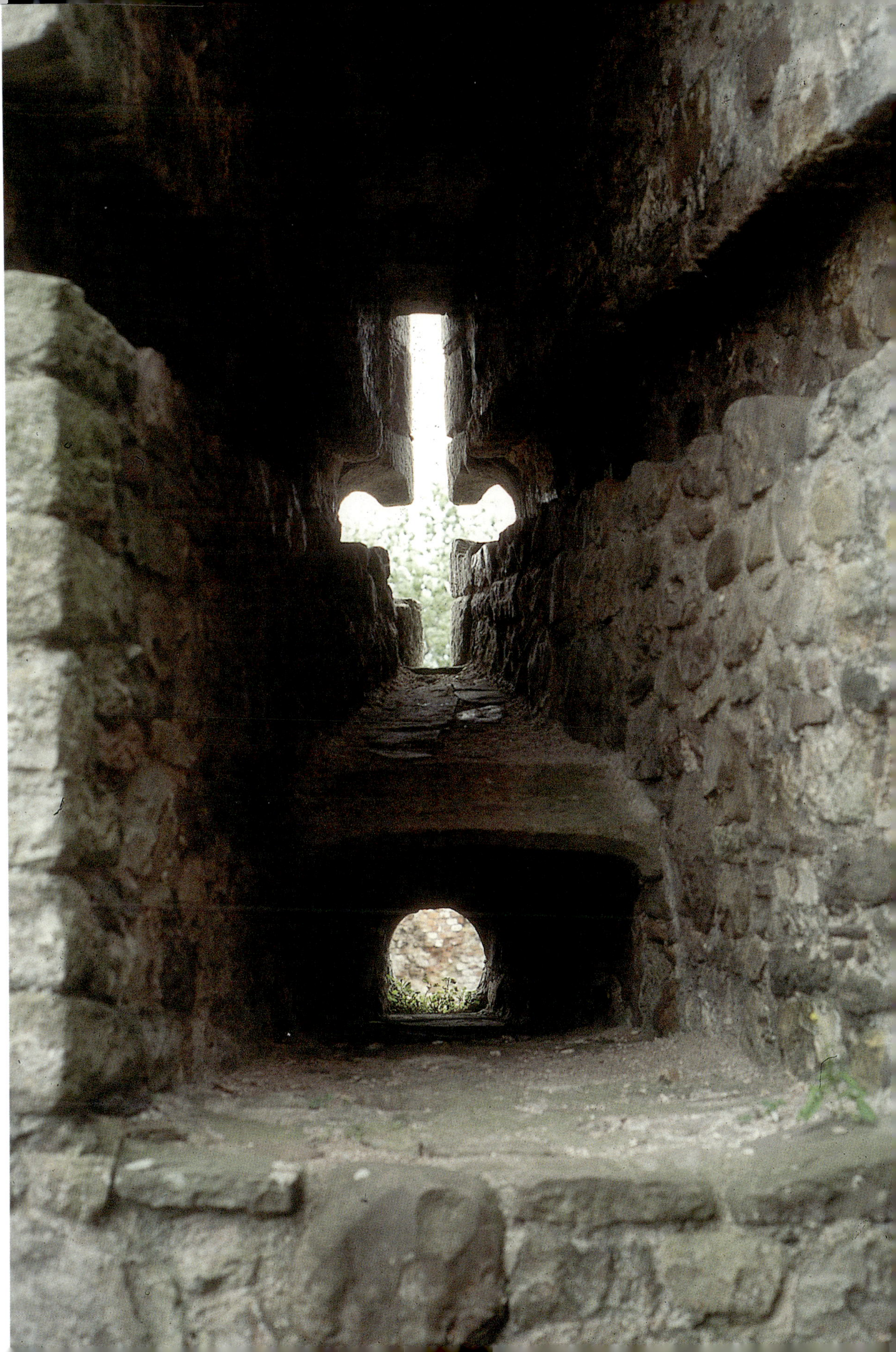

who lived and worked in the shadow of the great buildings of the medieval aristocracy. In 1240 Henry III's building of a new gateway the Tower of London suffered a set-back when the structure collapsed. Despite rebuilding, it collapsed for a second time exactly a year later to, according to Paris, much hilarity and ironic jeering from the citizens of London.[49] This topic is one for future academic study but, for now, it is intriguing to note that the peasantry were an integral part of the idealised landscape is seen in Langland's *Piers Plowman*:

> As I looked east high into the sun,
> I saw a tower on a toft strongly made;
> A deep dale below, a donjon within,
> With deep ditches, dark and dreadful to see.
> A fair field full of folk found I between,
> Of all manner of men, the poor and the rich;
> Working and wandering as the world demands,
> Some put themselves to the plough seldom at play
> In setting and sowing, working so hard.[50]

Conclusion

It would be incorrect to assume that the symbolic meaning inherent in castle-building was entirely for elite consumption; as icons of lordship castles were redolent to all sections of medieval society. The aftermath of the Peasants' Revolt in 1381, for example, saw an upsurge in seigneurial building in those areas most affected by the uprising, and it is possible to interpret the building or rebuilding of castles such as Cooling, Bodiam, Saltwood and North Elmham as an assertion of traditional forms of authority in a period of anxiety on the part of the aristocracy. This said, it is also likely that the very specific details of fortification were only ever intended to be understood in cultural terms. There has been a lively debate surrounding the nature of gunports, for example: how is it possible to understand a militarily-advanced feature placed in a location in a wall that rendered it unusable? One of the most convincing explanations resolves this potential contradiction in cultural terms. To the ignorant observer it might seem that a castle such as Raglan (Rhaglan) in Monmouthshire was equipped with highly effective and frightening military hardware (Figure 69). The more knowledgeable might note that the particular gunport was up-to-date and may have known something of the technology that lay behind its design. The well-informed guest, however, might notice the details of the feature, relate this to other buildings they had experienced and also note how difficult it would be to use in the event of a siege. If they offered this information to their host then they would thus reveal themselves as a true aristocrat, unquestionably one of 'those who fought'. Thinking such as this might profitably explain many of the aspects of castle-building that have been discussed in this book.

CHAPTER SEVEN

Rethinking the 'Castle Story'

Large parts of this book have sought to question some of the assumptions about castles with which many people (myself included) in this country were brought up and which are still maintained today in television programmes, heritage centres and in some books (Figure 70). In the process I have tried to refrain too much from saying that previous work was emphatically 'wrong'. It is rare for any academic work to remain 'right' for more than about thirty years and the strength and longevity of what has been termed here the 'castle story' is a testament to the scholarly insight, vigour and intellectual prowess of castle historians of the late nineteenth and twentieth centuries. While to some it now might seem that castle studies took a wrong turn it remains to be seen how (or indeed if) the new thinking on castles will develop.[1] Such has been the pace of change in the discipline that in some quarters even to mention the 'defence and defensibility' debate is regarded extremely outdated. Does this book represent another example of 'fighting yesterday's battle'?[2] I would suggest not and make no apology for dealing with the themes of form and function. While it might be the case that castle scholars need a more theoretically-aware approach to their subject, questions over why an individual built a castle at a given time and why a particular style was chosen are as relevant now as they were a century ago. The continued gathering of factual data (be it historical, archaeological or architectural) can only help us gain a fuller picture of what castles meant to contemporaries.

The study of castles has the potential to impact upon much broader themes and debates about medieval society. To discuss the military role of the castle and accept that the record of many is minimal inevitably leads us into questioning the nature of war in the Middle Ages. It could be contended that this book has offered a sanitized version of the past. I would argue that this is not the case and that we must try to recognise how much our perception of war in the Middle Ages is bound up in the legacy left to us by the twentieth century:[3] medieval warfare might in fact be more profitably be compared with that of Japan in the age of the Samurai or the Zulu culture of the mid nineteenth century. A good deal of writing over the past few years has seriously questioned aspects of the 'military' character of castles in 'conquest' phases of the history of, among other places, England, Ireland and the Holy Land, and this must beg further study.[4]

It has been argued here that the majority of crenellations found on castles were part of an architectural style which, while they could be pressed into use if necessary, primarily served to demonstrate aristocratic rank in a highly visually-orientated society. But as has also been pointed out, this style, by definition, referred to a military vocabulary. It must therefore follow that in order for this architectural style to make sense, at some level the building of fortifications equated with real military power. Even if some castles, perhaps most, are unquestionably 'non-defensive' in their design, there had to be some mechanism by which the building of a fortified residence carried meaning. With this in mind it is interesting to speculate about the existence of castles in Europe or beyond (ruling out short term campaign fortifications and siege works) where there indeed *was* a military purpose, where the architecture was unquestionably utilitarian in function and where sustained military action did occur. If such can be identified, their examination would illustrate the ways in which the majority are different and perhaps throw light upon the source from which the castles investigated here derived their meaning. Alternatively, if none is found then this would perhaps signal the death knell of the 'Real Castle', opening up a whole range of new issues about power, warfare, conquest and lordship. Most of the 'revisionist' arguments related in this book have been advanced with surprisingly little rigorous counter-argument from the academic community; time will tell if the 'castle story' has been changed for good.

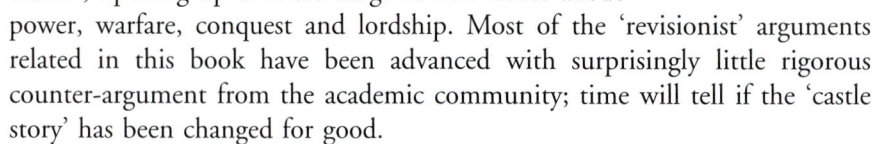

FIGURE 70. Reconstructed trebuchet at Caerphilly Castle, Glamorganshire. The 'military' perception of castles is still heavily embedded in the heritage industry.

Notes to the Chapters

Notes to Chapter 1: From Functionalism to Symbolism

1. M. W. Thompson (1994) 'The Military Interpretation of Castles', *Archaeological Journal* 151.
2. G. T. Clark (1884) *Mediaeval Military Architecture in England*, 2 vols, London.
3. E. S. Armitage (1912) *The Early Norman Castles of the British Isles*, London.
4. J. H. Round (1902) 'The Castles of the Conquest', *Archaeologia* 58.
5. A. Hamilton Thompson (1912) *Military Architecture in England During the Middle Ages*, Oxford.
6. ibid, p. 58.
7. C. L. H. Coulson (2003) *Castles in Medieval Society*, Oxford, Introduction.
8. C. Oman (1926) *Castles*, London; H. Braun (1936) *The English Castle*, London; S. Toy (1953) *The Castles of Great Britain*, London; S. Toy (1955) *A History of Fortification from 3000 BC to AD 1700*, London.
9. R. A. Brown, H. Colvin and A. Taylor (1963) *The History of the King's Works*, 2 vols, London; R. A. Brown (1955 and 2003) 'Royal Castle-Building in England, 1154–1216', *English Historical Review* 70, reprinted in R. Liddiard ed. *Anglo-Norman Castles*, Woodbridge; R. A. Brown (1959) 'A List of Castles, 1154–1216', *English Historical Review* 74.
10. D. Renn (1968) *Norman Castles in Britain*, London.
11. D. J. C. King (1983) *Castellarium Anglicanum*, New York; D. J. C. King (1988) *The Castle in England and Wales: An Interpretative History*, London.
12. R. A. Brown (1976) *English Castles*, 3rd edn, London, p. 172.
13. J. H. Beeler (1956) 'Castles and Strategy in Norman and Early Angevin England', *Speculum* 31; J. H. Beeler (1966) *Warfare in England, 1066–1189*, Cornell.
14. Brown, *Castles* pp. 14–16.
15. King, *Castellarium*, pp. xv–xxvii.
16. P. A. Faulkner (1958) 'Domestic Planning from the Twelfth to the Fourteenth Centuries', *Archaeological Journal* 115; P. A. Faulkner (1963) 'Castle Planning in the Fourteenth Century', *Archaeological Journal* 120.
17. King, *The Castle in England and Wales*, see discussion pp. 90–3.
18. Brown, *Castles* p. 172, an idea expressed early in his career; see C. Coulson (2001) 'Peaceable Power in Norman Castles', *Anglo-Norman Studies* 23, pp. 76–7.
19. D. J. C. King and L. Alcock (1969) 'Ringworks of England and Wales', *Château-Gaillard* 3.
20. B. K. Davison (1969) 'Early Earthwork Castles: a New Model', *Château-Gaillard* 3.
21. B. K. Davison (1967) 'The Origins of the Castle in England: The Institute's Research Project', *Archaeological Journal* 74.
22. R. A. Brown (1970) 'An Historian's Approach to the Origins of the Castle in England', *Archaeological Journal* 126.
23. C. Coulson (1979) 'Structural Symbolism in Medieval Castle Architecture', *Journal of the British Archaeological Association* 132.
24. ibid., p. 74.
25. This is certainly what Coulson himself believes: Charles Coulson *pers. comm.*

26. C. Coulson (1982) 'Hierarchism in Conventual Crenellation: An Essay in the Sociology and Metaphysics of Medieval Fortification', *Medieval Archaeology* **26**.
27. D. Austin (1984) 'The Castle and the Landscape', *Landscape History* **6**.
28. C. Platt (1982) *The Medieval Castle in England and Wales*, London.
29. M. W. Thompson (1987) *The Decline of the Castle*, Cambridge.
30. King, *Castle in England and Wales*; see, for example, criticism of Coulson especially at pp. 28–9.
31. D. Thackray (1991) *Bodiam Castle*, London, p. 59.
32. C. Coulson (1992) 'Some Analysis of Bodiam Castle, East Sussex', *Medieval Knighthood* **4**; D. J. Turner (1996) 'Bodiam, Sussex: True Castle or Old Soldier's Dream House?' in W. M. Ormrod ed. *England in the Fourteenth Century: Proceedings of the 1985 Harlaxton Symposium*, Woodbridge; C. Taylor, P. Everson and R. Wilson-North (1990) 'Bodiam Castle, Sussex', *Medieval Archaeology* **34**; J. Goodall (1998) 'The Battle for Bodiam Castle', *Country Life* (16 April); M. Johnson (2002) *Behind the Castle-Gate: From Medieval to Renaissance*, London.
33. D. Stocker (1992) 'The Shadow of the General's Armchair', *Archaeological Journal* **149**.
34. J. R. Kenyon (1990) *Medieval Fortifications*, Leicester; N. J. G. Pounds (1990) *The Medieval Castle in England and Wales: A Social and Political History*, Cambridge.
35. M. W. Thompson (1991) *The Rise of the Castle*, Cambridge.
36. T. McNeill (1992) *Castles*, London.
37. R. Higham and P. Barker (1992) *Timber Castles*, London.
38. C. Coulson (1996) 'Cultural Realities and Reappraisals in English Castle Study', *Journal of Medieval History* **22**.
39. T. A. Heslop (1991) 'Orford Castle and Sophisticated Living', *Architectural History* **34**.
40. P. Dixon (1998) 'Design in Castle-Building: The Control of Access to the Lord', *Château-Gaillard* **18**; P. Dixon and P. Marshall (1993 and 2003) 'The Great Tower at Hedingham Castle: A Reassessment', *Fortress* **18**, reprinted in Liddiard, *Anglo-Norman Castles*; P. Dixon (2002) 'The Myth of the Keep' in G. Meirion-Jones, E. Impey and M. Jones eds. *The Seigneurial Residence in Western Europe AD c.800–1600*, Oxford.
41. C. Coulson (1995) 'The French Matrix of the Castle Provisions of the Chester-Leicester Conventio', *Anglo-Norman Studies* **17**; C. Coulson (1994) 'Freedom to Crenellate by Licence: An Historiographical Revision', *Nottingham Medieval Studies* **38**; C. Coulson (1998) 'The Sanctioning of Fortresses in France: 'Feudal Anarchy' or Seigniorial Amity?', *Nottingham Medieval Studies* **41**.
42. O. H. Creighton (2002) *Castles and Landscapes*, London; Coulson, *Castles in Medieval Society*; Johnson, *Behind the Castle-Gate*.

Notes to Chapter 2: Castles, Conquest and Authority

1. E. Fernie (2000) *The Architecture of Norman England*, Oxford, p. 24.
2. J. Le Patourel (1976) *The Norman Empire*, Oxford; Brown, *Castles*.
3. J. Gillingham and R. Griffiths (2000) *Medieval Britain: A Very Short Introduction*, Oxford, pp. 1–2. This comment reflects a much wider body of literature, and this idea is explicitly stated by King in *The Castle in England and Wales*, p. 6: 'Peasants in revolt play an important part in some sorts of history; but in England they were not generally dangerous except at two periods: the years after the Norman Conquest, when the new lords appeared as upstart and tyrant foreigners ... and their lords found the shelter of a castle opportune' – the second was after the Peasants' Revolt.
4. D. Whitelock, D. C. Douglas and S. L. Tucker eds. (1961) *The Anglo-Saxon Chronicle*, London, p. 145; M. Chibnall ed. (1969) *The Ecclesiastical History of Orderic Vitalis*, vol. 2, Oxford, p. 219.
5. P. Hill and J. Wileman (2002) *Landscapes of War: the Archaeology of Aggression and Defence*, Stroud.

Notes to the Chapters

6. A. Williams (1995) *The English and the Norman Conquest*, Woodbridge, pp. 45–6.
7. R. Allen Brown (1969) *The Normans and the Norman Conquest*, Woodbridge query.
8. The literature on feudalism and on whether or not pre-Conquest England can be defined as such is vast, but see R. Allen Brown (1973) *The Origins of English Feudalism*, London; E. H. R. Brown (1974) 'The Tyranny of a Construct: Feudalism and Historians of Medieval Europe', *American Historical Review* 79; J. C. Holt (1984 and 1992) 'The Introduction of Knight Service in England', *Anglo-Norman Studies* 6, reprinted in M. Strickland ed. *Anglo-Norman Warfare*, Woodbridge; S. Reynolds (1994) *Fiefs and Vassals*, Oxford.
9. Williams, *English and the Norman Conquest*.
10. C. Drage (1987) 'Urban Castles', in J. Schofield and R. Leech eds. *Urban Archaeology in Britain*, London.
11. A. Williams (1992 and 2003) 'A Bell-House and a Burh-Geat: Lordly Residences in England before the Conquest', in C. Harper-Bill and R. Harvey eds. *Medieval Knighthood* 4, Woodbridge; reprinted in Liddiard, *Anglo-Norman Castles*.
12. D. Whitelock ed. (1955) *English Historical Documents, vol. 1 c. 500–1042*, London, pp. 431–2.
13. G. Beresford (1981) 'Goltho Manor, Lincolnshire: The Buildings and their Surrounding Defences, 850–1150', *Anglo-Norman Studies* 4; A. Saunders (1977) 'Five Castle Excavations: Reports on the Institute's Research Project into the Origin of the Castle in England', *Archaeological Journal* 134.
14. D. Renn (1994 and 2003) 'Burhgeat and Gonfanon: Two Sidelights from the Bayeux Tapestry', *Anglo-Norman Studies* 16, reprinted in Liddiard, *Anglo-Norman Castles*.
15. For a summary of excavated evidence see Higham and Barker, *Timber Castles*.
16. Williams, 'Bell House', *passim*.
17. Kenyon, *Medieval Fortifications*, p. 5.
18. P. Barker and R. Higham (2000) *Hen Domen, Montgomery. A Timber Castle on the English-Welsh Border: A Final Report*, Exeter.
19. Kenyon, *Medieval Fortifications*.
20. R. Eales (1990 and 2003) 'Royal Power and Castles in Norman England', in C. Harper-Bill and R. Harvey eds. *Medieval Knighthood* 3, Woodbridge, reprinted in Liddiard, *Anglo-Norman Castles*.
21. Eales, ibid.
22. For low estimates of numbers of new castles raised during Stephen's reign see C. Coulson (1994 and 2003) 'The Castles of the Anarchy' in E. King ed. *The Anarchy of Stephen's Reign*, Oxford, reprinted in Liddiard, *Anglo-Norman Castles*.
23. J. Green (1997) *The Aristocracy of Norman England*, Cambridge, p. 174.
24. B. English (1995) 'Towns, Mottes and Ring-Works of the Conquest', in A. Ayton and J. Price eds. *The Medieval Military Revolution*, London.
25. Davison, 'The Origins of the Castle in England'.
26. English, 'Towns, Mottes and Ring-Works'.
27. Creighton, *Castles and Landscapes*, p. 137.
28. C. Mahany (1977) 'Excavations at Stamford Castle, 1971–6', *Château-Gaillard* 8, pp. 223–45; C. Mahany and D. Roffe (1982) 'Stamford: the Development of an Anglo-Scandinavian Borough', *Anglo-Norman Studies* 5.
29. P. Holdsworth (1984) 'Saxon Southampton' in J. Haslam ed. *Anglo-Saxon Towns*, Chichester; A. G. Kinsley (1993) 'Excavations on the Saxo-Norman Town Defences at Slaughter House Lane, Newark-on-Trent, Nottinghamshire', *Transactions of the Thoroton Society of Nottinghamshire* 97; P. Marshall and J. Samuels (1994) 'Recent Excavations at Newark Castle, Nottinghamshire', *Transactions of the Thoroton Society of Nottinghamshire* 98.
30. K. S. B. Keats-Rohan (1986) 'The Devolution of the Honour of Wallingford, 1066–1148', *Oxoniensia* 65.
31. Chibnall, *Orderic Vitalis* vol. 2, pp. 212–13.
32. Whitelock *et al.*, *The Anglo-Saxon Chronicle*, p. 146.

33. A. Vince (1990) *Saxon London: An Archaeological Investigation*, London.
34. K. R. Potter ed. and trans. (1976) *Gesta Stephani*, Oxford, pp. 32–3. T. O'Keeffe (2001), *Romanesque Ireland: Architecture, Sculpture and Ideology in the Twelfth Century*, pp. 24–5.
35. Coulson, 'Peaceable Power'.
36. Whitelock *et al.*, *The Anglo-Saxon Chronicle*, p. 145.
37. Green, *Aristocracy of Norman England*, chapters 2–3.
38. King and Alcock, 'Ringworks of England and Wales'. The most obvious objection to this is the depiction of Hastings castle in the Bayeux Tapestry but a good case can be made for this reflecting the perception of castles in the 1070s when the Tapestry was commissioned.
39. B. K. Davison (1971–2) 'Castle Neroche: an Abandoned Norman Fortress in South Somerset', *Somerset Archaeological and Natural History Society* **116**.
40. Using Everson's dating of the site, P. Everson (1988) 'What's in a Name? Goltho, 'Goltho' and Bullington', *Lincolnshire History and Archaeology* **23**.
41. See comments by Higham and Barker, *Timber Castles*, p. 96: 'The accumulation of research suggests that, although there were regional differences in chronology, only as the eleventh century developed, and particularly from the early twelfth century, did society, and its environment, become more generally 'incastled'; and Eales, 'Royal Power and Castles': 'the argument from probability thus leads us back to the late eleventh century, the primary phase of Norman settlement in England, as the period in which the majority of pre-1200 castles were founded.'
42. M. Biddle (1970) 'Excavations at Winchester, 1969: Eighth Interim Report', *Antiquaries Journal* **50**, p. 291; M. Biddle (1975) 'Excavations at Winchester, 1971: Tenth and Final Interim Report: Part 1, *Antiquaries Journal* **55**, pp. 104–5.
43. Chibnall, *Orderic Vitalis* vol. 2, p. 237.
44. Eales, 'Royal Power', in Liddiard, *Anglo-Norman Castles*, p. 50
45. T. E. McNeill and M. Pringle (1997) 'A Map of Mottes in the British Isles', *Medieval Archaeology* **41**.
46. Beeler, *Warfare in England*.
47. N. P. Milner ed. (1993) *Vegetius: Epitome of Military Science*, Liverpool, p. 22.
48. See now the excellent discussion of castle siting in Creighton, *Castles and Landscapes*, Chapter 3.
49. R. Liddiard (2000) 'Population Density and Norman Castle-Building: Some Evidence from East Anglia', *Landscape History* **22**.
50. Compare P. Northeast (1999) 'Religious Houses' and E. Martin (1999) 'Medieval Castles' in D. Dymond and E. Martin eds. *An Historical Atlas of Suffolk* 3rd edn, Ipswich, pp. 59, 70.
51. T. Williamson (2000) *The Origins of Hertfordshire*, Manchester, Chapter 7.
52. I. J. Sanders (1960) *English Baronies: A Study of Their Origin and Descent 1086–1327*, Oxford, pp. 12–13.
53. D. Renn (1971) *Medieval Castles in Hertfordshire*, Chichester, p. 14.
54. J. Morris ed. (1976) *Domesday Book: Hertfordshire*, Chichester, 36, 7.
55. C. P. Lewis (1997) 'Joining the Dots: a Methodology for Identifying the English in Domesday Book' in K. S. B. Keats-Rohan ed. *Family Trees and the Roots of Politics: The Prosopography of Britain and France from the Tenth to the Twelfth Century*, Woodbridge.
56. For a summary of this evidence see Higham and Barker, *Timber Castles*, chapter 2.
57. R. Morris (1989) *Churches in the Landscape*, London, Chapter 6.
58. J. Blair ed. (1988) *Minsters and Parish Churches: The Local Church in Transition, 950–1200*, Oxford.
59. Pounds, *The Medieval Castle*, pp. 18–19; McNeill, *Castles*, pp. 39–40.
60. See Eales, 'Royal Power', n. 44, above; for further examples see Brown *et al.*, *King's Works*, pp. 24–5.
61. L. Butler (1992 and 2003) 'The Origins of the Honour of Richmond and its Castles', *Château-Gaillard* **16**, reprinted in Liddiard, *Anglo-Norman Castles*, pp. 91–103; Creighton, *Castles and Landscapes*.

Notes to the Chapters

62. P. H. Sawyer (1985) '1066–1086: a Tenurial Revolution?' in P. H. Sawyer ed. *Domesday Book: a Reassessment*, London.
63. As recently pointed out in Coulson, 'Peaceable Power'.
64. D. Renn (2000) 'The Norman Military Works', in R. Shoesmith and A. Johnson eds. *Ludlow Castle: Its History and Buildings*, Almeley, p. 136
65. Coulson, 'Peaceable Power'.
66. J. G. Coad and A. D. F. Streeton (1982) 'Excavations at Castle Acre Castle, Norfolk, 1972–1977: Country House and Castle of the Norman Earls of Surrey', *Archaeological Journal* **139**.
67. P. J. Drury (1982) 'Aspects of the Origins and Development of Colchester Castle', *Archaeological Journal* **139**.
68. T. A. Heslop, 'Constantine and Helena: The Roman in English Romanesque', forthcoming. I am grateful to Sandy Heslop for allowing me access to this paper prior to publication.
69. G. Parnell (1998) 'The White Tower, The Tower of London', *Country Life* (July 9); E. Impey and G. Parnell (2000) *The Tower of London: The Official Illustrated History*, London.
70. R. Turner (2002) *Chepstow Castle*, Cardiff.
71. D. Greenway and J. Sayers eds. (1989) *Jocelin of Brakelond, Chronicle of the Abbey of Bury St Edmunds*, Oxford, p. 123.
72. E. Impey (1999) 'The Seigneurial Residence in Normandy: An Anglo-Norman Tradition?', *Medieval Archaeology* **93**.
73. J. Morris ed. (1978) *Domesday Book: Buckinghamshire*, Chichester, 17,16.
74. H. Clover and M. Gibson eds. (1979), *The Letters of Lanfranc, Archbishop of Canterbury*, Oxford, pp. 166–7.
75. M. Swanton (1998) 'The Deeds of Hereward', in T. H. Ohlgren ed. *Medieval Outlaws: Ten Tales in Modern English*, Stroud.
76. D. Bates ed. (1997) *Regesta Regum Anglo-Normannorum: The Acta of William I*, Oxford, No. 117, pp. 410–17.
77. Fernie, *Architecture*, p. 154.
78. R. H. C. Davis and M. Chibnall eds. (1998), *The Gesta Guillelmi of William of Poitiers*, Oxford, pp. 147–9.
79. G. Garnett (1996) '"Franci et Angli": the Legal Distinctions between Peoples after the Conquest', *Anglo-Norman Studies* **8**.
80. C. P. Lewis (1988) 'An Introduction to the Herefordshire Domesday', in A. Williams and R. W. H. Erskine eds. *The Herefordshire Domesday*, London.
81. Whitelock *et al.*, *The Anglo-Saxon Chronicle* p. 119.
82. Round, 'The Castles of the Conquest'.
83. Williams, 'Bell-house'.
84. M. Chibnall (1986) *Anglo-Norman England, 1066–1166*, Oxford, pp. 161–86.
85. T. McNeill (1990 and 2003) 'Hiberna Pacata et Castellata', *Château-Gaillard* **14**, reprinted in Liddiard, *Anglo-Norman Castles*, p. 271.

Notes to Chapter 3: Architecture and Power

1. I base this on numerous conversations and correspondence with various colleagues over the past five years. The plentiful notes and short articles on this topic that have appeared annually in the Castle Studies Group Newsletter also, I think, support this statement.
2. Coulson, *Castles in Medieval Society*, Chapter 2.
3. T. A. Heslop (2000) '"Weeting Castle', A Twelfth-Century Hall House in Norfolk', *Architectural History* **43**.
4. The latter point is made in Creighton, *Castles and Landscapes*, Chapter 8.
5. M. Strickland ed. (1992) *Anglo-Norman Warfare*, Woodbridge, Introduction.

6. T. Jones ed. (1952) *Brut Y Tywysogyon Peniarth Version*, Cardiff, p. 57.
7. K. R. Potter trans. and E. King ed. (1998) *William of Malmesbury, Historia Novella*, Oxford, p. 24.
8. J. K. Knight (2000) *The Three Castles*, 2nd edn, Cardiff.
9. K. Norgate (1887) *England under the Angevin Kings*, vol. 2, London, p. 380.
10. Brown *et al., King's Works*, pp. 739–40.
11. Renn, 'The Norman Military Works', p. 125.
12. Coulson, 'Freedom to Crenellate by Licence'.
13. *Calendar of Patent Rolls* (1292–1307), p. 23.
14. Coulson, 'Hierarchism in Conventual Crenellation'; and Coulson, n. 12, above.
15. For the most recent discussion of Cooling see Johnson, *Behind the Castle Gate*, Preface.
16. For what follows see: J. Munby (1993) *Stokesay Castle*, English Heritage; D. Renn (2003) 'Two Views from the Roof: Design and Defence at Conwy and Stokesay', in J. R. Kenyon and K. O'Conor eds. *The Medieval Castle in Ireland and Wales*, Dublin.
17. J. R. Kenyon and M. W. Thompson (1994) 'The Origins of the Word 'Keep'', *Medieval Archaeology* **38**.
18. P. Marshall quoted in Coulson, 'Peaceable Power', p. 80.
19. T. McNeill (1997) *Castles in Ireland: Feudal Power in a Gaelic World*, London, pp. 20–4; for a different interpretation see D. Sweetman (1999) *The Medieval Castles of Ireland*, Woodbridge.
20. Potter, *Gesta Stephani*, p. 82.
21. Thompson, *The Rise of the Castle*, p. 108.
22. At Dover for example, it is likely that the great tower alone absorbed two-thirds of the total cost of Henry II's re-building. For totals of royal expenditure on castles see Brown, 'Royal Castle-Building in England'.
23. Dixon, 'The Myth of the Keep'.
24. T. A. Heslop (1994) *Norwich Castle Keep: Romanesque Architecture and Social Context*, Norwich.
25. Dixon and Marshall, 'The Great Tower at Hedingham Castle: A Reassessment'.
26. The investiture as earl was of some significance in this period; see D. Crouch (1992) *The Image of Aristocracy in Britain, 1000–1300*, London, pp. 72–5.
27. P. Marshall (2002) 'The Great Tower as Residence', in G. Meirion-Jones, E. Impey and M. Jones eds. *The Seigneurial Residence in Western Europe AD c800–1600*, Oxford.
28. ibid.
29. J. Gillingham (1999) *Richard I*, New Haven and London, pp. 301–5
30. R. K. Morris (1998) 'The Architecture of Arthurian Enthusiasm: Castle Symbolism in the Reigns of Edward I and his Successors', in M. Strickland ed. *Armies, Chivalry and Warfare in Medieval England and France*, Stamford, pp. 63–81.
31. A. Taylor (1987) *Rhuddlan Castle*, Cardiff, p. 12.
32. A. Taylor (1998) *Conwy Castle*, 4th edn, Cardiff, pp. 4–5.
33. N. Coldstream (2003) 'Architects, Advisors and Design at Edward I's Castles in Wales', *Architectural History* **46**.
34. J. R. Mathieu (1999) 'New Methods on Old Castles: Generating New Ways of Seeing', *Medieval Archaeology* **43**.
35. Brown *et al., King's Works*, pp. 369–95.
36. Morris, 'The Architecture of Arthurian Enthusiasm', p. 72.
37. P. Dixon and B. Lott (1993) 'The Courtyard and the Tower: Contexts and Symbols in the Development of Late Medieval Great Houses', *Journal of the British Archaeological Association* **146**; C. Coulson (2000) 'Fourteenth-Century Castles in Context: Apotheosis or Decline?' in N. Saul ed. *Fourteenth-Century England*, Woodbridge.
38. J. Goodall (1996) 'Tattershall Castle, Lincolnshire', *Country Life*; A. Emery (2000) *Great Medieval Houses of England and Wales vol. 2*, Cambridge, pp. 308–15.
39. Turner, *Chepstow Castle*.

Notes to the Chapters

40. A. Emery (1996) *Greater Medieval Houses of England and Wales vol. 1*, Cambridge, p. 64.
41. For what follows see C. M. Woolgar (1999) *The Great Household in Medieval England*, New Haven and London, pp. 51–8.
42. K. Mertes (1988) *The English Noble Household*, Oxford, p. 218.
43. B. Morley (1981) 'Aspects of Fourteenth-Century Castle Design', in A. Detsicas ed. *Collectanea Historica: Essays in Memory of Stuart Rigold*, Maidstone.
44. Emery, *Greater Medieval Houses vol. 1*, p. 293.
45. Faulkner, 'Domestic Planning from the Twelfth to the Fourteenth Centuries'; Faulkner, 'Castle Planning in the Fourteenth Century'.
46. Woolgar, *Great Household*, pp. 63–7.
47. As argued in Thompson, *The Decline of the Castle*.
48. A. Saunders (1989) *Fortress Britain*, Liphook.
49. Johnson, *Castle-Gate*.
50. J. Goodall (2000) 'Lulworth Castle, Dorset', *Country Life*, January 13th, pp. 34–9.
51. Johnson, *Behind the Castle Gate*, p. 182.
52. Crouch, *Image of Aristocracy*.
53. C. Coulson (1973) 'Rendability and Castellation in Medieval France', *Château-Gaillard* **6**.
54. J. Goodall, *English Castle Architecture, 1066–1640*, forthcoming.

Notes to Chapter 4: The Castle at War

1. J. Bradbury (1992) *The Medieval Siege*, Woodbridge; I. A. Corfis and M. Wolfe eds. (1995) *The Medieval City Under Siege*, Woodbridge; M. Prestwich (1996) *Armies and Warfare in the Middle Ages: The English Experience*, New Haven; M. Strickland (1996) *War and Chivalry: The Conduct and Perception of War in England and Normandy, 1066–1217*, Cambridge.
2. Probably best exemplified by C. Oman (1924) *The Art of War in the Middle Ages*, 2nd edn, 2 vols, London.
3. P. Contamine ed. and trans. M. Jones (1984) *War in the Middle Ages*, Oxford; J. Gillingham (1984 and 1992) 'Richard I and the Science of War in the Middle Ages' in J. Gillingham and J. C. Holt eds. *War and Government in the Middle Ages*, Woodbridge, reprinted in M. Strickland ed. *Anglo-Norman Warfare*, Woodbridge; Prestwich, *Armies and Warfare*; Strickland, *War and Chivalry*.
4. For 'inherent military probability' see A. H. Burne (1956) *The Agincourt War*, London; for a different approach, M. K. Jones (2002) 'The Battle of Verneuil (17 August 1424): Towards a History of Courage', *War in History* **9**.
5. For example, Pounds, *The Medieval Castle*, pp. 113–121.
6. S. Speight (1998) 'Castle Warfare in the Gesta Stephani', *Château-Gaillard* **19**.
7. R. Eales (1989 and 2003) 'Castles and Politics in England, 1215–1224', Thirteenth-Century England **2**, reprinted in Liddiard, *Anglo-Norman Castles*.
8. King, *Castellarium*.
9. D. Whitelock *et al.*, *The Anglo-Saxon Chronicle*, p. 173
10. J. R. Kenyon (1996 and 2003) 'Fluctuating Frontiers: Normano-Welsh Castle Warfare c. 1075 to 1240', *Château-Gaillard* **17**, reprinted in Liddiard, *Anglo-Norman Castles*, p. 251.
11. *Calendar of Inquisitions Miscellaneous* vol. 1 p. 367; King, *Castellarium*, p. 389.
12. R. Howlett ed. (1884–9) *Chronicles of the Reigns of Stephen, Henry II and Richard I*, Rolls Series, vol. 4, *The Chronicle of Robert de Torigni*, p. 172. The shame attached to his wife's actions led the Earl's early death anyway: Potter, *Gesta Stephani*, p. 235.
13. Potter, *Gesta Stephani*, p. 203.
14. M. Prestwich (1982) 'English Castles in the Reign of Edward II', *Journal of Medieval History* **9**; J. Gillingham (1981) *The Wars of the Roses: Peace and Conflict in Fifteenth-Century England*, London; A. Goodman (1981) *The Wars of the Roses*, London; Bradbury, *Medieval Siege*.

15. King, *Castellarium*, pp. 188–200. Totals for the Isle of Wight have not been included.
16. Potter, *Gesta Stephani*, pp. 213–15.
17. When actions during the Civil War are included this rises to 35.
18. J. France (1999) *Western Warfare in the Age of the Crusades, 1000–1300*, London, chapter 1.
19. Strickland, *Anglo-Norman Warfare*, Introduction.
20. M. Keen (1965) *The Laws of War in the Late Middle Ages*, London; M. Vale (1981) *War and Chivalry*, Norwich; M. Keen (1984) *Chivalry*, New Haven; R. Kaeuper (1999) *Chivalry and Violence in Medieval Europe*, Oxford.
21. A. Curry (1993) *The Hundred Years War*, Basingstoke, pp. 77–8.
22. R. Chamberlin (1985) *Carisbrooke Castle*, London, pp. 4–5.
23. A. Ayton and J. L. Price (1995) 'Introduction: The Military Revolution from a Medieval Perspective' in A. Ayton and J. L. Price eds. *The Medieval Military Revolution: State, Society and Military Change in Medieval and Early Modern Europe*, London, p. 10.
24. J. Gillingham (1989 and 1992) 'William the Bastard at War' in C. Harper-Bill, C. Holdsworth and J. Nelson eds. *Studies in History Presented to R. Allen Brown*, Woodbridge, reprinted in Strickland, *Anglo-Norman Warfare*; J. Bradbury (1984 and 1992) 'Battles in England and Normandy, 1066–1154', *Anglo-Norman Studies* 6, reprinted in Strickland, *Anglo-Norman Warfare*.
25. Prestwich, *Armies*, p. 12.
26. For a neat summary see King, *Castellarium*, p. xix.
27. F. C. Suppe (1994) *Military Institutions on the Welsh Marches Shropshire, 1066–1300*, Woodbridge, p. 20.
28. Knight, *The Three Castles*, p. 10.
29. Potter, *Gesta Stephani*, pp. 180–1.
30. Coulson, 'The Castles of the Anarchy', p. 181.
31. Pounds, *The Medieval Castle*, Chapter 2.
32. Suppe, *Military Institutions*, p. 31.
33. J. E. Lloyd (1911) *A History of Wales vol. 2*, London, pp. 673–4.
34. For details of a royal inquisition into the effects of raiding at Knaresborough in 1318 see, *Calendar of Inquisitions Miscellaneous* vol. 2 (1307–1349), p. 198.
35. Brown *et al., King's Works*, passim.
36. A. Taylor (1997) *Harlech Castle*, 3rd edn, Cardiff, p. 9.
37. M. Prestwich (2001) 'The Garrisoning of English Medieval Castles', in R. P. Abels and B. S. Bachrach eds. *The Normans and their Adversaries at War*, Woodbridge, p. 189.
38. ibid., p. 196.
39. R. Avent (1989) *Criccieth Castle*, Cardiff, p. 8.
40. Prestwich, 'English Castles', p. 164.
41. S. Painter (1934–5 and 2003) 'Castle Guard', *American Historical Review* 40, reprinted in Liddiard, *Anglo-Norman Castles*.
42. Prestwich, 'Garrisoning', p. 193; Coulson, *Castles in Medieval Society*, pp. 56–8, 277–9.
43. J. Moore (2000) 'Anglo-Norman Garrisons', *Anglo-Norman Studies* 22.
44. Pounds, *The Medieval Castle*, p. 117.
45. R. C. Smail (1995) *Crusading Warfare (1097–1193)*, 2nd edn, Cambridge.
46. M. Strickland (1989 and 1992) 'Securing the North: Invasion and the Strategy of Defence in Twelfth-Century Anglo-Scottish Warfare', *Anglo-Norman Studies* 11, reprinted in Strickland, *Anglo-Norman Warfare*.
47. See the excellent account in Strickland, *War and Chivalry*, Chapter 8.
48. Both quoted in Strickland, *War and Chivalry*, p. 207.
49. Prestwich, *English Armies*, p. 299.
50. J. Goodall (2000) 'Dover Castle and the Great Siege of 1216', *Château-Gaillard* 19.
51. Swanton, *The Deeds of Hereward* in Ohlgren, *Medieval Outlaws: Ten Tales in Modern English*, p. 50.
52. Jones, *Brut Y Tywysogyon*, p. 54.

Notes to the Chapters

53. Anon (1985) *Corfe Castle*, London, pp. 45–6.
54. Potter, *Gesta Stephani* p. 151–2. Robert had first entered into some kind of agreement with the castellan, William Pont-de L'Arche, as this is how he first gained entry to the castle. He eventually abandoned his relationship with the countess but the author of the *Gesta Stephani* relates how his lust led to him dying of a painful disease.
55. Keen, *The Laws of War*, chapter 8.
56. Jones, *Brut Y Tywysogyon*, p. 84.
57. D. Crouch (1990) *William Marshal: Court, Career and Chivalry in the Angevin Empire, 1147–1219*, London, pp. 16–17.
58. Prestwich, *Armies*, p. 291.
59. *Proceedings of the Privy Council* vol i. p. 275.
60. Potter, *Gesta Stephani*, p. 172
61. M. Chibnall (1989 and 2003) 'Orderic Vitalis on Castles' in C. Harper-Bill, C. Holdsworth and J. L. Nelson eds. *Studies in Medieval History Presented to R. Allen Brown*, Woodbridge, reprinted in Liddiard, *Anglo-Norman Castles*, p. 127.
62. F. Michel (1840) *Histoire des Ducs de Normandie et des Rois d'Angleterre*, Paris, p. 187.
63. R. Allen Brown (1986) *Rochester Castle*, 2nd edn, HMSO, p. 5.
64. Chibnall, *Orderic Vitalis*, vol. 6, pp. 520–2.
65. Brown, *Rochester*, pp. 10–11.
66. Goodman, *The Wars of the Roses*, p. 189.
67. A. J. Taylor (1998) *Conwy Castle and Town Walls*, 4th edn, Cardiff, p. 5.
68. J. R. Phillips (1874) *Memoirs of the Civil War in Wales and the Marches, 1642–1646*, vol. 2, London, p. 326.
69. K. Williams-Jones (1978) 'The Taking of Conwy Castle, 1401', *Transactions of the Caernarvonshire Historical Society* **39**.
70. R. R. Davies (1995) *The Revolt of Owain Glyn Dŵr*, Oxford, pp. 103–4.
71. For what follows see D. A. Carpenter (1990) *The Minority of Henry III*, London, pp. 360–70.
72. As now discussed at great length by Coulson, *Castles in Medieval Society*.
73. R. Allen Brown (1951) 'Framlingham Castle and Bigod, 1154–1216', *Proceedings of the Suffolk Institute of Archaeology* **25**.
74. W. L. Warren (1978) *King John*, 2nd edn, London, p. 249.
75. Brown, *Rochester*, pp. 10–11.
76. Prestwich, 'English Castles', p. 159.

Notes to Chapter 5: Lordly Landscapes

1. Creighton, *Castles and Landscapes*.
2. The literature on 'designed landscapes' is now extensive: C. Taylor (1989) 'Somersham Palace, Cambridgeshire: A Medieval Landscape for Pleasure?' in M. Bowden, D. Mackay and P. Topping eds. *From Cornwall to Caithness*, BAR British Series 209; P. Everson (1996) 'Bodiam Castle, East Sussex: Castle and its Designed Landscape', *Château-Gaillard* **17**; P. Everson (1998) "Delightfully Surrounded with Woods and Ponds": Field Evidence for Medieval Gardens in Britain' in P. Patterson ed. *There by Design: Field Archaeology in Parks and Gardens*, Oxford; R. Liddiard (2000) 'Castle Rising, Norfolk: A 'Landscape of Lordship', *Anglo-Norman Studies* **22**; C. Taylor (2000) 'Medieval Ornamental Landscapes', *Landscapes* **1.1**.
3. S. Landsberg (1995) *The Medieval Garden*, London, pp. 13–25.
4. Taylor, 'Medieval Ornamental Landscapes'.
5. P. Everson (2003) 'Medieval Gardens and Designed Landscapes', in R. Wilson-North ed. *The Lie of the Land: Aspects of the Archaeology and History of the Designed Landscape in the South West of England*, Exeter.
6. M. Beresford (1967) *New Towns of the Middle Ages*, London, p. 129.

7. Coulson, 'The Castles of the Anarchy', p. 188.
8. Beresford, *New Towns*, p. 128.
9. J. F. A Mason and P. Barker (1961–4) 'The Norman Castle at Quatford', *Transactions of the Shropshire Archaeological Society* **57**.
10. M. R. Eddy and M. R. Petchey (1983) *Historic Towns in Essex*, Chelmsford, p. 165.
11. C. G. Harfield (1991) 'A Hand List of Castles Recorded in the Domesday Book', *English Historical Review* **106**.
12. A. Rumble ed. (1986) *Domesday Book, Suffolk*, Chichester, 18,1.
13. Harfield, 'A Hand-List of Castles', pp. 375–6.
14. R. Liddiard (2000) *Landscapes of Lordship: The Castle and the Countryside in Medieval Norfolk, 1066–1200*, Oxford, p. 49.
15. R. Liddiard (2003) 'The Deer Parks of Domesday Book', *Landscapes* **4.1**.
16. J. Darlington ed. (2001) *Stafford Castle: Survey, Excavation and Research, 1978–1998 Vol. 1 The Surveys*, Stafford, p. 155; Liddiard, 'Castle Rising Castle, Norfolk'.
17. Austin, 'The Castle and the Landscape'.
18. R. Hoppitt (1992) 'A Study of the Development of Deer Parks in Suffolk from the Eleventh to the Seventeenth Century', unpublished PhD thesis, University of East Anglia.
19. *Calendar of Patent Rolls* (1350–1354), p. 165.
20. U. Albarella and S. J. M. Davis (1994) 'Mammals and Birds from Launceston Castle Cornwall: Decline in Status and the Rise of Agriculture, *Circaea* **12.1**.
21. Darlington, *Stafford Castle*, p. 155.
22. *Calendar of Inquisitions Miscellaneous*, vol. 2, (1307–1349), p. 6.
23. *The Register of the Black Prince, 1348–1365*, vol. 3, London, (1930–3), pp. 147, 273.
24. *CCR* (1318–1323), p. 43; J. Ridgard ed. (1985) *Medieval Framlingham: Select Documents, 1270–1524*, Woodbridge, p. 127.
25. Landsberg, *Medieval Garden*.
26. T. Wright ed. (1863) *Alexandri Neckham, De Naturis Rerum* Rolls Series 34, London, chapter 156, pp. 248–52.
27. C. C. J. Webb ed. (1909) *John of Salisbury, Policraticus*, Oxford, vol. 1 p. 23.
28. Much of the following is summarised from the excellent discussion in J. Cummins (1988) *The Hound and the Hawk: The Art of Medieval Hunting*, London.
29. *Calendar of Close Rolls* (1254–56), p. 90.
30. Norfolk Record Office MF 748/121 (Caister Tithe Award Map, c. 1843); MF 758/121 (Apportionment).
31. C. Harper-Bill ed. (1991) *The Cartulary of the Augustinian Friars of Clare*, Woodbridge, No. 32. (1262x1289) undated, but probably late 1260s.
32. Greenway and Sayers, *Jocelin of Brakelond*, p. 116.
33. J. R. H. Weaver ed. (1908) *The Chronicle of John of Worcester, 1118–40*, Oxford, pp. 56–7; D. Crouch (1986) *The Beaumont Twins*, Cambridge, pp. 46–7.
34. M. W. Thompson (1986) 'Monasteries and Castles', *Archaeological Journal* **143**.
35. D. Stocker and M. Stocker (1996) 'Sacred Profanity: The Theology of Rabbit Breeding and the Symbolic Landscape of the Warren', *World Archaeology* **28**.
36. Everson, 'Delightfully Surrounded', pp. 32–8.
37. R. Gilchrist (1999) *Gender and Archaeology: Contesting the Past*, London, Chapter 6.
38. Landsberg, *Medieval Garden*, p. 13.
39. D. Greenway ed. (1996) *Henry Archdeacon of Huntingdon, Historia Anglorum*, Oxford, p. 471.
40. J. S. Brewer, J. F. Dimock and G. F. Warner eds. (1861–91), *Giraldi Cambrensis Opera* Rolls Series 21, vol. 6, p. 92.
41. Brown, Colvin and Taylor, *King's Works* pp. 1016–7.
42. See Taylor, 'Medieval Ornamental Landscapes'.
43. R. A. B. Mynors ed. (1998) *William of Malmesbury, Gesta Regum Anglorum*, Oxford, p. 713.
44. Landsberg, *Medieval Garden*, pp. 21–5.

Notes to the Chapters

45. P. Everson, G. Brown and D. Stocker (2000) 'The Earthworks and Landscape Context', in P. Ellis ed. *Ludgershall Castle, Excavations by Peter Addyman, 1964–1972*, Wiltshire Archaeology and Natural History Society Monograph No. 2.
46. SRO (Bury St Edmunds) FL501/3/31 (Tithe Award Map, 1840).
47. Suffolk Record Office (Ipswich), (I)qSfra9, M. Brown and P. Patterson (1997) *RCHME Archaeological Field Survey Report: Framlingham Mere*.
48. B. Wadmore (1920) *The Earthworks of Bedfordshire*, Bedford.
49. Johnson, *Behind the Castle-Gate*, pp. 40–1.
50. P. Dixon (1990) 'The Donjon of Knaresborough: the Castle as Theatre', *Château-Gaillard* 14.
51. Everson *et al.*, 'The Earthworks and Landscape Context', n. 45, above.
52. Wright, *De Naturis Rerum*, chapter 12.
53. Quoted in Cummins, *Hound and Hawk*, p. 7.
54. I. Goch (1967) *The Court of Owain Glyndŵr at Sycharth* in A. Conran ed. *The Penguin Book of Welsh Verse*, London.
55. K. Thomas (1983) *Man and the Natural World: Changing Attitudes in England, 1500–1800*, London.
56. P. Matarasso ed. (1993) *The Cistercian World: Monastic Writings of the Twelfth Century*, Penguin, pp. 285–92.
57. K. D. Lilley (2002) *Urban Life in the Middle Ages, 1000–1450*, Basingstoke, Chapter 5.
58. J. Gillingham (2000) *The English in the Twelfth Century: Imperialism, National Identity and Political Values*, Woodbridge.
59. T. Williamson (1995) *Polite Landscapes: Gardens and Society in Eighteenth-Century England*, Stroud.
60. L. Watkiss and M. Chibnall eds. (1994) *The Waltham Chronicle*, Oxford, pp. 76–9.
61. A. Shopland, 'The Political Career of the D'Albini Earls of Sussex, 1088–1248', M.Phil in preparation, University of East Anglia.
62. Thompson, *The Rise of the Castle*, pp. 141–2.
63. Brown, *et al*, pp. 682–85; M. Leslie (1993) 'An English Landscape Garden before the 'English Landscape Garden?'', *Journal of Garden History* 13; Johnson, *Behind the Castle Gate*, Chapter 5.
64. J. Caley, H. Ellis and B. Bandinel eds. (1817–30) W. Dugdale, *Monasticon Anglicanum*, vol 6, 1, London, pp. 220–1, 'concessi canonicis ibidem regulariter Deo servientibus, totam planam terram ipsius Chenilleuardae et boscum et reliqua omnia praedictae villae pertinentia, excepta particula quae ego inde retinui ad castellum et parcum meum faciendum'.
65. L. Butler (1990) *Denbigh Castle*, Cardiff, p. 7.
66. J. A. Wight (1972) *Brick Building in England from the Middle Ages to 1550*, London, p. 94.
67. See, for example, licences for Drayton (Northants), 1328, *Calendar of Patent Rolls* (1322–30), p. 319; Burton Constable (Yorkshire), 1338, *Calendar of Patent Rolls* (1338–40), p. 94; Slyngesby (Yorkshire), 1344, *Calendar of Patent Rolls* (1343–45), p. 190.
68. Taylor, 'Medieval Ornamental Landscapes', see n. 42, above.
69. J. Phibbs (1998) 'Recording What Isn't There: Three Difficulties with Eighteenth-Century Landscapes' in P. Patterson ed. *There by Design: Field Archaeology in Parks and Gardens*, Oxford.

Notes to Chapter 6: Experiencing Castles: Iconography and Status

1. W. Van Emden (1984) 'The Castle in Some Works of Medieval French Literature' in K. Reyerson and F. Powe eds. *The Medieval Castle, Romance and Reality*, Dubuque, Iowa; M. A. Whitaker (1984) 'Otherworld Castles in Middle English Arthurian Romance' in *The Medieval Castle, Romance and Reality*, Dubuque, Iowa.
2. Brewer *et al.*, *Giraldi Cambrensis Opera* vi, p. 92.
3. J-L. Leclanche ed. (1983) *Le Conte de Floire et Blancheflor*, Paris, vv. 1799–802.

4. W. Frescoln ed. (1983) *The Romance of Fergus*, Philadelphia, vv. 345–9.
5. L. Constans ed. (1904) *Roman de Troie*, Paris, vv. 3050–3094.
6. P. Herring (2003) 'Cornish Medieval Deer Parks' in R. Wilson-North ed. *The Lie of the Land: Aspects of the Archaeology and the History of the Designed Landscape in the South West of England*, Exeter.
7. Giovanna Michaelson *pers. comm.*
8. R. A. Higham, J. P. Allan and S. R. Blaylock (1982) 'Excavations at Okehampton Castle, Devon Part II: The Bailey', *Devon Archaeology Society Proceedings* 40.
9. ibid., p. 72.
10. Emery, *Greater Medieval Houses*, vol. 2, pp. 383–91.
11. ibid., p. 383
12. A. J. Taylor (1986) *The Welsh Castles of Edward I*, London, pp. 35–7.
13. N. Johnstone (1997) 'An Investigation into the Location of the Royal Courts of Thirteenth-Century Gwynedd' in N. Edwards ed. *Landscape and Settlement in Medieval Wales*, Oxford.
14. *Calendar of Patent Rolls*, (1313–1317), p. 576.
15. R. R. Davies (1991) *The Age of Conquest: Wales 1063–1415*, Oxford, p. 336.
16. For what follows see G. Jones (2001) 'Aspects of a Medieval Landscape: Ruthin Castle and the Lordship of Dyffryn-Clywd', unpublished BA dissertation, University of Wales.
17. D. Pratt (1990) 'The Marcher Lordship of Chirk, 1329–1330', *Denbighshire Society Transactions* 39.
18. For the excavations at Castle Acre, Coad and Streeton, 'Excavations at Castle Acre Castle'; J. G. Coad, A. D. F. Streeton and R. Warmington (1987) 'Excavations at Castle Acre Castle, Norfolk, 1975–1982: The Bridges, Lime Kilns, and Eastern Gatehouse', *Archaeological Journal* 144; for a discussion of the landscape context see Liddiard, *'Landscapes of Lordship'*.
19. Brown *et al.*, *King's Works*, pp. 629–41.
20. And not, as is often said (including by myself), a term invented by Matthew Paris. My thanks are due to Stephen Church for bringing this to my attention.
21. J. Goodall (1999) 'The Key of England', *Country Life*; J. Goodall (1999) 'In the Powerhouse of Kent', *Country Life*.
22. Quoted in Coulson, 'Structural Symbolism in Castle Architecture' p. 75.
23. Chibnall, *Orderic Vitalis*, pp. 232–3.
24. Heslop, *Norwich Castle Keep*.
25. Fergus, vv. 1515–9.
26. A. J. Holden ed. (1984) *Roman de Waldef*, Geneva, vv. 337–9.
27. Waldef, vv. 38–44.
28. W. R. J. Barron ed. (1974) *Sir Gawain and the Green Knight*, Manchester, pp. 69–73.
29. ibid., p. 139.
30. J. Gildea ed. (1967) *Partonopeu de Blois*, Villanova, vv. 787–792.
31. ibid., vv. 827–30.
32. ibid., vv. 931–953.
33. Van Emden, 'The Castle', pp. 1–36.
34. Anon (1996) *Restormel Castle*, London, p. 5.
35. C. Coulson (1995) 'Battlements and Bourgeoisie: Municipal Status and the Apparatus of Urban Defence in Later-Medieval England' in S. Church and R. Harvey eds. *Medieval Knighthood* 5, Woodbridge.
36. Avent, *Criccieth Castle*, p. 1.
37. D. Renn (1993) *Goodrich Castle*, London.
38. J. Weaver (1998) *Middleham Castle*, London, p. 12.
39. O. J. Padel (1988) 'Tintagel in the Twelfth and Thirteenth Centuries', *Cornish Studies* 16.
40. Johnson, *Behind the Castle Gate*, Introduction.
41. Turner, *Chepstow Castle*, p. 17.
42. Avent, *Criccieth Castle*; A. D. Carr (1995) *Medieval Wales*, Macmillan, p. 64.
43. F. Suppe (1989 and 2003) 'Castle Guard and the Castlery of Clun', *Haskins Society Journal* 1,

Notes to the Chapters

reprinted in Liddiard, *Anglo-Norman Castles*.
44. BL MS Harley 2110 (Castle Acre Cartulary), f. 5v.
45. Van Emden, 'The Castle', p. 15.
46. A. Taylor (1985) *Studies in Castles and Castle-Building*, London, pp. 179–84.
47. L. Butler (1993) *Pickering Castle*, London, p. 25.
48. King, *Castellarium*, p. 30.
49. Brown *et al., King's Works*, p. 712.
50. Quoted in Austin, 'The Castle and the Landscape'.

Notes to Chapter 7: Rethinking the Castle Story

1. Coulson, *Castles in Medieval Society*.
2. See comments by C. Coulson (2003–4) 'Orthodoxy or Opportunity?', *Castle Studies Group Bulletin*.
3. This idea is not so methodologically impossible as it may first appear; see K. R. Dockray (1979) 'Japan and England During the Fifteenth Century: The Onin War and the Wars of the Roses' in C. Ross ed. *Patronage, Pedigree and Power in Later Medieval England*, Gloucester.
4. For Ireland see McNeill, *Castles in Ireland*; for the suggestion that European fortress customs may have been present in the Crusader kingdoms in the twelfth century see P. Edbury (1999) 'Warfare in the Latin East' in M. Keen ed. *Medieval Warfare: A History*, Oxford, pp. 89–112.

Further Reading

The starting point for researching a particular castle is D. J. Cathcart King, *Castellarium Anglicanum* (New York, 1983), which contains lists of castles in England and Wales together with an extensive bibliography. For comprehensive bibliographical information see J. R. Kenyon, *Castles, Town Defences, and Artillery Fortifications in Britain and Ireland: A Bibliography* Vol. *i* (CBA, 1978); *ii* (CBA, 1983); *iii* (CBA, 1990). The Castles Studies Group also publishes annual bibliographies and details of this excellent forum can be found at www.castlestudiesgroup.org.uk. Useful information can also be found in the *Victoria County History* series, the various inventories of the *Royal Commissions* in England and Wales and, for the later medieval period, in Emery's vast surveys contained in A. Emery, *Greater Medieval Houses of England and Wales Vol. 1: Northern England* (Cambridge, 1996) and *Vol. 2: Midlands, East Anglia and Wales* (Cambridge, 2000). The following list of works is intended as a guide only, but should prove a useful starting point.

Early works

Armitage, E. S. (1912) *The Early Norman Castles of the British Isles*, John Murray, London.
Clark, G. T. (1884) *Mediaeval Military Architecture in England*, 2 vols, Wyman, London.
Hamilton Thompson, A. (1912) *Military Architecture in England During the Middle Ages*, Oxford University Press, Oxford.

General works

Brown, R. A. (1976) *English Castles*, 3rd edn, Batsford, London, reprinted by Boydell Press, Woodbridge, 2004.
Coulson, C. L. H. (2003) *Castles in Medieval Society*, Oxford University Press, Oxford.
Creighton, O. and Higham, R. (2003) *Medieval Castles*, Shire Archaeology, Princes Risborough.
 – by far the best introduction to the subject.
Kenyon, J. R. (1990) *Medieval Fortifications*, Leicester University Press, Leicester.
Kenyon, J. R. and Avent, R. eds (1987) *Castles in Wales and the Marches: Essays in Honour of D. J. Cathcart King*, University of Wales Press, Cardiff.
McNeill, T. (1992) *Castles*, Batsford and English Heritage, London.
McNeill, T. (1997) *Castles in Ireland: Feudal Power in a Gaelic World*, Routledge, London.
Morris, M. (2003) *Castle: A History of the Buildings that Shaped Medieval Britain*, Channel 4, London.
Platt, C. (1982) *The Castle in Medieval England and Wales*, Secker and Warburg, London.
Pounds, N. J. G. (1990) *The Medieval Castle in England and Wales: A Social and Political History*, Cambridge University Press, Cambridge.
Tabraham, C. (1986) *Scottish Castles and Fortifications*, H.M.S.O., Edinburgh.
Thompson, M. W. (1991) *The Rise of the Castle*, Cambridge University Press, Cambridge.

Further Reading

The Norman Conquest and early castles

Brown, R. A. (1969) *The Normans and the Norman Conquest*, Boydell Press, Woodbridge.
Fernie, E. (2000) *The Architecture of Norman England*, Oxford University Press, Oxford.
Higham, R. and Barker, P. (1992) *Timber Castles*, Batsford, London.
Higham, R. and Barker, P. (2000) *Hen Domen, Montgomery. A Timber Castle on the English-Welsh Border: A Final Report*, University of Exeter Press and the Royal Archaeological Institute, Exeter.
Impey, E. and Parnell, G. (2000) *The Tower of London: The Official Illustrated History*, Merrell Holberton, London.
Liddiard, R. ed. (2003) *Anglo-Norman Castles*, Boydell Press, Woodbridge. – a collection of important essays on castles in the eleventh and twelfth centuries.
Meirion-Jones, G., Impey, E. and Jones, M. eds (2002) *The Seigneurial Residence in Western Europe AD c800–1600*, BAR International Series 1088, Oxford.
Renn, D. (1968) *Norman Castles in Britain*, Baker, London.
Williams, A. (1995) *The English and the Norman Conquest*, Boydell Press, Woodbridge.

Castle landscapes

Creighton, O. H. (2002) *Castles and Landscapes*, Continuum, London.
Everson, P., Brown, G. and Stocker, D. (2000) 'The Earthworks and Landscape Context' in P. Ellis ed. *Ludgershall Castle, Excavations by Peter Addyman, 1964–1972*, Wiltshire Archaeology and Natural History Society Monograph No. 2, 97–115.
Liddiard, R. (2000) *Landscapes of Lordship: The Castle and the Countryside in Medieval Norfolk, 1066–1200*, BAR British Series 309, Oxford.

Warfare

Bradbury, J. (1992) *The Medieval Siege*, Boydell Press, Woodbridge.
France, F. (1999) *Western Warfare in the Age of the Crusades, 1000–1300*, UCL Press, London.
Keen, M. ed. (1999) *Medieval Warfare: A History*, Oxford University Press, Oxford.
Prestwich, M. (1996) *Armies and Warfare in the Middle Ages: The English Experience*, Yale University Press, New Haven.
Strickland, M. ed. (1992) *Anglo-Norman Warfare*, Boydell Press, Woodbridge.
Strickland, M. (1996) *War and Chivalry: The Conduct and Perception of War in England and Normandy, 1066–1217*, Cambridge University Press, Cambridge.

Later medieval castles

See General Works, above, but also:
Johnson, M. (2002) *Behind the Castle Gate: From Medieval to Renaissance*, Routledge, London.
Taylor, A. J. (1986) *The Welsh Castles of Edward I*, Hambledon Press, London.
Thompson, M. W. (1987) *The Decline of the Castle*, Cambridge University Press, Cambridge.

Bibliography

Manuscript sources

British Library
MS Harley 2110 (Castle Acre Cartulary)

Norfolk Record Office
MF 748/121 (Caister by Yarmouth Tithe Award Map, c. 1843)
MF 758/121 (Caister by Yarmouth Tithe Apportionment)

Suffolk Record Office (Bury St Edmunds)
FT 146/2 (Clare Tithe Award Map, 1840)

Suffolk Record Office (Ipswich)
(I)qSfra9 Brown, M. and Patterson, P. (1997) *RCHME Archaeological Field Survey Report: Framlingham Mere*.

Bibliography

Albarella, U. and Davis, S. J. M. (1994) 'Mammals and Birds from Launceston Castle Cornwall: Decline in Status and the Rise of Agriculture, *Circaea* **12.1**, 1–56.

Anon (1985) *Corfe Castle*, National Trust, London.

Anon (1996) *Restormel Castle*, English Heritage, London.

Armitage, E. S. (1912) *The Early Norman Castles of the British Isles*, John Murray, London.

Austin, D. (1984) 'The Castle and the Landscape', *Landscape History* **6**, 69–81.

Avent, R. (1989) *Criccieth Castle*, Cadw, Cardiff.

Ayton, A. and Price, J. L. (1995) 'Introduction: The Military Revolution from a Medieval Perspective' in A. Ayton and J. L. Price eds. *The Medieval Military Revolution: State, Society and Military Change in Medieval and Early Modern Europe*, I. B. Tauris, London, 1–22.

Barker, P. and Higham, R. (2000) *Hen Domen, Montgomery. A Timber Castle on the English–Welsh Border: A Final Report*, University of Exeter Press and the Royal Archaeological Institute, Exeter.

Barron, W. R. J. ed. (1974) *Sir Gawain and the Green Knight*, Manchester University Press, Manchester.

Bates, D. ed. (1997) *Regesta Regum Anglo-Normannorum: The Acta of William I*, Clarendon Press, Oxford.

Beeler, J. H. (1956) 'Castles and Strategy in Norman and Early Angevin England', *Speculum* **31**, 581–601.

Beeler, J. H. (1966) *Warfare in England, 1066–1189*, Cornell University Press, Cornell.

Beresford, G. (1981) 'Goltho Manor, Lincolnshire: The Buildings and their Surrounding Defences, 850–1150', *Anglo-Norman Studies* **4**, 13–36.

Beresford, M. (1967) *New Towns of the Middle Ages*, Lutterworth Press, London.

Biddle, M. (1970) 'Excavations at Winchester, 1969: Eighth Interim Report', *Antiquaries Journal* **50**, 277–326.

Biddle, M. (1975) 'Excavations at Winchester, 1971: Tenth and Final Interim Report: Part 1,' *Antiquaries Journal* **55**, 96–126.

Blair, J. ed. (1988) *Minsters and Parish Churches: The Local Church in Transition, 950–1200*, Monograph 17, Oxford University Committee for Archaeology, Oxford.

Bradbury, J. (1984 and 1992) 'Battles in England and Normandy, 1066–1154', *Anglo-Norman Studies* **6**, 1–12, reprinted in M. Strickland ed. *Anglo-Norman Warfare*, Boydell Press, Woodbridge, 182–93.

Bradbury, J. (1992) *The Medieval Siege*, Boydell Press, Woodbridge.

Braun, H. (1936) *The English Castle*, Batsford, London.

Brewer, J. S., Dimock, J. F. and Warner, G. F. eds. (1861–91) *Giraldi Cambrensis Opera*, Rolls Series, 21.

Brown, E. H. R. (1974) 'The Tyranny of a Construct: Feudalism and Historians of Medieval Europe', *American Historical Review* **79**, 1063–88.

Brown, R. A. (1951) 'Framlingham Castle and Bigod, 1154–1216', *Proceedings of the Suffolk Institute of Archaeology* **25**, 127–48.

Brown, R. A. (1955 and 2003) 'Royal Castle-Building in England, 1154–1216', *English Historical Review* **70**, 353–98, reprinted in R. Liddiard ed. *Anglo-Norman Castles*, Boydell Press, Woodbridge, 133–77.

Brown, R. A. (1959) 'A List of Castles, 1154–1216', *English Historical Review* **74**, 249–80.

Brown, R. A. (1985) *The Normans and the Norman Conquest*, 2nd edn, Boydell Press, Woodbridge.

Brown, R. A. (1970) 'An Historian's Approach to the Origins of the Castle in England', *Archaeological Journal* **126**, 13–48.

Brown, R. A. (1973) *The Origins of English Feudalism*, Allen and Unwin, London.

Brown, R. A. (1976) *English Castles*, 3rd edn, Batsford, London.

Brown, R. A. (1986) *Rochester Castle* 2nd edn, H. M. S. O., London.

Brown, R. A., Colvin, H. and Taylor, A. (1963) *The History of the King's Works*, 2 vols, H. M. S. O., London.

Burne, A. H. (1956) *The Agincourt War*, Eyre and Spottiswoode, London.

Butler, L. (1990) *Denbigh Castle*, Cadw, Cardiff.

Butler, L. (1992 and 2003) 'The Origins of the Honour of Richmond and its Castles', *Château-Gaillard* **16**, 69–80, reprinted in R. Liddiard ed. *Anglo-Norman Castles*, Boydell Press, Woodbridge, 91–103.

Butler, L. (1993) *Pickering Castle*, English Heritage, London.

Calendar of Inquisitions Miscellaneous

Calendar of Patent Rolls

Caley, J., Ellis, H. and Bandinel, B. eds. (1817–30) W. Dugdale, *Monasticon Anglicanum*, 6 vols in 8, Longman, London.

Carpenter, D. A. (1990) *The Minority of Henry III*, Methuen, London.

Carr, A. D. (1995) *Medieval Wales*, Macmillan, Basingstoke.

Chamberlin, R. (1985) *Carisbrooke Castle*, English Heritage, London.

Chibnall, M. ed. (1969–80) *The Ecclesiastical History of Orderic Vitalis*, 6 vols, Clarendon Press, Oxford.

Chibnall, M. (1986) *Anglo-Norman England, 1066–1166*, Blackwell, Oxford.

Chibnall, M. (1989 and 2003) 'Orderic Vitalis on Castles', in C. Harper-Bill, C. Holdsworth and J. L. Nelson eds. *Studies in Medieval History Presented to R. Allen Brown*, Boydell Press, Woodbridge, 43–56, reprinted in R. Liddiard ed. *Anglo-Norman Castles*, Boydell Press, Woodbridge, 119–132.

Clark, G. T. (1884) *Mediaeval Military Architecture in England*, 2 vols, Wyman, London.

Clover, H. and Gibson, M. eds. (1979) *The Letters of Lanfranc, Archbishop of Canterbury*, Clarendon Press, Oxford.

Coad, J. G. and Streeton, A. D. F. (1982) 'Excavations at Castle Acre Castle, Norfolk, 1972–1977: Country House and Castle of the Norman Earls of Surrey', *Archaeological Journal* **139**, 138–301.

Coad, J. G., Streeton, A. D. F. and Warmington, R. (1987) 'Excavations at Castle Acre Castle, Norfolk, 1975–1982: The Bridges, Lime Kilns, and Eastern Gatehouse', *Archaeological Journal* **144**, 256–307.

Coldstream, N. (2003) 'Architects, Advisors and Design at Edward I's Castles in Wales', *Architectural History* **46**, 19–35.

Conran, A. ed. (1967) *The Penguin Book of Welsh Verse*, Penguin, Harmondsworth.

Constans, L. ed. (1904) *Roman de Troie*, Firmin-Didot et cie, Paris.

Contamine, P. ed. and trans. M. Jones (1984) *War in the Middle Ages*, Blackwell, Oxford.

Corfis, I. A. and Wolfe, M. eds (1995) *The Medieval City Under Siege*, Boydell Press, Woodbridge.

Coulson, C. (1973) 'Rendability and Castellation in Medieval France', *Château-Gaillard* **6**, 59–67.

Coulson, C. (1979) 'Structural Symbolism in Medieval Castle Architecture', *Journal of the British Archaeological Association* **132**, 73–90.

Coulson, C. (1982) 'Hierarchism in Conventual Crenellation: An Essay in the Sociology and Metaphysics of Medieval Fortification', *Medieval Archaeology* **26**, 69–100.

Coulson, C. (1992) 'Some Analysis of Bodiam Castle, East Sussex', in C. Harper-Bill and R. Harvey eds. *Medieval Knighthood* **4**, Boydell Press, Woodbridge, 51–107.

Coulson, C. (1994) 'Freedom to Crenellate by Licence: An Historiographical Revision', *Nottingham Medieval Studies* **38**, 86–137.

Coulson, C. (1994) 'The Castles of the Anarchy' in E. King ed. *The Anarchy of Stephen's Reign*, Clarendon Press, Oxford, 67–92, reprinted in R. Liddiard ed. *Anglo-Norman Castles*, Boydell Press, Woodbridge, 179–202.

Coulson, C. (1995) 'Battlements and Bourgeoisie: Municipal Status and the Apparatus of Urban Defence in Later-Medieval England' in S. Church and R. Harvey eds. *Medieval Knighthood* **5**, Boydell Press, Woodbridge, 119–95.

Coulson, C. (1995) 'The French Matrix of the Castle Provisions of the Chester-Leicester Conventio', *Anglo-Norman Studies* **17**, 65–86.

Coulson, C. (1996) 'Cultural Realities and Reappraisals in English Castle Study', *Journal of Medieval History* **22**, 171–208.

Coulson, C. (1998) 'The Sanctioning of Fortresses in France: 'Feudal Anarchy' or Seigniorial Amity?', *Nottingham Medieval Studies* **41**, 38–104.

Coulson, C. (2000) 'Fourteenth-Century Castles in Context: Apotheosis or Decline?' in N. Saul ed. *Fourteenth-Century England*, Boydell Press, Woodbridge, 133–51.

Coulson, C. (2001) 'Peaceable Power in Norman Castles', *Anglo-Norman Studies* **23**, 69–95.

Coulson, C. L. H. (2003) *Castles in Medieval Society*, Oxford University Press, Oxford.

Coulson, C. (2003–4) 'Orthodoxy or Opportunity?', *Castle Studies Group Bulletin*, 115–6.

Creighton, O. H. (2002) *Castles and Landscapes*, Continuum, London.

Crouch, D. (1986) *The Beaumont Twins*, Cambridge University Press, Cambridge.

Crouch, D. (1990) *William Marshal: Court, Career and Chivalry in the Angevin Empire, 1147–1219*, Longman, London.

Crouch, D. (1992) *The Image of Aristocracy in Britain, 1000–1300*, Routledge, London.

Cummins, J. (1988) *The Hound and the Hawk: The Art of Medieval Hunting*, Weidenfeld and Nicolson, London.

Curry, A. (1993) *The Hundred Years War*, Macmillan, Basingstoke.

Darlington, J., ed. (2001) *Stafford Castle: Survey, Excavation and Research, 1978–1998 Vol. 1 The Surveys*, Stafford Borough Council, Stafford.

Davies, R. R. (1991) *The Age of Conquest: Wales 1063–1415*, Oxford University Press, Oxford.

Davies, R. R. (1995) *The Revolt of Owain Glyn Dwr*, Oxford University Press, Oxford.

Davis, R. H. C. and Chibnall, M. eds. (1998) *The Gesta Guillelmi of William of Poitiers*, Clarendon Press, Oxford.

Davison, B. K. (1967) 'The Origins of the Castle in England: The Institute's Research Project', *Archaeological Journal* **124**, 202–11.

Davison, B. K. (1969) 'Early Earthwork Castles: A New Model', *Château-Gaillard* **3**, 37–47.

Davison, B. K. (1971–2) 'Castle Neroche: An Abandoned Norman Fortress in South Somerset', *Somerset Archaeological and Natural History Society* **116**, 16–58.

Dixon, P. (1990) 'The Donjon of Knaresborough: The Castle as Theatre', *Château-Gaillard* **14**, 121–39.

Dixon, P. (1998) 'Design in Castle-Building: The Control of Access to the Lord', *Château-Gaillard* **18**, 47–57.

Dixon, P. (2002) 'The Myth of the Keep' in G. Meirion-Jones, E. Impey and M. Jones eds. *The Seigneurial Residence in Western Europe AD c.800–1600*, BAR International Series 1088, Oxford, 9–13.

Dixon, P. and Lott, B. (1993) 'The Courtyard and the Tower: Contexts and Symbols in the Development of Late Medieval Great Houses', *Journal of the British Archaeological Association* **146**, 93–101.

Dixon, P. and Marshall, P. (1993 and 2003) 'The Great Tower at Hedingham Castle: A Reassessment', *Fortress* **18**, 16–23, reprinted in R. Liddiard ed. *Anglo-Norman Castles*, Boydell Press, Woodbridge, 297–306.

Dockray, K. R. (1979) 'Japan and England During the Fifteenth Century: The Onin War and the Wars of the Roses' in C. Ross ed. *Patronage, Pedigree and Power in Later Medieval England*, A. Sutton, Gloucester, 143–170.

Drage, C. (1987) 'Urban Castles' in J. Schofield and R. Leech eds. *Urban Archaeology in Britain*, CBA Report No. 61, London, 117–32.

Drury, P. J. (1982) 'Aspects of the Origins and Development of Colchester Castle', *Archaeological Journal* **139**, 302–419.

Dymond, D. and Martin, E. eds (1999) *An Historical Atlas of Suffolk*, 3rd edn, Archaeology Service, Suffolk County Council, Ipswich.

Eales, R. (1989) 'Castles and Politics in England, 1215–1224', *Thirteenth-Century England* **2**, 23–4, reprinted in R. Liddiard ed. *Anglo-Norman Castles*, Boydell Press, Woodbridge, 367–88.

Eales, R. (1990) 'Royal Power and Castles in Norman England', in C. Harper-Bill and R. Harvey eds *Medieval Knighthood* **3**, Boydell Press, Woodbridge, 49–78, reprinted in R. Liddiard ed. *Anglo-Norman Castles*, Boydell Press, Woodbridge, 41–67.

Edbury, P. (1999) 'Warfare in the Latin East' in M. Keen ed. *Medieval Warfare: A History*, Oxford University Press, Oxford, 89–112.

Eddy, M. R. and Petchey, M. R. (1983) *Historic Towns in Essex*, Essex County Council Planning Department, Chelmsford.

Emery, A. (1996) *Greater Medieval Houses of England and Wales Vol. 1: Northern England*, Cambridge University Press, Cambridge.

Emery, A. (2000) *Greater Medieval Houses of England and Wales Vol. 2: East Anglia, Central England and Wales*, Cambridge University Press, Cambridge.

English, B. (1995) 'Towns, Mottes and Ring-Works of the Conquest' in A. Ayton and J. Price eds *The Medieval Military Revolution*, I. B. Tauris, London, 43–62.

Everson, P. (1988) 'What's in a Name? Goltho, 'Goltho' and Bullington', *Lincolnshire History and Archaeology* **23**, 92–9.

Everson, P. (1996) 'Bodiam Castle, East Sussex: Castle and its Designed Landscape', *Château-Gaillard* **17**, 66–72.

Everson, P. (1998) ''Delightfully Surrounded with Woods and Ponds': Field Evidence for Medieval Gardens in Britain' in P. Patterson ed. *There by Design: Field Archaeology in Parks and Gardens*, BAR British Series 267, Oxford, 32–8.

Everson, P. (2003) 'Medieval Gardens and Designed Landscapes', in R. Wilson-North ed. *The Lie of the Land: Aspects of the Archaeology and History of the Designed Landscape in the South West of England*, Devon Gardens Trust, Mint Press, Exeter, 24–33.

Everson, P., Brown, G., and Stocker, D. (2000) 'The Earthworks and Landscape Context' in P. Ellis ed. *Ludgershall Castle, Excavations by Peter Addyman, 1964–1972*, Wiltshire Archaeology and Natural History Society Monograph No. 2, 97–115.

Faulkner, P. A. (1958) 'Domestic Planning from the Twelfth to the Fourteenth Centuries', *Archaeological Journal* **115**, 150–83.

Faulkner, P. A. (1963) 'Castle Planning in the Fourteenth Century', *Archaeological Journal* **120**, 215–35.

Fernie, E. (2000) *The Architecture of Norman England*, Oxford University Press, Oxford.

France, F. (1999) *Western Warfare in the Age of the Crusades, 1000–1300*, UCL Press, London.

Frescoln, W. ed. (1983) *The Romance of Fergus*, W. H. Allen, Philadelphia.

Garnett, G. (1996) '"Franci et Angli": The Legal Distinctions between Peoples after the Conquest', *Anglo-Norman Studies* **8**, 109–37.

Gilchrist, R. (1999) *Gender and Archaeology: Contesting the Past*, Routledge, London.

Gildea, J. ed. (1967) *Partonopeu de Blois*, Villanova University Press, Villanova.

Gillingham, J. (1981) *The Wars of the Roses: Peace and Conflict in Fifteenth-Century England*, Weidenfeld and Nicolson, London.

Gillingham, J. (1984 and 1992) 'Richard I and the Science of War in the Middle Ages', in J. Gillingham and J. C. Holt eds. *War and Government in the Middle Ages*, Boydell Press, Woodbridge, 78–91, reprinted in M. Strickland ed. *Anglo-Norman Warfare*, Boydell Press, Woodbridge, 194–207.

Gillingham, J. (1989 and 1992) 'William the Bastard at War', in C. Harper-Bill, C. Holdsworth and J. Nelson eds *Studies in History Presented to R. Allen Brown*, Boydell Press, Woodbridge, 141–58, reprinted in M. Strickland ed. *Anglo-Norman Warfare*, Boydell Press, Woodbridge, 143–60.

Gillingham, J. (1999) *Richard I*, Yale University Press, New Haven and London.

Gillingham, J. (2000) *The English in the Twelfth Century: Imperialism, National Identity and Political Values*, Boydell Press, Woodbridge.

Gillingham, J. and Griffiths, R. (2000) *Medieval Britain: A Very Short Introduction*, Oxford University Press, Oxford.

I. Goch (1967) *The Court of Owain Glyndŵr at Sycharth* in A. Conran ed. *The Penguin Book of Welsh Verse*, Penguin, Harmondsworth, 153–6.

Goodall, J. (1996) 'Tattershall Castle, Lincolnshire', *Country Life* (10 October), 50–5.

Goodall, J. (1998) 'The Battle for Bodiam Castle', *Country Life* (16 April), 58–63.

Goodall, J. (1999) 'The Key of England', *Country Life*, 45–7.

Goodall, J. (1999) 'In the Powerhouse of Kent', *Country Life* (25 March), 110–13.

Goodall, J. (2000) 'Dover Castle and the Great Siege of 1216', *Château-Gaillard* **19**, 91–102.

Goodall, J. (2000) 'Lulworth Castle, Dorset', *Country Life* (13 January), 34–9.

Goodall, J. *English Castle Architecture, 1066–1640*, forthcoming.

Goodman, A. (1981) *The Wars of the Roses*, Routledge and Kegan Paul, London.

Green, J. (1997) *The Aristocracy of Norman England*, Cambridge University Press, Cambridge.

Greenway, D. and Sayers, J. eds (1989) *Jocelin of Brakelond, Chronicle of the Abbey of Bury St Edmunds*, Oxford University Press, Oxford.

Greenway, D. ed. (1996) *Henry Archdeacon of Huntingdon, Historia Anglorum*, Clarendon Press, Oxford.

Hamilton Thompson, A. (1912) *Military Architecture in England During the Middle Ages*, Oxford University Press, Oxford.

Harfield, C. G. (1991) 'A Hand List of Castles Recorded in the Domesday Book', *English Historical Review* **106**, 371–92.

Harper-Bill, C. ed. (1991) *The Cartulary of the Augustinian Friars of Clare*, Suffolk Charters 11, Suffolk Records Society, Boydell Press, Woodbridge.

Herring, P. (2003) 'Cornish Medieval Deer Parks' in R. Wilson-North ed. *The Lie of the Land: Aspects of the Archaeology and the History of the Designed Landscape in the South West of England*, Devon Gardens Trust, Mint Press, Exeter, 34–50.

Heslop, T. A. (1991) 'Orford Castle and Sophisticated Living', *Architectural History* **34**, 36–58.

Heslop, T. A. (1994) *Norwich Castle Keep*, Centre of East Anglian Studies, Norwich.

Heslop, T. A. (2000) '"Weeting Castle", A Twelfth-Century Hall House in Norfolk', *Architectural History* **43**, 42–57.

Heslop, T. A. 'Constantine and Helena: The Roman in English Romanesque', forthcoming.

Higham, R. A., Allan, J. P. and Blaylock, S. R. (1982) 'Excavations at Okehampton Castle, Devon Part II: The Bailey', *Devon Archaeology Society Proceedings* **40**, 19–151.

Higham, R. and Barker, P. (1992) *Timber Castles*, Batsford, London.

Hill, P. and Wileman, J. (2002) *Landscapes of War: The Archaeology of Aggression and Defence*, Tempus, Stroud.

Holden, A. J. ed. (1984) *Roman de Waldef*, Fondation Martin Bodmer, Geneva.

Holdsworth, P. (1984) 'Saxon Southampton' in J. Haslam ed. *Anglo-Saxon Towns*, Phillimore, Chichester, 331–43.

Holt, J. C. (1984 and 1992) 'The Introduction of Knight Service in England', *Anglo-Norman Studies* **6**, 89–106, reprinted in M. Strickland ed. *Anglo-Norman Warfare*, Boydell Press, Woodbridge, 128–42.

Hoppitt, R. (1992) 'A Study of the Development of Deer Parks in Suffolk from the Eleventh to the Seventeenth Century', unpublished PhD thesis, University of East Anglia, Norwich.

Howlett, R. ed. (1884–9) *Chronicles of the Reigns of Stephen, Henry II and Richard I*, Rolls Series.

Impey, E. (1999) 'The Seigneurial Residence in Normandy: An Anglo-Norman Tradition?', *Medieval Archaeology* **93**, 45–73.

Impey, E. and Parnell, G. (2000) *The Tower of London: The Official Illustrated History*, Merrell Holberton, London.

Johnson, M. (2002) *Behind the Castle Gate: From Medieval to Renaissance*, Routledge, London.

Johnstone, N. (1997) 'An Investigation into the Location of the

Royal Courts of Thirteenth-Century Gwynedd' in N. Edwards ed. *Landscape and Settlement in Medieval Wales*, Oxbow Monograph 81, Oxford, 55–69.

Jones, G. (2001) 'Aspects of a Medieval Landscape: Ruthin Castle and the Lordship of Dyffryn-Clywd', unpublished BA dissertation, University of Wales, Bangor.

Jones, M. K. (2002) 'The Battle of Verneuil (17 August 1424): Towards a History of Courage', *War in History* **9**, 375–411.

Jones, T. ed. (1952) *Brut Y Tywysogyon or The Chronicle of the Princes: Peniarth MS. 20 version*, University of Wales Press, Cardiff.

Kaeuper, R. (1999) *Chivalry and Violence in Medieval Europe*, Oxford University Press, Oxford.

Keats-Rohan, K. S. B. (1986) 'The Devolution of the Honour of Wallingford, 1066–1148, *Oxoniensia* **65**, 311–18.

Keen, M. H. (1965) *The Laws of War in the Late Middle Ages*, Routledge and Kegan Paul, London.

Keen, M. (1984) *Chivalry*, Yale University Press, New Haven.

Kenyon, J. R. (1990) *Medieval Fortifications*, Leicester University Press, Leicester.

Kenyon, J. R. (1996) 'Fluctuating Frontiers: Normano-Welsh Castle Warfare c. 1075 to 1240', *Château-Gaillard* **17**, 119–26, reprinted in R. Liddiard ed. *Anglo-Norman Castles*, Boydell Press, Woodbridge, 247–257.

Kenyon, J. R. and Thompson, M. W. (1994) 'The Origins of the Word 'Keep'', *Medieval Archaeology* **38**, 175–6.

King, D. J. C. (1983) *Castellarium Anglicanum*, Kraus International Publications, New York.

King, D. J. C. (1988) *The Castle in England and Wales: An Interpretative History*, Croome Helm, London.

King, D. J. C. and Alcock, L. (1969) 'Ringworks of England and Wales', *Château-Gaillard* **3**, 90–127.

Kinsley, A. G. (1993) 'Excavations on the Saxo-Norman Town Defences at Slaughter House Lane, Newark-on-Trent, Nottinghamshire', *Transactions of the Thoroton Society of Nottinghamshire* **97**, 14–63.

Knight, J. K. (2000) *The Three Castles*, 2nd edn, Cadw, Cardiff.

Landsberg, S. (1995) *The Medieval Garden*, British Museum Press, London.

Leclanche, J. L. ed. (1980) *Le Conte de Floire et Blancheflor*, H. Champion, Paris.

Le Patourel, J. (1976) *The Norman Empire*, Clarendon Press, Oxford.

Leslie, M. (1993) 'An English Landscape Garden before the 'English Landscape Garden'?', *Journal of Garden History* **13**, 2–18.

Lewis, C. P. (1988) 'An Introduction to the Herefordshire Domesday' in A. Williams and R. W. H. Erskine eds *The Herefordshire Domesday*, Alecto Historical Editions, London. Page numbers?

Lewis, C. P. (1997) 'Joining the Dots: A Methodology for Identifying the English in Domesday Book' in K. S. B. Keats-Rohan ed. *Family Trees and the Roots of Politics: The Prosopography of Britain and France from the Tenth to the Twelfth Century*, Boydell Press, Woodbridge, 69–87.

Liddiard, R. (2000) *Landscapes of Lordship: The Castle and the Countryside in Medieval Norfolk, 1066–1200*, BAR British Series 309, Oxford.

Liddiard, R. (2000) 'Castle Rising, Norfolk: A 'Landscape of Lordship', *Anglo-Norman Studies* **22**, 169–86.

Liddiard, R. (2000) 'Population Density and Norman Castle-Building: Some Evidence from East Anglia', *Landscape History* **22**, 37–46.

Liddiard, R. (2003) 'The Deer Parks of Domesday Book', *Landscapes* **4.1**, 4–23.

Liddiard, R. ed. (2003) *Anglo-Norman Castles*, Boydell Press, Woodbridge.

Lilley, K. D. (2002) *Urban Life in the Middle Ages, 1000–1450*, Palgrave, Basingstoke.

Lloyd, J. E. (1911) *A History of Wales*, vol. 2, Longmans, London.

Mahany, C. (1977) 'Excavations at Stamford Castle, 1971–6', *Château-Gaillard* **8**, 223–45.

Mahany, C. and Roffe, D. (1982) 'Stamford: The Development of an Anglo-Scandinavian Borough', *Anglo-Norman Studies* **5**, 197–219.

Marshall, P. (2002) 'The Great Tower as Residence' in G. Meirion-Jones, E. Impey and M. Jones eds *The Seigneurial Residence in Western Europe AD c800–1600*, BAR International Series 1088, Oxford, 27–44.

Marshall, P. and Samuels, J. (1994) 'Recent Excavations at Newark Castle, Nottinghamshire', *Transactions of the Thoroton Society of Nottinghamshire* **98**, 49–57.

Mason, J. F. A. and Barker, P. (1961–4) 'The Norman Castle at Quatford', *Transactions of the Shropshire Archaeological Society* **57**, 37–62.

Matarasso, P. ed. (1993) *The Cistercian World: Monastic Writings of the Twelfth Century*, Penguin, London.

Mathieu, J. R. (1999) 'New Methods on Old Castles: Generating New Ways of Seeing', *Medieval Archaeology* **43**, 115–42.

McNeill, T. (1990 and 2003) 'Hiberna Pacata et Castellata', *Château-Gaillard* **14**, 261–75, reprinted in R. Liddiard ed. *Anglo-Norman Castles*, Boydell Press, Woodbridge, 257–71.

McNeill, T. (1992) *Castles*, Batsford and English Heritage, London.

McNeill, T. (1997) *Castles in Ireland: Feudal Power in a Gaelic World*, Routledge, London.

McNeill, T. E. and Pringle, M. (1997) 'A Map of Mottes in the British Isles', *Medieval Archaeology* **41**, 220–2.

Mertes, K. (1988) *The English Noble Household*, Blackwell, Oxford.

Michel, F. (1840) *Histoire des Ducs de Normandie et des Rois d'Angleterre*, J. Renouard et cie, Paris.

Milner, N. P. ed. (1993) *Vegetius: Epitome of Military Science*, Liverpool University Press, Liverpool.

Moore, J. (2000) 'Anglo-Norman Garrisons', *Anglo-Norman Studies* **22**, 205–59.

Morley, B. (1981) 'Aspects of Fourteenth-Century Castle Design' in A. Detsicas ed. *Collectanea Historica: Essays in Memory of Stuart Rigold*, Kent Archaeological Society, Maidstone, 104–13.

Morris, J. ed. (1976) *Domesday Book: Hertfordshire*, Phillimore, Chichester.

Morris, J. ed. (1978) *Domesday Book: Buckinghamshire*, Phillimore, Chichester.

Morris, R. (1989) *Churches in the Landscape*, Dent, London.

Morris, R. K. (1998) 'The Architecture of Arthurian Enthusiasm: Castle Symbolism in the Reigns of Edward I and his Successors' in M. Strickland ed. *Armies, Chivalry and Warfare in Medieval England and France*, Paul Watkins, Stamford, 63–81.

Munby, J. (1993) *Stokesay Castle*, English Heritage, London.

Mynors, R. A. B. ed. (1998) *William of Malmesbury, Gesta Regum Anglorum*, Clarendon Press, Oxford.

Norgate, K. (1887) *England under the Angevin Kings*, vol. 2, Macmillan, London.

O'Keeffe, T. (2001) *Romanesque Ireland: Architecture, Sculpture and Ideology in the Twelfth Century*, Four Courts Press, Dublin.

Oman, C. (1924) *A History of Art of War in the Middle Ages*, 2 vols, 2nd edn, Methuen and Co., London.

Oman, C. (1926) *Castles*, Great Western Railway, London.

Padel, O. J. (1988) 'Tintagel in the Twelfth and Thirteenth Centuries', *Cornish Studies* 16, 61–6.

Painter, S. (1934–5 and 2003) 'Castle Guard', *American Historical Review* 40, 450–9, reprinted in R. Liddiard ed. *Anglo-Norman Castles*, Boydell Press, Woodbridge, 203–10.

Parnell, G. (1998) 'The White Tower, The Tower of London', *Country Life* (July 9), 86–9.

Phibbs, J. (1998) 'Recording What Isn't There: Three Difficulties with Eighteenth-Century Landscapes' in P. Patterson ed. *There by Design: Field Archaeology in Parks and Gardens*, BAR British Series 267, Oxford, 27–31.

Phillips, J. R. (1874) *Memoirs of the Civil War in Wales and the Marches, 1642–1649*, 2 vols, Longmans, Greene and Co., London.

Platt, C. (1982) *The Medieval Castle in England and Wales*, Secker and Warburg, London.

Potter, K. R. ed. and trans. (1976) *Gesta Stephani*, Clarendon Press, Oxford.

Potter, K. R. trans. and King, E. ed. (1998) *William of Malmesbury, Historia Novella*, Clarendon Press, Oxford.

Pounds, N. J. G. (1990) *The Medieval Castle in England and Wales: A Social and Political History*, Cambridge University Press, Cambridge.

Pratt, D. (1990) 'The Marcher Lordship of Chirk, 1329–1330', *Denbighshire Society Transactions* 39, 5–41.

Prestwich, M. (1982) 'English Castles in the Reign of Edward II', *Journal of Medieval History* 9, 159–78.

Prestwich, M. (1996) *Armies and Warfare in the Middle Ages: The English Experience*, Yale University Press, New Haven.

Prestwich, M. (2001) 'The Garrisoning of English Medieval Castles' in R. P. Abels and B. S. Bachrach eds *The Normans and their Adversaries at War*, Boydell Press, Woodbridge, 185–200.

Proceedings of the Privy Council.

Register of the Black Prince, The, 1348–1365, 3 vols (1930–3), H. M. S. O., London.

Renn, D. (1968) *Norman Castles in Britain*, Baker, London.

Renn, D. (1971) *Medieval Castles in Hertfordshire*, Phillimore for the Hertfordshire Local History Council, Chichester.

Renn, D. (1993) *Goodrich Castle*, English Heritage, London.

Renn, D. (1994 and 2003) 'Burhgeat and Gonfanon: Two Sidelights from the Bayeux Tapestry', *Anglo-Norman Studies* 16, 178–98, reprinted in R. Liddiard ed. *Anglo-Norman Castles*, Boydell Press, Woodbridge, 69–90.

Renn, D. (2000) 'The Norman Military Works' in R. Shoesmith and A. Johnson eds. *Ludlow Castle: Its History and Buildings*, Logaston Press, Almeley, 125–38.

Renn, D. (2003) 'Two Views from the Roof: Design and Defence at Conway and Stokesay' in J. R. Kenyon and K. O'Conor eds. *The Medieval Castle in Ireland and Wales*, Four Courts, Dublin, 163–75.

Reynolds, S. (1994) *Fiefs and Vassals*, Oxford University Press, Oxford.

Ridgard, J. ed. (1985) *Medieval Framlingham: Select Documents, 1270–1524*, Suffolk Records Society 27, Boydell Press, Woodbridge.

Round, J. H. (1902) 'The Castles of the Conquest', *Archaeologia* 58, 313–40.

Rumble, A. ed. (1986) *Domesday Book, Suffolk*, Phillimore, Chichester.

Sanders, I. J. (1960) *English Baronies: A Study of Their Origin and Descent 1086–1327*, Clarendon Press, Oxford.

Saunders, A. (1977) 'Five Castle Excavations: Reports on the Institute's Research Project into the Origin of the Castle in England', *Archaeological Journal* 134, 1–156.

Saunders, A. (1989) *Fortress Britain*, Beaufort, Liphook.

Sawyer, P. H. (1985) '1066–1086: A Tenurial Revolution?' in P. H. Sawyer ed. *Domesday Book: A Reassessment*, Edward Arnold, London, 71–85.

Shopland, A. 'The Political Career of the D'Albini Earls of Sussex, 1088–1248', M. Phil thesis in preparation, University of East Anglia, Norwich.

Smail, R. C. (1995) *Crusading Warfare 1097–1193*, 2nd edn, Cambridge University Press, Cambridge.

Speight, S. (1998) 'Castle Warfare in the Gesta Stephani', *Château-Gaillard* 19, 269–74.

Stocker, D. (1992) 'The Shadow of the General's Armchair', *Archaeological Journal* 149, 415–20.

Stocker, D. and Stocker, M. (1996) 'Sacred Profanity: The Theology of Rabbit Breeding and the Symbolic Landscape of the Warren', *World Archaeology* 28, 265–72.

Strickland, M. (1989 and 1992) 'Securing the North: Invasion and the Strategy of Defence in Twelfth-Century Anglo-Scottish Warfare', *Anglo-Norman Studies* 11, 37–58, reprinted in M. Strickland ed. *Anglo-Norman Warfare*, Boydell Press, Woodbridge, 208–29.

Strickland, M. ed. (1992) *Anglo-Norman Warfare*, Boydell Press, Woodbridge.

Strickland, M. (1996) *War and Chivalry: The Conduct and Perception of War in England and Normandy, 1066–1217*, Cambridge University Press, Cambridge.

Suppe, F. (1989 and 2003) 'Castle Guard and the Castlery of Clun', *Haskins Society Journal* 1, 123–34, reprinted in R. Liddiard ed. *Anglo-Norman Castles*, Boydell Press, Woodbridge, 211–21.

Suppe, F. C. (1994) *Military Institutions on the Welsh Marches : Shropshire, AD 1066–1300*, Boydell Press, Woodbridge.

Swanton, M. (1998) 'The Deeds of Hereward', in T. H. Ohlgren ed. *Medieval Outlaws: Ten Tales in Modern English*, Sutton, Stroud, 12–60.

Sweetman, D. (1999) *The Medieval Castles of Ireland*, Boydell Press, Woodbridge.

Taylor, A. (1985) *Studies in Castles and Castle-Building*, Hambledon Press, London.

Taylor, A. (1987) *Rhuddlan Castle*, Cadw, Cardiff.

Taylor, A. (1997) *Harlech Castle*, 3rd edn, Cadw, Cardiff.

Taylor, A. (1998) *Conwy Castle*, 4th edn, Cadw, Cardiff.

Taylor, A. J. (1986) *The Welsh Castles of Edward I*, Hambledon Press, London.

Taylor, A. J. (1998) *Conway Castle and Town Walls*, 4th edn, Cadw, Cardiff.

Taylor, C. (1989) 'Somersham Palace, Cambridgeshire: A Medieval Landscape for Pleasure?' in M. Bowden, D. Mackay and P. Topping eds *From Cornwall to Caithness*, BAR British Series 209, Oxford, 211–24.

Taylor, C. (2000) 'Medieval Ornamental Landscapes', *Landscapes* 1.1, 38–55.

Taylor, C., Everson, P. and Wilson-North, R. (1990) 'Bodiam Castle, Sussex', *Medieval Archaeology* 34, 155–57.

Thackray, D. (1991) *Bodiam Castle*, National Trust, London.

Thomas, K. (1983) *Man and the Natural World: Changing Attitudes in England, 1500–1800*, Allen Lane, London.

Thompson, M. W. (1986) 'Monasteries and Castles', *Archaeological Journal* 143, 305–21.

Thompson, M. W. (1987) *The Decline of the Castle*, Cambridge University Press, Cambridge.

Thompson, M. W. (1991) *The Rise of the Castle*, Cambridge University Press, Cambridge.

Thompson, M. W. (1994) 'The Military Interpretation of Castles' *Archaeological Journal* 151, 439–45.

Toy, S. (1953) *The Castles of Great Britain*, William Heinemann, London.

Toy, S. (1955) *A History of Fortification from 3000 BC to AD 1700*, William Heinemann, London.

Turner, D. J. (1996) 'Bodiam, Sussex: True Castle or Old Soldier's Dream House?' in W. M. Ormrod ed. *England in the Fourteenth Century: Proceedings of the 1985 Harlaxton Symposium*, Boydell Press, Woodbridge, 267–77.

Turner, R. (2002) *Chepstow Castle*, Cadw, Cardiff.

Vale, M. (1981) *War and Chivalry*, Duckworth, London.

Van Emden, W. (1984) 'The Castle in Some Works of Medieval French Literature' in K. Reyerson and F. Powe eds *The Medieval Castle: Romance and Reality*, Kendall/Hunt, Dubuque, Iowa, 1–36.

Vince, A. (1990) *Saxon London: An Archaeological Investigation*, Seaby, London.

Wadmore, B. (1920) *The Earthworks of Bedfordshire*, The Bedfordshire Standard, Bedford.

Warren, W. L. (1978) *King John*, 2nd edn, Eyre Methuen, London.

Watkiss, L. and Chibnall, M. eds (1994) *The Waltham Chronicle*, Clarendon Press, Oxford.

Weaver, J. (1998) *Middleham Castle*, English Heritage, London.

Weaver, J. R. H. ed. (1908) *The Chronicle of John of Worcester, 1118–40*, Clarendon Press, Oxford.

Webb, C. C. J. ed. (1909) *John of Salisbury, Policraticus*, Clarendon Press, Oxford.

Whitaker, M. A. (1984) 'Otherworld Castles in Middle English Arthurian Romance' in K. Reyerson and F. Powe eds. *The Medieval Castle: Romance and Reality*, Kendall/Hunt, Dubuque, Iowa, 27–46.

Whitelock, D. ed. (1955) *English Historical Documents, vol. 1 c.500–1042*, Eyre and Spottiswoode, London.

Whitelock, D., Douglas, D. C. and Tucker, S. L. eds (1961) *The Anglo-Saxon Chronicle*, Eyre and Spottiswoode, London.

Wight, J. A. (1972) *Brick Building in England from the Middle Ages to 1550*, J. Baker, London.

Williams, A. (1992 and 2003) 'A Bell-House and a Burh-Geat: Lordly Residences in England before the Conquest' in C. Harper-Bill and R. Harvey eds *Medieval Knighthood* 4, Boydell Press, Woodbridge, 221–40, reprinted in R. Liddiard ed. *Anglo-Norman Castles*, Boydell Press, Woodbridge, 23–40.

Williams, A. (1995) *The English and the Norman Conquest*, Boydell Press, Woodbridge.

Williams-Jones, K. (1978) 'The Taking of Conway Castle, 1401', *Transactions of the Caernarvonshire Historical Society* 39, 7–43.

Williamson, T. (1995) *Polite Landscapes: Gardens and Society in Eighteenth-Century England*, Sutton, Stroud.

Williamson, T. (2000) *The Origins of Hertfordshire*, Manchester University Press, Manchester.

Woolgar, C. M. (1999) *The Great Household in Medieval England*, Yale University Press, New Haven and London.

Wright, T. ed. (1863) *Alexandri Neckam, De Naturis Rerum*, Rolls Series 34, London.

Index

Aachen, 22
Aberconwy, Caernarfonshire, 55
Aberystwyth, Cardigan, 55
Acton Burnell, Shropshire, 73
Aelmer, thane of King Edward's, 27–8
Alexander, Bishop of Lincoln, 101
Alexander Neckham, 105, 115
Alfred, the Great, 15
Alric, 35
'Anarchy' of Stephen's Reign, 18, 95, 107, 119, 139
Anglo–Saxon Chronicle, 12, 20, 22, 36, 37, 73, 148
Armitage, E. S., 3, 6
Arthurian imagery, 56–8, 145
Arundel, Sussex, 101
artillery forts, 2, 40, 64–5, 73
Aubrey de Vere III, 52–3
Audley End, Essex, 66
Austin, D., 7

Baconsthorpe, Norfolk, 64
Bamburgh, Northumberland, 87
Barker, P., 10
Barnard, Co. Durham, 103
Barnwell Chronicle, 94
Basing House, Hampshire, 75
bastard feudalism, 63
Battle Abbey, Sussex, 30
Bayeux Tapestry, 16
Beaumaris, Anglesey, 2, 54, 55, 56, 143
Bedford, Bedfordshire, 91–3, 94, 96
Beeler, J., 5, 78
Beeston, Cheshire, 24, 25, 44, 95, 104, 147
Benington, Hertfordshire, 26–8
Berkeley, Gloucestershire, 59

Berkhamsted, Hertfordshire, 88, 111, 112
Berwick, Northumberland, 84
Black Prince, 104
Blickling Hall, Norfolk, 66–7
Blitzkreig, 13, 78
Bodiam, Sussex, 7–11, 39, 61–2, 64, 150
Bolingbroke, Lincolnshire, 26, 44
Bolton, Yorkshire, 58, 62
bookland, 31
Bramber, Sussex, 31, 33
Braun, H., 5
Bridgnorth, Shropshire, 87, 101
Brompton, Shropshire, 82
Brown, R. A., 5, 6, 78
Brut y Tywysogyon, 76
burh, 15, 17, 23, 30, 31
burh-geat, 15, 16, 21, 31, 33, 34, 67
Bury St Edmunds, Suffolk, 25, 107

Cadell ap Gruffudd, prince of Deheubarth, 42
Caernarvon, Caernarvonshire, 46, 54, 55–6, 57, 58
Caerphilly, Glamorgan, 56, 152
Caesar's Camp, Kent, 22, 24
Caister, Norfolk, 62, 63, 107
Camber, Sussex, 65
Cambridge, Cambridgeshire, 13, 19
cannon, 64, 86–7
Canterbury, Kent, 19, 20, 141
Carisbrooke, IoW, 64, 69, 77, 79
Carmarthen, Carmarthen, 42
Carreg Cennen, Carmarthen, 127, 128
Castle Acre, Norfolk, 28, 33, 107, 134–9, 147
Castle Bromwich, Warwickshire, 28
Castle Camps, Cambridgeshire, 126

Castle Hedingham, Essex, 51, 52–3, 54, 95, 113, 127, 139
Castle Neroche, Somerset, 28
Castle Rising, Norfolk, 51, 53, 54, 103, 113–14, 117, 119, 139
castles,
  approach routes, 45, 131–41
  attacks on, 71–8
  and churches, 29–30, 36
  castle 'story', 1–2, 40–1, 67, 151–2
  distribution, 23–6
  definition of, 39–40, 46, 68, 122
  labour services on, 30–31
  numbers, 18
  siting, 24–5, 29, 123–7
  strategic network, 23–4
Castle Guard, 83
Catterick, Yorkshire, 30
Cawood, Yorkshire, 62
cellular lodgings, 62–3
Château-Gaillard, 42, 54
Chepstow, Monmouth, 34, 51, 59, 61, 147
Chirk, Denbigh, 134
chivalry in castle architecture, 7, 57–8, 70
Christchurch, Hampshire, 75
Civil War, English, 75, 86, 89, 95
Clare, Suffolk, 41, 103, 107, 109, 114
Clarendon, Wiltshire, 41
Clark, G. T., 3
Clavering, Essex, 37
Clun, Shropshire, 49, 50, 59, 81, 83, 147
Cnut, king of England, 13
Cockermouth, Cumberland, 83
Cockfield, Suffolk, 34
Colchester, Essex, 33–4, 47, 83, 95, 141
Coldstream, N., 56

175

conditional respite, *see* sieges
Conisborough, Yorkshire, 50, 54
Constantinople, 56
Conway, Caernarvonshire, 2, 55, 82, 89–91, 148
Cooling, Kent, 44, 64, 145, 150
Corfe, Dorset, 24, 85, 86, 87, 88
Coulson, C., 6, 7, 8, 11, 22
courtyard castle, 59–62
Creighton, O., 11, 19
Criccieth, Caernarvonshire, 55, 82, 145, 146, 147
Cromwell's Castle, Isles of Scilly, 65
Crondall, Hampshire, 75
Crowmarsh, Oxfordshire, 88
Cunobelin, king, 34

Dartington, Devon, 62
Davison, B. K., 6, 19
Deal, Kent, 65
decline of the castle, 58–64
Deddington, Oxfordshire, 74
deer parks, 97, 98, 99, 100, 102–3, 111, 114, 118, 134
Denbigh, Denbigh, 46, 120
Devizes, Wiltshire, 100, 102
Dinas Brân, Denbighshire, 125, 126
Dixon, P., 11
Dolbadarn, Caernarvonshire, 56
Dolwyddelan, Caernarvonshire, 56, 57
Domesday Book, 19, 27, 35
donjon, 11, 17, 33, 34, 42, 46–51
    debate over function of, 48–51, 119, 138
dovecotes, 107
Dover, Kent, 6, 11, 19, 50, 54, 64, 73, 83, 86, 96, 139–41
Dunster, Somerset, 109
Durham, 36

Eadric, the Wild, 14
Eleanor of Castile, 98, 110
Eales, R., 18
Edgar, *aetheling*, 13
Edward I, king of England, 9, 42, 54, 55, 89, 98, 131–2
Edward II, king of England, 75
Edward, the Confessor, 13, 22, 37
Edwin, earl of Mercia, 13

Elizabeth de Burgh, 115
Ely, Cambridgeshire, 86
Ely 'plea', 36
Epitome Rei Militaris, 24, 79
Everson, P., 8
Ewyas Harold, Herefordshire, 37
Exeter, Devon, 13, 20, 21, 22, 85
Eynesford, Kent, 16, 28, 35

Faringdon, Oxfordshire, 81
Faulkner, P., 6, 62
Fawkes de Bréauté, 91–3
feudalism, 1, 14
fieldworks, 81
First Crusade, 70
fishponds, 45, 106, 114, 132
Flint, Flintshire, 55, 59, 132
Folkestone, Kent, 22
forebuilding, 51
Framlingham, Suffolk, 6, 47, 83, 92, 93–5, 104, 106, 114–5

gardens, 98, 104, 110, 132
Garden of Eden, 105
garderobes, 60, 61, 64
garrisons, 82–3
gatehouse, 47, 61
Gaucher de Châtillon, 139–40
Geoffrey de Clinton, 120
Geoffrey of Monmouth, 145
Gerald of Wales, 111, 123
Gesta Herewardi, 35
Gesta Stephani, 71
Gilbert de Clare, 41
Gilbert de Tonbridge, *see* Gilbert de Clare
Gilbert Fitz Richard, 74
Gilchrist, R., 110
Gisors, 49
gloriette, 98
Gloucester, Gloucestershire, 19, 80, 106
Goodall, J., 68, 139
Goodrich, Herefordshire, 59–62
Goltho, Lincolnshire, 15, 22, 28
great parks, 102–3, 113
Grosmont, Monmouthshire, 42, 80
Guines, 47
gunports, 64, 150
Gwilym ap Tudor, 89–91

Gyrth, 79

Haddon Hall, Derbyshire, 62, 129–30
halls, 35, 46, 60, 62, 115, 142
Hardwick Hall, Derbyshire, 66
Harewood, Yorkshire, 111
Harold Godwineson, king of England, 79
Harold Hardrada, king of Norway, 79
Harlech, Merioneth, 54, 55, 82
harrying of the north, 13
Hastings, 1, 22, 79
Haverah, Yorkshire, 106
Hen Domen, Montgomeryshire, 17, 43, 73
Hengrave Hall, Suffolk, 66
Henry I, king of England, 105, 111, 112
Henry II, king of England, 11, 42, 47, 54, 80, 88, 139
Henry III, king of England, 43, 139
Henry IV, king of England, 87, 90
Henry V, king of England, 70, 84
Henry VIII, king of England, 2, 64
Henry de Braybrooke, 91–2
Henry of Huntingdon, 111
Henry Fitz Hugh II, 98
Hereford, Herefordshire, 37
Hereward, the Wake, 35
Herstmonceux, Sussex, 58, 64
Hertford, Hertfordshire, 88
Heslop, T. A., 11
Higham, R., 10
households, 60–3,
Hubert de Burgh, 42, 87
Hugh Bigod, 93
Hugh de Bolbec, 148
Hugh de Frene, 43
Hugh de Lacy, 50
Hundred Years War, 8, 9, 47
hunting, 100, 105–6
Huntingdon, Huntingdonshire, 13
Hywel, of the axe, 145

Iolo Goch, 145
'inherent military probability', 70
Ivanhoe, 14
Ivo Tallibois, 26

Joan de Valence, 60

Jocelin of Brakelond, 107
John, king, 75, 94–5
John Fitz Gilbert, 86
John of Salisbury, 105
John of Worcester, 107
Johnson, M., 11, 65, 118

Kenilworth, Warwickshire, 73, 85, 96, 106, 111, 120
Kenyon, J., 10
keeps, *see donjon*
King, D. J. C., 5, 6, 7, 73, 74, 75, 78
Kirby Muxloe, Leicestershire, 61, 120
Knaresborough, Yorkshire, 59, 82, 103, 104, 115

Launceston, Cornwall, 101, 103, 126
Lawrence de Ludlow, 44–6, 145
Leeds, Kent, 97, 98, 110, 127
Leicester, Leicestershire, 19
Leofwine, 79
licence to crenellate, 7, 9, 43–5, 120, 145
Lilley, K., 118
Lincoln, Lincolnshire, 13, 36
Lincoln, battle of, 79
literature, depiction of castles in, 122–6, 142–4
little park, 106, 113, 115–16, 133
Llandovery, Carmarthenshire, 86
Llanstephen, Carmarthenshire, 86
Llywelyn ap Gruffudd, 147
Llywelyn ap Iorwerth, 132
Llywelyn, the Great, 43, 55
London, 19
Louis VIII, king of France, 83, 94
Ludgershall, Wiltshire, 114, 115
Ludlow, Shropshire, 22, 31, 32, 129
Lulworth Castle, Dorset, 66, 68
Lydham, Shropshire, 82

Mabinogion, 58
Magnus Maximus, 58
Manorbier, Pembrokeshire, 106, 107, 111, 123, 125
Marshall, P., 11
Marsh Gibbon, Buckinghamshire, 35
Master James of St George, 55, 56
Matthew Paris, 148
Maxstoke, Warwickshire, 61

Mayette, 87
McNeill, T., 10
Middleham, Yorkshire, 111, 145
Middleton Stoney, Oxfordshire, 28
Mileham, Norfolk, 113
military architecture, 2, 39
military interpretation of castles, 39–40
Moccas, Herefordshire, 43
monastic houses, 109–110
Montecute, Somerset, 35
Montgomery, Montgomery, 43, 82, 148
Morcar, earl of Northumbria, 13
Morris, R., 55
mottes, 3, 19, 23, 29
motte and bailey, 1, 6, 17, 18, 22, 30
murdrum fine, 35, 36

Nefyn, 58
Newark, Nottinghamshire, 19, 101
Newbury, Berkshire, 86
New Buckenham, Norfolk, 49, 101, 114, 139
Newcastle, Northumberland, 50, 54, 84
Norham, Northumberland, 84
Norman Conquest, of England, 1, 12–15, 23, 30–6
Norman Conquest, of Ireland, 38
Northgate, church of, Oxford, 16
North Elmham, Norfolk, 150
Norwich, Norfolk, 36, 43, 47, 50–1, 119, 142
Nottingham, Nottinghamshire, 13, 15, 82, 83
Nunney, Somerset, 58

Odiham, Hampshire, 75, 105
Odo of Bayeux, 22
Okehampton, Devon, 127, 128
Old Wardour, Wiltshire, 62, 105, 111
Oman, C., 5
Ongar, Essex, 101
Orderic Vitalis, 12, 20, 37, 38
Orford, Suffolk, 11, 47–8, 50, 53, 54, 93, 101
origins of castle, 6, 19, 36–9
Oswestry, Shropshire, 80, 83
Owain Glyn Dŵr, 75, 90, 116
Oxborough, Norfolk, 64

palaces, 41, 110
Palladianism, 66
Partonopeu of Blois, 143–4
Peasants' Revolt, 118
Peckforton park, Cheshire, 104
Pembroke, Pembrokeshire, 47
Peter Heynoe, 79
Peter of Valognes, 26–8
Pickering, Yorkshire, 148
Pickhill, Yorkshire, 30
Piers Ploughman, 150
'Phoney' Castle, 39–40
Platt, C., 7
Pontefract, Yorkshire, 62, 95
Portchester, Hampshire, 6, 16, 28, 75, 86
Pounds, N. J. G., 10
Prestwich, M., 96

Quatford, Shropshire, 101

Raglan, Monmouth, 113, 149, 150
Ralph, Lord Cromwell, 59
Ralph of Coggeshall, 92
Ranulf, the king's chancellor, 111
Ravensworth, Yorkshire, 98–9
'real' castle, 39–40
Reformation, 65, 66
Reginald de Grey, 132
Renaissance, 66
Renn, D., 5, 31
Restormel, Cornwall, 51, 144
Rhuddlan, Denbigh, 55, 56, 110, 132
Rhys ap Tudor, 89–91
Richard I, 42, 54, 70
Richard's Castle, Herefordshire, 37
Richard, Earl of Cornwall, 126, 145
Richard of Brionne, *see* Gilbert de Clare
Richard Marshal, 80
Richmond, Yorkshire, 30, 31, 33, 59
ringwork, 6, 17, 18, 19
ritual in siege warfare, 72, 84–9
Robert, Count of Mortain, 101
Robert Fitz Hildebrand, 86
Robert Malet, 101
Robert of Bellême, 101
Robert, Earl of Gloucester, 81, 107
Robert Walpole, 119
Rochester, Kent, 85, 88–9, 94, 96
Roger Bigod, 93–4

Roger Bigod III, 59, 61, 147
Roger, Bishop of Salisbury, 42, 100
Rouen, 112
Round, J. H., 3
Ruthin, Denbigh, 131–4

Saltwood, Kent, 58, 64, 115, 150
Scarborough, Yorkshire, 40, 50, 54
Scott, Sir Walter, 2
Segontium, 58
Sherborne, Dorset, 22
Sheriff Hutton, Yorkshire, 61
Shrewsbury, Shropshire, 80, 88
sieges,
    aristocratic attitude to, 78
    conventions of, 84–9
    numbers of, 71–8
    regional variation of, 76
    preparation for, 82
    siege castles, 87–8
Skenfrith, Monmouth, 42
Skipton, Yorkshire, 104
Southampton, Hampshire, 19, 59, 75
South Wingfield, Derbyshire, 62
Spalding, Lincolnshire., 26
St Albans, Hertfordshire, 25
St Oswald, 36
Stafford, Staffordshire, 103
Stamford, Lincolnshire, 15, 19
Stamford Bridge, Yorkshire, 79
Statute of Rhuddlan, 55
Stephen, king, 74, 86, 88
Stigand, archbishop of Canterbury, 13
Stocker, D., 10
Stokesay, Shropshire, 44–6, 145

Stow, Lincolnshire, 110, 111
Sulgrave, Northamptonshire, 15, 16, 28, 35, 36
Sycharth, Denbighshire, 116

Tattershall, Lincolnshire, 4, 59
Taylor, A., 5, 56
Taylor, C., 8
Tetbury, Gloucestershire, 87
Thomas Becket, 54, 141
Thomas, Lord Bindon, 66
Thompson, A. H., 3
Thompson, M. W., 7, 10
'Three Castles', 42
Tintagel, Cornwall, 124, 126, 145
Tonbridge, Kent, 41, 56, 74
Topcliffe, Yorkshire, 30
Torrington, Devon, 50
Tostig, 79
Trematon, Cornwall, 101
Toy, S., 5
trial by battle, 78
Trim, 50
Trowbridge, Wiltshire, 28

urban castles, 16, 18, 19

Valence family, 59–61

Waleran, Count of Meulan, 107
Wallingford, Oxfordshire, 19
Walmer, Kent, 65
Wareham, Dorset, 19
warfare,
    aristocratic mentality, 78–80

castle-based warfare, 80–4
nature of, 76–9
ritual in, 72, 84–9
Wark, Northumberland, 84
Wars of the Roses, 2, 75, 89, 95
Warwick, Warwickshire, 13, 58, 59, 62, 74
Warkworth, Northumberland, 87, 129
Weeting, Norfolk, 42
White Castle, Monmouth, 42, 51
White Tower, 33, 34, 47, 51, 54, 142, 150
William I, king of England, 1, 12, 13, 18, 20, 22–3, 33, 36, 54, 105, 141
William, II, king of England, 51, 87, 105
William de Valence, 60, 145
William Fitz Odo, 50
William Fitz Osbern, 22
William, lord Hastings, 120
William of Malmesbury, 112
William of Newburgh, 18, 42
William of Poitiers, 38
William of Warenne, 33
Winchester, Hampshire, 19, 23, 75
Windsor, Berkshire, 62, 83, 101
Wolvesey, Hampshire, 75
Woodstock, Oxfordshire, 41, 111
Worcester, Worcestershire, 36, 107
Wulfstan II, Lupus, bishop of Worcester and York, 15
Wulfstan II, St, bishop of Worcester, 36

Yielden, Bedfordshire, 115
York, Yorkshire, 13, 19, 35, 141